CW00740704

Praise for *In Each Other's Care*

"Reading Stan Tatkin is like listening to your favorite wise uncle armed with the latest developments in brain research. Smart, practical, blessedly specific, *In Each Other's Care* asks: What would our relationships be like if we remembered, even in stressful moments, that we are actually in a relationship? When we feel threatened, we lose each other and revert to I, me, mine—forgetting, that our very well-being depends on the emotional ecosystem we're a part of. Stan reminds us that taking care of one another, of our union, is taking care of ourselves. He offers actionable tools, like how to speak up and care for your partner at the same time. This book is a revolution. It has the power to transform your relationship and your life."

TERRENCE REAL
New York Times bestselling author of *Us* and founder of the Relational Life Institute

"Solidly grounded in cutting edge neuroscience and attachment research, Stan Tatkin's new book, *In Each Other's Care*, is a wonderful, clear, practical book that challenges its readers to get serious about truly nurturing their adult love relationships and shows them how to do it. Informed by his extensive experience with countless couples, Stan Tatkin takes head-on the conflicts that not only threaten to break a relationship but can also sour it, leaving partners resigned, embittered, and feeling alone, pining for the lost intimacy of earlier days. This book is knowing, loving, and no-nonsense, challenging us to do what it takes to nurture our adult romantic love relationships. In a non-sentimental way, Stan says if you want your relationship to survive and thrive, it is in your self-interest to take care of your partner and learn how to interact when conflicts arise.

"This is for after the infatuation and early in love have gotten you in a serious relationship or marriage, when 'in love' turns into love and being in a committed relationship, and conflicts arrive and stay. Stan Tatkin is serious about the hard work needed and challenges us to give up our pet peeves (usually about our partners), look at ourselves, and together with our partner(s), do the hard work of the relationship.

"Stan Tatkin means business. This 'purpose-centered, action-oriented' book takes every imaginable typical conflict committed partners get into, analyzes them, breaks them down, and actually answers the question: Why is this happening? And then he concretely and in step-by-step detail describes 'the correction,' i.e., what to do—not what the partner must do, but what I must do, and what we must do.

"Follow these concrete, eminently understandable and doable steps, and you will have a solid relationship and a loving, grateful partner. Save the complaining about your partner for your friends. As a couple, roll up your sleeves and get to work. In it together, in each other's care, this is a wonderful, practical, no-nonsense resource for those serious about wanting their love relationship to endure."

DIANA FOSHA, PHD
developer of AEDP and editor of *Undoing Aloneness and the Transformation of Suffering into Flourishing*

"In *In Each Other's Care*, Stan Tatkin, with the voice of a brilliant, compassionate master therapist, deconstructs with clarity and insight how to repair the often-paradoxical vulnerabilities of relationships. Through poignant examples, we learn the power of presence and attention in recovering the important role of mutual safety in fostering the recovery of the shared trust that enables couples to co-regulate and their relationships to flourish. The message is brilliantly insightful—both partners must experience safety and trust in their relationship. Without this mutual trust, their ability to fulfill their biological imperative of connectedness will be compromised."

STEPHEN W. PORGES, PHD
distinguished university scientist, founding director of the Traumatic Stress
Research Consortium at the Kinsey Institute, Indiana University Bloomington,
and professor of psychiatry at University of North Carolina at Chapel Hill

"Since, as couples, we are 'in each other's care' and since, according to the author, we are all difficult to live with, it makes sense that we need a guide to help us take care of each other. And that is what Stan Tatkin, a relationship scholar and seasoned therapist, has provided. If you find yourself in one or several of the conflict scenarios he has provided, you have a ready-to-hand guide for its resolution. If you do not find yourself there, the solution process applies anyway, and we encourage you to use it. We recommend this book to all couples for achieving their optimal care of each other."

HARVILLE HENDRIX, PHD, AND HELEN LAKELLY HUNT, PHD
authors of *Getting the Love You Want*

"Dr. Stan Tatkin's brilliance as a practitioner is his ability to see past the 'content' couples present—the disagreements, slights, and intractable arguments—to diagnose the underlying dynamic: Are you a secure-functioning couple or not? And if not, why? In *In Each Other's Care*, Tatkin outlines how to both achieve and then concretize a commitment to being secure-functioning, and moves readers through typical scenarios that threaten relationships, like thirds (infidelity, illness, addiction, distancing), a tendency to act as a single (bullying, dominating, acting unilaterally), and avoidance. What he's ultimately offering are tools and scripts for redirecting all of us away from our desire to be 'right' back to the sanctity and health of our relationships, because by protecting each other, we are ultimately protecting ourselves. *In Each Other's Care* should be required reading for anyone who wants to build skill in love and intimacy and experience true interdependence with the person they've chosen to do life alongside."

ELISE LOEHNEN
author, host of the podcast *Pulling the Thread*, and former chief content officer of Goop

"If your partnership needs a visit to the repair shop, read this book. With Tatkin's wisdom and experience, your complaints may finally come to rest and you'll be laughing together again. People in happy partnerships live over five years longer. Tatkin may even extend your life!"

HELEN FISHER, PHD
author of *Anatomy of Love* and senior research fellow at the Kinsey Institute

"Inclusive, practical, and inspiring! Stan Tatkin is a master at his craft. *In Each Other's Care* has the recipes we need for effective repair, healing, and a happier life. This is a gift you will be genuinely thrilled to give to yourself and your relationship."

ELISHA GOLDSTEIN, PHD
psychologist and author of *Uncovering Happiness*

"The best question you will have after reading this book is: What will we do with the money we saved by not going to couples therapy? The second question you will ask is: How did Stan know he was talking to us? Stan has probably heard every marital problem on the planet. His knowledge, skills, and intuition will x-ray specific marriage problems and then go one better. You find solutions to specific problems and then function as a team to create loving resolutions. There is a lot of pain from unfulfilled dreams. But Stan gives you the escape hatch from that pain to an inspired future. I'm proud to recommend this marvelous book."

PETER PEARSON, PHD
cofounder of The Couples Institute and trainer of couple therapists in 63 countries

"To improve appearances, use a mirror. To improve relationships, use an expert guide. In this book, renowned couple therapist Stan Tatkin presents the essential principles and practices that enhance relationships. Want advice that is easy to understand and readily applicable? *In Each Other's Care* contains practical solutions to the problems that couples commonly encounter."

JEFFREY K. ZEIG, PHD
director of The Milton H. Erickson Foundation

"Good relationships require a lot of work. But what kind of work? What are the skills and tools required to successfully negotiate and sustain long-term love and commitment? This insightful and engaging book offers the insight and concrete direction required to keep intimate relationships vibrant and healthy. It is an essential guide designed to help couples gain mutual respect, acceptance, and shared appreciation. For those committed to deepening and expanding the love they share, this book offers tools and guidance toward doing just that."

ROBERT WEISS, PHD, LCSW
author of *Prodependence*

"*In Each Other's Care*, by Stan Tatkin, is the most comprehensive book for couples I've seen anywhere. It addresses numerous life dilemmas—money, kids, messiness, prenups, cheating, arguments, and more—with warmth and understanding, and offers readers practical suggestions and solutions to them.

"Couples wanting to 'get along' better, become more intimate, heal from slights or wounds, and develop better ways and skills at interacting will find it extremely useful. Tatkin is careful to ensure that each person in the couple feels safe and open.

"As a couple therapist working with a primarily LGBTQ clientele, I was particularly struck by this guide: most books on couples address heterosexual couples either mainly or exclusively, and Tatkin's work is designed for all couples, no matter how they identify. That, combined with the excellent, useful content, makes this book a significant contribution to the field."

RICK MILLER, LICSW
couple and family therapist specializing in LGBTQ-related issues

"Only an exceptionally skilled and experienced couple therapist could have written this book! Be sure to take this journey as Stan exposes all the many ways partners hurt and challenge one another. And then apply his lens to rise above these conflicts, prevent unnecessary pain, and create a loving and secure-functioning union."

ELLYN BADER, PHD
cofounder of The Couples Institute and co-creator of The Developmental Model of couples therapy

"Our expectations of love relationships are more demanding than at any time in history. If ever there was a manual for how to create and keep a successful, long-term, committed relationship that's sexual over time—this is it! With great precision and clarity about the psychobiological patterns that drive people in committed relationships, Tatkin illuminates an explicit and skillful approach that demands that all parties meet the conditions necessary to create a securely functioning relationship. *In Each Other's Care* is a love letter that should not be missed!"

ALEXANDRA KATEHAKIS, PHD
author of *Mirror of Intimacy*

"Stan Tatkin to the rescue! *In Each Other's Care* offers thoughtful solutions to the greatest hits of what brings couples to therapy. It's organized in a way that saves time and sanity: partners can go to the page where Stan explores whatever issue they are interested in and learn different ways to view it and handle it. It's an excellent resource for any couple looking for another tool to add to their secure-functioning arsenal."

KARA HOPPE, MFT
coauthor of *Baby Bomb*

"Stan Tatkin's new book, *In Each Other's Care*, does exactly what it says it will do—it teaches readers to care for their partner, even when it's seemingly impossible, like in those times when arguments and disagreements create a breach that seems too great. Tatkin shows us that when we turn toward our partner, and if we follow the cues, we can learn to take care of ourselves as well as the one we love. For anyone who has ever been in a relationship and knows the difficulties of making corrections after a conflict and how hard it is not to blame the other, this book shows us exactly how to repair even the biggest disputes and differences. In his most important book yet, the author brings his many years of experience with couples and his commitment to his own long-term relationship to show readers how we, too, can learn to grow closer to our partners. We see in each chapter common complaints we all experience and ways to turn things around to create the most desirable intimate and long-term connections. Everyone needs to read this book."

TAMMY NELSON, PHD
sex and relationship therapist, TEDx speaker, author of *Open Monogamy*, and host of *The Trouble with Sex* podcast

"This is the guide couples have been waiting for! *In Each Other's Care* feels like a warm, accessible, and personal conversation intent on saving us from a world of hurt, one couple at a time. Only a master clinician like Stan Tatkin could distill what is known about secure attachment, self-regulation, and the neuroscience of threat and safety, and offer it up in bite-size nuggets of truly useful wisdom for couples and therapists alike. Chock full of actionable steps to go from conflict and frustration to a secure two-person team, Stan Tatkin's latest gem has my highest recommendation for anyone seeking better relationships and a more secure-functioning society."

CHERYL ARUTT, PSYD
clinical and forensic psychologist and author of *Healing Together: A Program for Couples*

"We forget that creating secure relationships is like copiloting a plane. If one partner goes unconscious or acts erratically consistently, all passengers are in for a world of hurt. Stan covers almost every conceivable conflict situation with explicit scenarios that guide us out of everyday swamps. Transparency is crucial but unlikely if partners don't actively collaborate to reduce shame and fear. Stan teaches us how to satisfy mutual needs by reading bodily signals, listening keenly, and responding quickly.

"The only downside to reading this book is that you'll wish you'd read it sooner! I immediately used some of Stan's suggestions with my psychotherapy clients and my husband. I love Stan's passion for the highest quality relationships possible and his courage to tell us we'll have to work ceaselessly, take risks, and compromise to bring our shared plane to a safe landing."

SUSAN WARREN WARSHOW, LCSW
founder of DEFT Institute and author of *A Therapist's Handbook to Dissolve Shame and Defense*

In Each Other's
CARE

Also by Stan Tatkin

What Every Therapist Ought to Know:
Attachment, Arousal Regulation, and Clinical
Techniques in Couple Therapy (audiobook)

We Do:
Saying Yes to a Relationship of Depth, True
Connection, and Enduring Love

Your Brain on Love:
The Neurobiology of Healthy Relationships (audiobook)

Wired for Love:
How Understanding Your Partner's Brain and Attachment Style
Can Help You Defuse Conflict and Build a Secure Relationship

The Relationship Rx:
Insights and Practices to Overcome Chronic
Fighting and Return to Love (audiobook)

Baby Bomb:
A Relationship Survival Guide for New Parents (with Kara Hoppe)

Love and War in Intimate Relationships:
Connection, Disconnection, and Mutual Regulation
in Couple Therapy (with Marion Solomon)

In Each Other's
CARE

A Guide to the Most Common
Relationship Conflicts and
How to Work Through Them

Stan Tatkin

BOULDER, COLORADO

Sounds True
Boulder, CO 80306

Published 2023

Book design by Meredith Jarrett
Illustrations by Lin Chen

Printed in Canada

BK05050

Library of Congress Cataloging-in-Publication Data

Names: Tatkin, Stan, author.
Title: In each other's care : a guide to the most common relationship
   conflicts and how to work through them / Stan Tatkin.
Description: Boulder, CO : Sounds True, 2023. | Includes bibliographical
   references and index.
Identifiers: LCCN 2022030204 (print) | LCCN 2022030205 (ebook) | ISBN
   9781622039012 (hardcover) | ISBN 9781622039029 (ebook)
Subjects: LCSH: Interpersonal relations. | Couples—Psychology.
Classification: LCC HM1106 .T358 2023 (print) | LCC HM1106 (ebook) | DDC
   158.2—dc23/eng/20220922
LC record available at https://lccn.loc.gov/2022030204
LC ebook record available at https://lccn.loc.gov/2022030205

10 9 8 7 6 5 4 3 2 1

FSC
www.fsc.org
MIX
Paper from
responsible sources
FSC® C016245

This book is dedicated to all the couples who have enriched my life and have taught me to be a better clinician, better partner, and better father.

And to my primary inspiration as my lifelong partner in all things, Dr. Tracey Boldemann-Tatkin.

Contents

Introduction

Why We Are in Each Other's Care

PACT began with one simple shift in thinking: in couple therapy, partners are in each other's care and not simply in their own. The basis for this is psychobiological. The human primate is the only species we know of that excels at interactive regulation, particularly in close proximity. It's easier for us to read each other in the moment than it is to read ourselves.

Stan Tatkin
developer of A Psychobiological Approach to Couples Therapy® (PACT)

The central concept of my work with couples is that human beings are, by nature, dependent creatures who group together, unite, for interdependent purposes. This book for couples bears that out. When we join a union, an alliance, a troupe, or a team, we should each share a common purpose, vision, and culture as equal investors in whatever that shared purpose, vision, and culture is to be. Only unions in which members are governed by autocrats, dictators and slave owners must forego their interests for that of another.

The human primate is a selfish animal. Unless an individual mutual stake in a union with others, they will surely take of opportunities to serve self-interests. That's not evil, will nat- Unless people orient toward being in each other's ers and act urally revert to ideas of self-care to the exclusion ings to gain accordingly. Our interdependency—having th f fair play, jus- and the same things to lose—is our greatest tice, and sensitivity to one another.

Get ready to examine the specific complaints I commonly hear in my couple clinics, particularly in the United States. In the course of this book, you and your partner will discover how arguments get triggered, why they keep happening, and what you really can do to get better at communicating what you want without the drama. Even the seemingly simple changes require a willingness from the both of you—open minds and hearts and a commitment to heal your relationship—as I offer my perspective as a couple therapist on injury and repair. If your goal is to work on preventing the blistering arguments that boil over and burn, you've opened the right book.

In my previous books, I wrote extensively about attachment, developmental neuroscience, and secure functioning. Think of this book as more of a hands-on repair manual. Unlike my other relationship books, this one gets into the common complaints partners level against each other. If you don't find your exact complaint here, you'll likely find one related or adjacent to it that will satisfy you. I'm excited about this project as it's radically different from my earlier writings. Rather than reiterate what I've already said, this format allows you to look through specific areas of conflict that most couples will encounter at some point in time. You can read it from cover to cover, scan for what interests you, or use the index to find keywords that match your curiosities.

The complaints in section 2 contain various scenarios that I have heard in my couple clinic. I have been careful to mask gender, location, ethnicity, religion, race, and other identifiers that may distract from the focus of this book, which is two-person interdependent relationships that are romantically oriented. Therefore, we focus on the similarities between human primates and not their differences.

Though you will notice cultural references throughout this book, I believe a good amount of what you'll read will apply to you regardless of your cultural heritage, ethnicity, race, gender identity, sexual orientation, or religion. Differences aside, complaints come in all shapes. Yet, within romantic partnerships, couples tend to share what I call a limited variety of problems. Reassuring or not, that's what I can see as a couple therapist from thirty thousand feet.

You might view your relationship troubles in terms of subject matter, such as money, timeliness, messiness, sexuality, and children—or other issues, such as conflicting interests, religious diversities, political disparities, financial quandaries, and stepfamily challenges. Details will vary, but I believe you will begin to see those details, like the complaints themselves, reappear and repeat in most if not all subjects.

If you're new to my work, I encourage you to read *Wired for Love* and/ or *We Do* before embarking on this one, as both provide much of the background information you might need to make the best use of this book.

An Important Note about Primary Partners

Secure functioning, a term used throughout this book, refers to any system where primary partners exist. Primary partners are not limited to twosomes but can include three or more adult individuals engaged in a committed relationship. Note that I say "adult individuals" to mean that primary partners do not include children or those unable to operate with full autonomy and ability to fully consent.

Secure functioning can include consensual, ethical nonmonogamy of any kind, be it an open relationship, swinging, polyamorous relationship, or any other configuration that involves primaries who are engaged with secure-functioning principles of equal power and authority, parity, collaboration, cooperation, justice, fairness, and mutual sensitivity. Full stop.

This book is purposely written to be gender-neutral, and it focuses on a two-person system, also known as a dyadic system, of adults, be they gay, straight, nongendered, or trans. I want to make this abundantly clear to readers of various sensitivities regarding inclusion, as most relationship books do not make clear that relationships come in a great many forms and configurations and have since our species began.

This is a vital message to the reader as this book frequently mentions couples, obviously referring to a two-person system. I did not include examples of three-or-more-person systems in this book. However, those readers who are in ethical, consensual nonmonogamous relationships will be able to take principles of secure functioning and apply them to a multiple-person system. Please enjoy the words here in the spirit with which they are intended and bend them to your particular situation, as I believe they will apply if you wish them to.

Structure of Chapters

Since this is a repair manual, I have organized the chapters according to common complaints partners bring to couple sessions. Each chapter contains the following sections relating to its particular complaints:

- The Complaint in Action
- Why Does This Keep Happening?
- The Central Culprit: The Interaction
- Corrections
- Variations of This Complaint

You can also make liberal use of the book's back matter, including references and an index for searching ideas that may not be in the table of contents.

The Complaint in Action

This section illustrates the dialogue between partners about the complaint. To simplify matters around gender identity, race, ethnicity, age, or other identifiers, partners are labeled as Partner A and Partner B. Some of the complaints may appear to describe one's education level, socio-economic status, or other identifier. Not all identifying elements are intentional.

Why Does This Keep Happening?

Here I attempt to explain why this complaint repeats and can feel like an endless battle. My aim is to help you recognize this repetition when it occurs around similar complaints.

The Central Culprit: The Interaction

In this important section, I break down the couple's inter-action as presented in the "Complaint in Action" segment. My premise in this book is that unskilled interactions repeated and unrepaired during stressful moments are a principal cause of mutual dysregulation, dissatisfaction, threat inflammation, resentment, and avoidance in all relationships. How complaints become conflicts should interest everyone since the point of this book isn't really complaints, subject matters, or areas of importance. I have come to recognize—over many years of studying my own and other relationships—that microaggressions expressed and perceived during stressful interpersonal interactions are a leading cause of coregulatory dysfunction in couples and eventual relationship disso-lution. Poor interactions, therefore, are a central culprit.

Corrections

In this section, I clarify ways in which the interaction could go that would make it more successful. These corrections should serve as examples for all similar inter-actions when partners are under stress.

Variations of This Complaint

I've attempted to cover as many variations of the com-plaint as possible without repeating or overstating a point. I welcome you to apply your own variations to the ones provided and use the same guiding principles. If I've missed yours, look at a similar complaint or see if your concern is addressed in other chapters.

Secure Functioning Defined

Secure functioning is a social contract between two individuals of equal power and authority to remain fair, just, and sensitive at all times, while also remaining fully collaborative and cooperative. As such, secure-functioning individuals orient themselves toward a *two-person psychology*, whereby they are fully autonomous, differentiated people entering a relationship of inter-dependence—two people with a shared sense of purpose and vision for the future and a shared stake in all things. Their main purpose is to survive and thrive as a couple and as individuals.

Secure-functioning partners are tied together and their fates are shared. They move in lockstep through a variety of means that ensure well-informed, good outcomes for both. Partners bargain, negotiate, reason, influence, and otherwise seduce each other to win-win results. They work together as a team, not as solo players.

These couples understand that they are in each other's care and not simply their own. The partners take care of each other and themselves at the same time, rarely sacrificing one for the other. Secure partners tend to put their relationship first above all other things because the relationship is an energy source for all other things. If the relationship is not in good order, nothing else functions well. The couple's oxygen masks go on first, then they tend to everybody else. They are in charge of each other and everyone else. Two bosses, two generals, two monarchs, two executives, two governors, two legislators, two enforcers, two leaders; neither of them is simply a passenger, follower, or domestic.

Secure functioning assumes symmetry, conditionality, and terms for unionizing. Two strangers coming together for purposes beyond feelings and emotions, physical attraction, or other fleeting factors beyond human control. Their terms are measurable, and their behavior is guided by agreed-upon principles that govern both of them.

Principles of governance contain actionable behaviors and attitudes that ensure mutual protection of safety and security, love and affection, growth and potential, health and well-being, and any other good they both can envision. These principles are mutual justifications for limiting and pushing each other as partners to do the right thing (as agreed upon) when the right thing is the hardest thing to do.

Compared to insecure-functioning partners, secure-functioning partners get things done. They work out big life problems and little daily frustrations quickly and keep interpersonal stress to an absolute minimum. They are happier—more adaptive, flexible, creative, friendly, and healthy. They even look younger due to reduced allostatic load (Brooks 2012; Entringer and Epel 2020; Guidi et al 2021; Saxbe et al 2020).

Agreements and Guardrails

Agreements are to secure-functioning relationships what beams and supports are to a house structure. Without agreements—which are based on shared interests—a relationship, like a house, won't hold up. The better the agreements, the stronger the structure in good weather and bad. In order to make a pact or agreement, both parties have to articulate their personal reasons for getting on board. It must be good for both parties or the agreement is worthless.

All free unions consist of what we must do and what we must never do—so say we all. In couples it's simpler because it's so say we both. An agreement is a guardrail, or something I further define below as a shared principle of governance; that is, a way to govern each other whenever necessary.

Agreements can inhibit behavior or produce behavior, depending on the purpose or principle the couple wants installed. Where are we going to set the bar for this or that purpose or shared vision? Say that we never want to threaten to end the relationship and we both agree, after much discussion, that it is in our mutual best interest to abstain from using that cudgel to correct behavior or get what we want. Threatening the relationship has too many downsides. It creates an existential crisis, for one. For another, it threatens abandonment, so it becomes a whip that frightens and bullies another into submission and therefore leads to resentment, threat memory, and other bad consequences that will blow back and forth. And it has terrible downstream effects that make repair difficult. So, we decide to take that option off the table, which means we'll have to correct behavior in some other way.

In order for this to work, both parties must agree that threatening to end the relationship is to be avoided, and both must have personal stakes in its prevention. If either is unsure or still thinks it can or should be used if deemed necessary, the agreement should be nullified. It will be impossible to enforce.

Here's another example. Why be monogamous or polyamorous or have an open relationship? I don't personally care if partners agree fully with any of these arrangements. But they *must* agree and agree properly. Whatever their preference, partners must have both personal and mutual reasons for making the social contract. Both partners must be thoughtful, thorough, and honest. Each must consider conditions, long-term effects, downsides, and upsides. The agreement—all agreements—must be explicit, declarative, and without any room for misinterpretation or ambiguity.

Keep in mind that a couple's cocreated culture, structure, and guardrails maintain ease, peace, well-being, and safety. The sculpting of these lifesaving features requires full collaboration and cooperation by both parties. Cooperation will only occur if partners have a personal stake in the agreements they make.

If an agreement serves only one party, it won't work. It must serve both partners' interests to a high degree, or it's a waste of time and effort and enforcement *will* fail.

My wife, Tracey, and I choose monogamy. I have a personal reason to be monogamous. I decided that I want to experience one person deeply. Same with my career. I decided I wanted to study couples exclusively. Previously, my interests were too scattered. I found late in life that focusing on *one* thing allowed me to intensify both my understanding of myself and that "one thing." Chasing novelty proved both exhausting and fruitless. I learned to find novelty in the familiar, the extraordinary in the ordinary.

Mine was a personal pursuit of depth over coverage, discipline over impulse, and profound appreciation of the tricks my mind constantly plays to convince me I must run from or to something because the present moment may seem unsatisfactory. I know my mind is constantly comparing and contrasting, is always aware of what's missing and what I don't have, and my own fears and negativism relentlessly seek relief. Like everyone else, I'm addicted to my own thinking and feeling and can easily get trapped in my own mental movie. Don't get me wrong; I still do very stupid things, but far fewer as I become more purpose centered.

Nonmonogamy wouldn't work for me, not because I could get caught or because it would hurt Tracey or because someone else said it was wrong, but because I would let *myself* down if I broke the agreement. I would no longer be who I said I was. I would betray myself.

To violate the agreement would be to self-harm. *And*, it would violate my vow to keep Tracey safe and secure.

I use my own example here as a demonstration of what I mean by personal stake. I make agreements that serve my own interests as well as my partner's. A purpose or principle is, for me, different from a rule or law. The latter is usually created by a small or very large group and leads to a *dominant end*—such as to obey the law, to serve God, or to be loyal to a group or cause. Serving a principle or purpose is more personal and often leads to a relative end, which is more painstakingly considered and reflected upon than absolute (Kohlberg and Ryncarz 1990).

When making agreements, be certain the two of you first look to where you agree. Partners too often focus on where they disagree and how they are different from each other. That is a mistake. Find where you agree first and then work your way down.

For instance, do we both want to feel loved, valued, wanted, cherished, chosen, appreciated, respected? If the answer is yes, then go further. How often do we want to feel that way? Perhaps it's every day. Good. How do we wish to be treated in order to feel those things? (Feelings are never guaranteed, by the way.) We're different people so we may want to be treated differently. No problem. That can be arranged.

Now, under what conditions should these actions take place? Remember, we are constructing a purpose-centered, action-oriented vision for cocreating an experience for us both. Be careful when discussing conditions. If the conditions are feeling-centered, your results will suffer. Therefore, the answer to the question of whether we do these things that lead to the other's experience of feeling loved, valued, wanted, cherished, chosen, appreciated, and respected every day regardless of how we feel should be yes. If it isn't, the agreement is not purpose-centered.

When purpose-centered, we focus on what must be done whether or not we feel like it. Why? Because we've decided it is the best thing we can do even when the best thing is the hardest to do. That's awesome! That's setting the bar high, and you will now get the best. Pay to play, remember? Pay to play. Set the bar low and you will get exactly what you paid for.

Consider the following for each of your purpose-centered agreements:

- Where do you both agree? If you get stuck, move up a level to where you can agree (i.e., "I want apples, and you want oranges, but we both want fruit").

- What are your and your partner's personal and mutual reasons for wanting this? You both must have them (i.e., you both need to be pointing in the same direction), or it won't work.

- "Why do you want this for yourself?" Clarify the want fully when asking each other this question.

- How do you want to manifest it behaviorally? Only purpose and behavior protect and produce feeling and experience, not the other way around.

- What are the conditions under which these behaviors must happen? Do not use feelings or state of mind as a condition.

- What, if any, downsides are there to this agreement?

- What, if any, bad downstream effects could occur as a result of this agreement?

- If either of you should fail to follow through on the agreement, what guardrails will you put in place to enforce it so that the agreement holds? My recommendation for a guardrail is a prompt, reminder, or cue if either partner should forget or misstep. The forgetful or misstepping partner *must* immediately apologize, yield, and cooperate without delay, defense, or explanation. This *will* work, but only if the other fully cooperates.

The stakes are very high. Impulsive, reflexive, or forgetful misbehavior is okay. However, pushback or resistance when cued or prompted is a serious matter as it represents a breach of trust and is evidence that this partner will not be governed by their own or anyone else's principles. That amounts to a fatal error in judgment and therefore is insecure functioning to a T. This now becomes a safety issue.

To avoid this disastrous outcome, make your agreements thoughtfully, thoroughly, and with certainty. Faulty agreements cause the most problems with follow-through and enforcement.

Shared Purpose, Shared Vision, and Shared Principles of Governance

My friends, most love relationships do not last exceptionally long. There are a good many reasons for this. Let's start at the very top with a lack of shared purpose, vision, and principles of governance. The following material refers only to human unions among freethinking, independent adults in a conditions-based volunteered venture. It does not apply to dictatorships, master-slave arrangements, or parent-child relationships.

Shared Purpose

Shared purpose is your foundational "together" statement; the oath you create together and live by each day. Without a shared purpose between united humans, there is nothing to hold people together over time, particularly hard times. Review these examples with your partner. As you read this book, work together to create a shared purpose for your relationship.

> *Together we survive and thrive in this life.*
>
> *Together we stand in all things and against all odds.*
>
> *Together we share all burdens and all bounties.*
>
> *Together we lead each other and everyone in our care.*

Shared Vision

Shared vision comprises the highest actions you agree to take together. Without a shared vision pointing them in the same direction, people will go off in their own directions. Along with your shared purpose, think about how you want to craft the shared vision for your relationship. Use these examples to get started on your own:

> *Our vision is to remain in love, grow as individuals, do good things, and leave the world a better place.*

Our vision is to raise our children to be good citizens and empathic human beings who are self-respecting, earnest, morally straight, ethically unimpeachable, resilient, and loving.

Our vision is to serve one another and to establish each other's ongoing felt sense of safety and security, happiness and well-being.

Our vision is to be a secure-functioning couple.

Shared Principles of Governance

Shared principles of governance (SPGs) are the unbreakable "we" agreements that protect each of you and the essence of your relationship. Without shared principles by which to govern people in union, there is unfairness, injustice, social insensitivity, and misbehavior along with a lack of accountability, safety, security, and prosperity in that union. Here are a few SPGs to help you craft the shared principles for your relationship:

We have each other's backs at all times, without exception.

We repair, correct, fix, or make amends without explanation, condition, excuse, or defense when the other experiences hurt, misunderstanding, or any other injury—and we do so within one hour without exception.

We make all decisions that would affect each other together by getting each other fully on board before acting.

We protect each other's interests in public and private at all times.

We do loving, romantic, and affectionate deeds for each other throughout every day without exception.

We consider our own interests, concerns, and troubles as we consider the other's interests, concerns, and troubles, and we do so simultaneously.

When working together on SPGs, come up with big-ticket items that cover large swaths of what you both wish to protect or promote. For instance, if you're thinking of adding, "We never lie to each other about money spent," consider expanding that agreement to cover every facet of your life by stating, "We are fully transparent, truthful, and forthcoming with each other." Why think small when you can think big? Bigger is better because it covers more ground.

The Rules of Shared Principles of Governance:

- Start each item with the word "We."

- Avoid using emotions, feelings, vague language, or other nonactionable, measurable qualifications. Remember, you cannot legislate thoughts, feelings, moods, attitudes, or other results you cannot directly control by will alone.

- Keep it short and simple enough for a five-year-old to understand.

- You both must fully buy into the shared principle and be able to defend why it is a good idea *personally* before arguing why it is a good idea *mutually*. If a partner cannot defend how this or that principle pays off personally—having nothing to do with the other person—the principle will not hold when it becomes most necessary.

- Consider your principles *perfect* and *incontrovertible* but yourself as neither. Principles, once they are in place and fully agreed upon, shall no longer be debated unless later amended by both partners. If a partner fails to meet an SPG, the only option open to them is to make amends and make it right. In other words, beg for forgiveness and fix it stat! SPGs make relationships easier as everyone knows what they can and cannot do in order to keep the relationship securely functioning. SPGs also allow partners to enforce limits on each other (we don't do that) or promote gains with each other (we must do this).

- Each principle is met regardless of mood, attitude, feelings, desire, or any other mitigating factor people use to avoid doing what is best over what is convenient or in line with how they feel. This makes life together much easier, safer, and more secure. Without SPGs, you and your partner are risking your relationship in the Wild West, where anything goes.

- If you both find yourself in the weeds, battling over a principle and seemingly unable to agree, move up a level and think through something bigger and more overarching. For example, if you and I are arguing over whether we should eat bananas or grapes and we cannot agree, we can go up a level and ask, "Should we eat fruit? Would that be a good idea?" Perhaps we will agree there.

- When working on SPGs, consider your roles as policy makers. If you begin to work on each other instead of the policy, you have gone off track and off task. If you fail to complete a policy and find that there are several issues now on the table, you both have again gone off task. Your jobs are to get something done. Create policies that provide protection and gains for you both. These principles or policies constitute your relationship character, ethics, and culture. What do we stand for? If we have children, what do we want to show and not simply tell about relationship, communication, humility, respect, honesty, shared power, conflict resolution, making amends, character, and reliability?

We humans either forget or do not know that nature does not care about relationships—at all. We care, especially now that we live longer than fifteen years. In the incredibly old days, it did not matter that we died early, even if it was by killing each other. Nature drives us to replenish the species through procreation. What we do after that is our business—and problem. Nature is indifferent; we are not. Nature repeats itself; we often elect to change, if even only a little.

Unless we are in an enriched environment where we can learn and grow socially-emotionally, we are going to do as we know, and what we know is what we've experienced thus far. Full stop. Suffering sometimes leads to insight, self-reflection, learning, and growth in the social-emotional realm. For instance, the shattering experience of divorce can sometimes lead one to learn and grow through regret. That person may start on a path toward greater self-awareness and discovery that may never have been kindled if not for suffering loss. While some will learn much, others will learn nothing, regret nothing, and never benefit from their suffering. Unfortunately, even many of those who bask in an enriched social-emotional environment learn nothing and, as a result, see no reason to change.

Some of us are limited by personality, psychobiological development, and neurobiological functioning. Some of us are limited by early trauma, leading to brain and body changes that hold us hostage to our own adaptations to a dangerous world.

Having said all this, I do believe that despite our limitations we can get along with others if we share purpose, vision, and guardrails that bring out our inner angels and harness our inner devils. Human history has continually proven this to be true. We call this possibility of getting along, surviving, and prospering together with all our differences *civilization*.

Section One

What You Need to Know

Chapter 1

The Problem of Being Human
(A.K.A. We Are All Pains in the Ass)

L et me start here with a heads-up that I repeat myself throughout this book, and that repetition is entirely purposeful. The
concepts in the book, though simple and straightforward,
are incredibly difficult to metabolize and implement. Repetition is
the only way we learn what we may already know in some measure
but don't understand enough to put into regular play. That is called
vertical learning. Psychotherapy is vertical learning. It's a process of
repetition that deepens your understanding of yourself as well as
the complexities in your life and how to integrate other people into
it. Although the information itself is not *new*, through repetition,
what you know or think you know becomes more useable rather
than simply an idea in your head that goes, *Oh yeah*, and is forgotten
about a minute later. You may not believe it now but you *need* the
repetition in this book to make it as valuable as I believe it will be for
you and your partnership.

Before we launch into the various complaints listed in this book, we need to understand a few points about communication, memory, and perception. Let us start first with communication.

Communication

Human communication, even on a good day, is really terrible. It really is. We misunderstand each other much of the time.

Do you really know whether your partner understands what you are saying? Does your partner get the nuances or understand the purpose of the words you are using? Do you think they know exactly how you feel about your words or the meaning of the words? When you're listening to someone, do you think you really understand them? Do you understand their mind? Their context? More often than not, you are approximating each other. You're getting close.

Most of our communication is implicit, nonverbal. Our verbal communication, which we all love and adore and depend on, is really the culprit. It gets us into a lot of trouble.

When you were dating, I'm sure you were much more careful about the words you used. How careful are you now? Many couples grow sloppy with each other in terms of their verbal communication. They take shortcuts because they think they know each other.

You're probably taking a lot of shortcuts, assuming your partner understands the meaning of your words, and you're getting into trouble. Do you even have each other's attention when you are communicating? Many times, you don't. You both are busy, you are moving, and your lives are only getting busier. And then you find yourselves saying, as many couples do, "Oh, it's my partner's problem. They're not listening." Right?

When it comes to communication, you both must take responsibility for making sure that your speech is clear and understood by the other person. As you will read in this section, just because you say something, doesn't mean your partner is translating it as you intend. Here's an example:

Partner A I want more intimacy in our relationship.
Partner B I want that, too!

The problem here is that to Partner A *intimacy* means "more sex." Partner B, on the other hand, thinks that agreeing to intimacy will mean more interpersonal talk. What is more is that *sex* actually means "only intercourse," and *interpersonal talk* specifically means "more questions about how I'm doing." That is how we talk to each other—as if the other person knows *exactly* what we mean. Much of the time, *we* don't even know exactly what we mean.

Remember the good old days (of course you don't) when speech was simpler? We would just say, "Duck!" or "Eat!" or "Sleep!" or "Run!" or "Lion!" Fast forward to today's linguistic complexities and consider for a moment all the nuances in our talk, all the lingo, all the changing meanings for regular words. Take the word *sick*, for example. Today it could mean physically ill, mentally ill, disgusting, or amazing. And the language couples use with each other can seem even more confusing. "I want to know you deeply" could mean many different things. "I want you to show me your soul" could make a person's head spin. "I want you to say what you really feel" can, for some, seem like a trick or an insurmountable task. We use a great many words and phrases that mean a great many things, none of which partners clarify with each other. This is a terrific error.

The human brain is always trying to conserve energy; it does as little as possible until it must. Most people, particularly partners, will treat clarification as unnecessary and, in fact, frustrating. "You should know what I mean," a partner might say. "My meaning is obvious." Or, "Everyone knows what that means." Both speaker and listener feel persecuted by the chasm between meaning and understanding. Minds misattune, which leads to heightened arousal (faster heartbeat, higher blood pressure), which leads to threat perception, which leads to fight, flight, or freeze.

Rinse and repeat.

Grice's Maxims and Miller's Law

If you are done with all that and ready to practice a new approach so the need for repair turns out to be less and less frequent, absorb and remember these few potent drops of science and wisdom from Paul Grice and George Miller:

Paul Grice, a British philosopher, is best known for his maxims of cooperative speech. **Grice's maxims assert that a speaker, who has a** listener, must talk in a manner that is fully cooperative with their audience. The speaker must remain true to the maxims of *quality, quantity, manner, and relevance*. Any other approach would be considered uncooperative and noncollaborative (Grice 1996).

For instance, for a speaker-partner to use words, phrases, or names that are unfamiliar, obscure, or ambiguous to their listener would violate maxims of quality and manner. A speaker-partner who is saying too much or too little, or providing too much or too little information, would be violating the maxim of quantity. When a speaker-partner provides too little information for which there is no evidence and which makes them seem to be withholding, misleading, or otherwise deceiving, they would be violating the maxim of quality. And, when a speaker-partner's narrative turns tangential, goes off topic, or in any way loses the listener's train of thought, that partner is violating the maxim of relevance.

George Miller, a professor of psychology at Princeton and one of the founders of cognitive psychology and psycholinguistics, believed the listener could radically change the way people get along. **Miller's law instructs us to suspend judgment about what someone is saying so that we can first understand them without infusing their meaning with our own personal interpretations. Miller's law states "that in order to understand what someone is telling you, it is necessary for you to assume the person is being truthful, then imagine what could be true about it"** (Miller and Isard 1963).

Please memorize both Grice's maxims and Miller's law. Hold to these two valuable guides for collaborative and cooperative speech and listening, and you will remain at peace, get a lot accomplished, protect your relationship's safety and security system, and likely promote love, affection, appreciation, and respect.

Check and Recheck

The brain relies on memory, speed, and energy conservation for ordinary tasks. Communication is considered ordinary when it comes to couples. The exception to this rule is when dating or courting. In the beginning, we are extremely cautious about our communication; more formal. We do not want to lose the gig, so we don't introduce risk by taking shortcuts, assuming the other knows what we're talking about or that they understand our meaning. Recklessness in the beginning can mean the end. All this changes once we *think* we know each other, become overly familiar, even familial, and start getting sloppy. We say things in shorthand, assuming the other hears and understands, or we act as if we heard and understood. Neither of us is checking and rechecking on either the listener's or the speaker's side.

In my clinical experience as a couple therapist, this type of carelessness in communication is the most common error of all. Partners will disregard the fact that they are mostly misunderstanding each other much of the time without realizing it. They will also take for granted the complexity and error potential of verbal and nonverbal communication and will blame each other for their mutually imposed malfeasance.

This common and frankly annoying error is easily avoidable by returning to the formality likely present at the beginning of the relationship. Check in with simple, nonthreatening questions or requests:

- "Are you saying . . . ?"
- "I want your eyes because this is important . . ."
- "Let me make sure I understand . . ."
- "Say back what you heard . . ."
- "Let me repeat that."
- "What do you think I meant by . . . ?"
- "We may not be talking about the same thing. Are you saying . . . ?"

Checking and rechecking is *vital* to daily governance and the proper running of a two-person system. If you were two astronauts communicating out in space while tethered to the mothership, would you be incredibly careful with your communication? You bet you would. Your lives would be at stake. If you were two generals deciding a war plan, would you talk in shorthand or assume you were on the same page? If you did, people would die.

You are no different. If you and your partner continue to use shoddy communication to share information, your relationship will suffer badly. These errors, if repeated again and again, go right into your respective personal narratives about what's wrong with the other partner and why you're unhappy. Remember, our personal narratives form to protect our interests only and are almost always based on faulty data—like errors in communication!

Be orderly. Be precise. Be responsible. Be a two-person system.

Microcommunication

The following are examples of what we call microcommunications, which are quick explanations intended to fill in blanks that would otherwise be filled by the observing person's negatively biased brain.

I get up from a conversation to retrieve some object without telling my partner what I'm doing. This leaves the mystery up to my partner's brain to fill in the blank. Since I and my partner were born with brains having a negativity bias, my partner will now fill in the blank with a negative possibility, perceiving my behavior as being rude, inattentive, uncaring, disinterested, or bored, which I'll likely pay for later unless I close the communication gap.

"I'm still listening; I'm just grabbing my coffee," I say before I move. I have foreclosed on my partner's ability to fill in a blank by filling it in myself. No negative consequences.

My partner asks me a question, and I just sit there for a long spell without a peep. I've just allowed them to fill in the blank with something negative. That will come back to hurt me unless I quickly uncover what's going on internally.

"Hold on a second; I'm thinking," I say. My partner's anxiety and fantasies about my silence are forestalled because I filled in the blank. Nothing to come back to hurt me.

I get up from the bed after lovemaking without saying anything. My partner is free to make up any reason for this, and it's not going to be good.

"Honey, I'm just running to the bathroom; I'll be right back," I say and give my partner a kiss. This probably will go without incident.

I'm thinking about something disturbing while I look at my partner without saying anything. My partner predictively thinks I'm upset with them. I'm going to hear about it *right now* unless I catch the thread first.

"Honey, I was just thinking about something upsetting having nothing to do with you," I say, thus depriving my partner of any other idea. I may want to go further and say what I was thinking about. That would save time, wouldn't it?

Microcommunications are small but significant bridges in communication that make relationships safer, easier, and less likely to devolve into back-and-forths that waste valuable time and energy. I think it's also respectful, elegant, thoughtful, and considerate. But mostly, I believe it's smart! Leaving blank spaces for another to fill is simply self-harming.

Can you hear yourself? If nothing else, this section should convince you that your communication is ready for an overhaul. It is terrible, especially if you think it's terrific. If you are not using Grice's maxims and Miller's law, you are not connecting. If you're not checking and rechecking meaning and understanding, you're not doing well—and your partner's suffering, too. If you are not using microcommunications to close all gaps that could be filled in by your partner, you're not anywhere near good to go.

Now, about your sharp memory: that does not work as you might think, either. Often, you rely on your memory; you think it's correct, don't you? Think again.

Memory—State—Perception

We are memory animals. Just about everything we do throughout each day is memory based. That is how we conserve energy. If we did not do this, we would never get out of a corner of the room, for we would have to rediscover everything from scratch. Procedural memory is our automation blueprint for daily life and interaction. Our state of mind is linked to memory, and memories enhance our state of mind. When we feel happy, we tend to remember happy times. While feeling happy, remembering happy things, we act happy, look happy, and perceive others as happier. Our state of mind directly affects our perceptions, which affects our outward behavior toward others. We get positive feedback that further enhances our state of mind. And so, we're in a happy loop.

The same is true when we are unhappy. I'm in an unhappy state of mind. Perhaps I'm reminded of something that made me unhappy, and now my current state reflects that. I start perceiving through a lens of unhappiness, and my behavior follows in tow. I get feedback from the environment, and it amplifies my unhappy state. I start to perceive more unhappiness around me. Or, I perceive a disturbing dissonance between my own state of mind and that of others who seem happy, further driving me into my own unhappiness. And so, I'm in an unhappy loop.

My state of mind drives my memory, and my memory drives my state of mind. That is part of the loop. Additionally, my state of mind alters my perception like a funhouse mirror, distorting my seeing, hearing, smelling, tasting, and tactile experience. It's wild but true. Check it out for yourself.

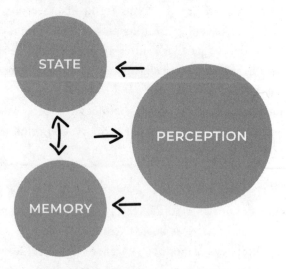

Figure 1. Memory—State—Perception

Memory

You're probably pretty sure about what you've remembered, and if your partner disagrees with you, they're wrong. If you both came into my office and started to argue about a memory, about what happened last week with whom, where, and in what sequence, I can pretty much guarantee you that you'd both be wrong.

How do I know this?

First, each person's experience is recorded differently, depending on their current states of mind and body. Your mental-emotional condition could be angry, sad, frightened, depressed, anxious, sleepy, agitated, drunk, or stoned, while your physical condition might be sleep deprived, hungry, fighting an illness, in pain, sitting, standing, or lying down. If you're particularly startled or frightened, your visual focus narrows, failing to notice and record various details and surrounding elements. The environment may also play a part in how you record the moment. In other words, the recording of experience is highly variable to begin with, and then you have memory and recall, which is all faulty.

Let's divide memory into three basic parts:

1. **Working memory** is very brief and dependent upon a resourced brain with certain structures that are able to operate properly and in concert with other structures.

2. **Short-term memory** is fairly volatile, variable, and subject to poor recording and recall. For example, under certain levels of stress, the hippocampus,[1] a brain structure important for retaining short-term memory, can become temporarily impaired. Such is the case when partners grow to be hyperaroused, in fight or flight, and dysregulated. Their ability to accurately recall these events is highly compromised, often with confusion around context, meaning, and sequence. During dysregulated events, blank spots in time appear in each partner's memory.

3. Then there's **long-term memory**, largely formed at nighttime during sleep. Memory traces are copied throughout the brain as your daytime experiences are processed, and your body repairs itself.

Now, memory does not operate like a video recorder. There is no exact replication of experience. Rather, memory fills in blanks and

---

1   In the movie *Memento* (2000), the main character suffers permanent short-term memory loss, likely due to a damaged hippocampus.

embellishes with emotion, context, and meaning. In other words, memory contains nonmemory elements each time an experience is recalled. What's more, our current mental-emotional state alters our memory recall and changes it each time. As far as anyone knows, the original memory is overwritten, so to speak, by the next recall.

Therefore, memory is plastic and influenced by the mind we have at the moment, just as the experience was recorded by the mind we had at that moment. If memory were, in fact, static and unchanging, psychoanalysis or any other process of learning about oneself and others would change nothing about our past. But this is untrue, as anyone who has gone through a process of increased understanding can attest.

As a person who initially claims little memory of their childhood progresses in psychotherapy, they will frequently begin to recall more and more people and events with increasing detail. The past is, therefore, changing as one's present changes. Same is true for couples who are on their last leg. They've accrued so many bad memories that the good ones become eclipsed. Even some of their good memories, such as how they met or their wedding day, take on a more negative cast. Conversely, couples who had a terrible start but are currently happy often recall their early catastrophic experiences as more positive and even humorous.

When I am angry with my partner, Tracey, I may begin to remember all the times I've been angry with her. When I feel in love with Tracey (99.9 percent of the time), I may begin to remember all the loving moments I've enjoyed with her. Memory and current state of mind are mutually influencing and reinforcing.

Let me say that once again because it is really important for you to . . . ah . . . remember: memory influences state, and state influences memory.

Perception

Are you with me so far? Remember what I just said to you? **Memory and state continuously influence each other, and state alters perception.** What does that mean, and why should you care?

Take my above example of when I'm angry with Tracey. If it's connected to a repeating experience, I will remember every time I've had that experience, including similar past non-Tracey experiences, and my angry state can increase. This angry state of mind alters my visual, auditory, kinesthetic, tactile, olfactory, and gustatory perception of Tracey in a manner that is consistent with that particular angry mental-emotional state. I may interpret her voice, her face, her touch, her words, her smell and, yes, even her taste through this distorted filter. It is as if my memory and sense perception are aligned with my internal experience of danger or safety.

Perception is wild, isn't it? Yet this is how we, as animals, roll, and failure to understand these aspects of the human condition can be disastrous for our relationships.

Automation

As I have said, the human brain conserves energy to avoid overtaxing the system. One of the brain's main energy-conserving features is *automation*. While our brains love novelty (and moving objects, as do cats), new experiences, though often delightful and exhilarating, are energy expending and therefore must soon be relegated to the "known." Learning to drive is exciting and anxiety producing, but our brains soon automate the procedures involved, meaning we cease to see them as novel, and we eventually become in danger of multitasking while driving. A vacation to a new and different land can be lots of fun, adventurous, and enlivening but also stressful and sometimes nerve-racking. Revisit the same place several times and the luster may diminish, as what was once novel transitions to the ordinary.

We automate everything, including our partners. Nothing anyone can do about this normal, absolutely gonna-happen neurobiological reality. What's new will soon become old. That's nature's way of saying, "Now that you know this, it's on to more novelty." What you know is easier and less energy-expending than what you don't know. It makes sense.

Yet in romantic relationships, this can be a real big problem. For one, automated partners will operate under the illusion that they actually know each other. They will naturally come to be less attentive, less present, less curious, less formal, less thoughtful, and much more reflexive and memory based. They become so familiar as to be family, and that's a big fat mistake.

The only remedy for automation is *presence* and *attention*. One finds novelty in the ordinary; the unknown in the known; the "strangerness" in the familiar other. This is a discipline that arises from an awareness that automation, while easy, is robotic, thoughtless, and deadening and leads us to feeling bored, disappointed, perplexed, and deprived of vitality. Automation is not living or experiencing, it's simply remembering through sensory-motor recognition systems that provide unconscious instruction for doing ordinary things.

Prompting Method

Because we are memory animals, most everything we do is by memory and blazing fast recognition systems in the brain. Throughout most days, we are incredibly unconscious; that is to say, we are operating routinely, reflexively, mindlessly. Therefore, we are going to do the same—sometimes stupid—things again and again. That is why it is foolish to tell your partner, "Don't do that again," or for the partner to say, "I'll never do that again." If you understand how our brain works, it is almost guaranteed that we will automatically repeat a reflexive behavior without thought.

This is where a two-person system comes in handy. We cannot remember much or even remain aware of much during our day-to-day lives. This is especially true when we are under the least bit of stress. So, partners must use the *prompting method*, whereby one partner prompts the other to remember to do or not to do something that has been automatic.

Here is the caveat: **the prompting method can only be used with prior agreement and permission by the offending partner.** For instance, if I do something that is annoying, hurtful, distracting, or threatening that my partner perceives as such, I acknowledge this causes her distress. Either I or she can say, "Do I have your permission to prompt you next time when you do that? And do you agree to yield immediately if I do?" Both parts are important, as she cannot feel relieved unless I get fully on board with this idea. If I say yes, then I *must* yield when prompted without pushback of any kind. I cannot complain (verbally or nonverbally), defend, attack, withdraw, or otherwise be difficult. After all, I will want my partner to do the same when I am bothered by one of her behaviors. Good for me, good for her.

This method absolutely works if both partners are fully on board and play by the rules without exception. Human beings are difficult, but nobody should want to be too difficult. A partner who agrees to be prompted and to yield (shift, change tone, lower voice, stop, go, hold, apologize) and then does *not* do so when prompted is now categorically *too difficult*. Not only that, but now they have a credibility problem. Can that person be trusted going forward? That's a legitimate concern for the betrayed partner.

So take this seriously. It is not a game. **The prompting method is the only way to stop or start problematic behavior without relying on memory. Additionally, the prompting method is how we learn new behaviors and train out old ones.** Partners literally train each other—by permission and agreement—to become better partners and, perhaps, people.

The following tool is a valuable one for using what did not work this time as a way to construct guardrails for dealing with the same problem next time.

Predict—Plan—Prepare—Revise (PePPeR)

If you really think about it, your partner is predictable (as are you). Are you actively predicting them ahead of time? This is not to be confused with anticipatory threat, whereby you fear your partner's reaction. That's a threat memory response and is definitely not your friend. Anticipatory threat will alter your behavior—your voice, movements, facial expressions, posture, and word choice—just enough to appear threatening to your partner. As such, that will not work, and that is not what I mean by predicting.

Predicting your partner means you know their vulnerabilities, fears, and concerns and what makes them feel happy, safe and secure, appreciated, respected, loved, and wanted. You are an expert on your partner—the animal you chose. You can *predict* what they are likely to do or say or how they will react in this moment or that moment. You have tried many strategies, and you've found several that work when your partner is in a particular state of mind.

You are your partner's whisperer. It's your job. Theirs, too. You *plan* your approach or your response in advance. You also plan for the worst and what you will do if it happens. You practice for it as you would for a job interview. You *prepare* the scene so that you have an edge, an advantage, because you know things your partner does not. You are going to use attraction—meaning skill, calm, clarity, kindness, affection, bargaining, persuasion, and seduction (not fear, threat, guilt, or shame)—to handle them. If your plan does not work, you revise your strategy and make changes for the next time.

PePPeR works and should be used by the two of you when thinking ahead about any potential challenge, event, or childrearing issue. Again, human beings are energy conserving and therefore do the least necessary, including predicting, planning, and preparing for the obvious. Do it and tell me it does not work.

Done and Next

One day I was watching Norman Lear being interviewed for his ninety-eighth birthday. When asked what his secret for happiness was, he said, "Know the difference between what's done and what's next. I put my mind on what's next."

To my "island" fellows—those who I have identified in previous books as distancing, dismissive, and avoidant—Lear's motto is not the same as "Forget about the past and only look forward." No. His advice is to take what was done and learn from it as you determine what should be next. In other words, the past is done, but if nothing is learned from the wreckage of the past, what's next will simply be a repetition of the past.

Secure-functioning couples focus on what's next and only on what's done if something needs to be learned and put in place for the next time. That is the smart way to deal with mistakes, injuries, misdeeds, and other offenses. The exception to this case may be substantial acts of betrayal. We will get to betrayals later in this book.

Too many couples become embroiled in the past by rehashing events, relitigating events, and remembering events to the point where they are in a loop they cannot exit or resolve. The loop again involves pesky memory and our attempts to sequence, contextualize, and factualize events that have already been relegated to personal narratives that have radically altered the original experience. Neither partner can actually claim their version is the correct one. It is a waste of time and energy and worse, it consolidates each partner's confirmation biases because the rehashing is inflammatory and adds to threat perception going forward.

The best way to handle the past is to fix it in the present. Both partners admit their part in the debacle, apologize, and scramble to find ways to prevent that event from recurring. The past is always present—there is no getting away from it. We change the past by changing the present and the future. Only new experiences can quell old memories, and those new experiences must be devoid of elements reminiscent of previous misdeeds or events.

Chapter 2

Threat Reduction

Threat perception is the single most underrated cause of relationship distress. Most people, including researchers, target sexual compatibility, finances, childrearing, gender roles, and affairs as leading causes of relationship dissatisfaction. However, a deeper cross-cultural and human element involving survival of the species is responsible for most conflict between individuals and groups.

As all animals possess an instinct to survive, the human primate is similarly organized on a very primitive level. The nervous system with its sensitive sensory-motor faculties and brain regions is dedicated to detecting possible threat or danger. Our nervous systems create continuous tension between our conscious, reasoning, and contingency-dependent brain areas and those primitive areas that will shoot first and ask questions later. In previous books, I have referred to these two generalized areas as *primitives* and *ambassadors* and get into the nuts and bolts of this particularly fascinating topic. Suffice it to say here, for this book's purpose, that human beings, like all animals, will resort to self-preserving impulses whenever their nervous system deems it necessary.

True, we've probably all met people with more heightened threat-perception responses than others. Many of those individuals have good reason. Since we humans are memory animals, we mostly operate every day according to blazing-fast recognition and procedural-memory systems that allow us to go about our daily routines. We are mainly automatic creatures. Memories of hurt feelings, danger, life threat, and other negative experiences encode more readily than pleasant experiences. The reason should be obvious: I must remember what to avoid, fight, or flee in the future for the sake of my survival.

Take Care of Yourself and Your Partner at the Same Time

Secure-functioning couples operate as a two-person psychological system; that is, they orient themselves as being in each other's care and view each other as mutual shareholders in their ongoing felt sense of safety and security. Therefore, how partners *interact with each other*, particularly when either is under stress, determines that felt sense of safety and security. Problems couples encounter that involve threat perception are centered on their interactions—facial expressions, physical movements, posturing, vocal volume and tone, word choices, and lack of immediate or quick relief.

Here's the thing: human beings can only be influenced while under conditions of safety. By that I mean, interpersonal safety. Scared, angry, or sad individuals can be influenced by others with whom they currently feel safe. If the person (or persons) attempting to persuade, convince, or influence is perceived as threatening, they don't have an audience. When partners are feeling unsafe or insecure, and nothing is done about that right away, no one shares or receives anything other than defensiveness.

Regardless of what makes us who we are—our culture, our history, our intelligence, our reasonableness—absolutely none of us will be understanding, generous, empathic, compassionate, or be able to give the benefit of doubt if we feel unsafe or insecure in the relationship in the present moment. When stressed or threatened, we produce glucocorticoids along with adrenalin as we move toward fight or flight.

Glucocorticoids affect several brain areas, including the prefrontal cortex and various limbic areas, altering our perception and our ability to think relativistically and remain friendly and loving (Belanoff, Gross, Yager, and Schatzberg 2001; Sapolsky 2017).

Insecure functioning involves individuals who orient as one person only, which is expressed by conveying personal interests only in the language of *me, my, I*. This will present as unfriendly and threatening to the other. For instance, I will talk and act like I care only about my concerns, fears, feelings, thoughts, wishes, and needs. As soon as I do, you get the message that you'd better do the same as I clearly do not have you in mind at all. Quickly we both square off, forced to defend ourselves, our honor, our reputation, our own needs and wants, and now we are adversaries. In essence, it's game over. We both walk away with nothing except more threat, frustration, and memory with which to kindle the next episode.

Remember the last blowout you and your partner had? While under the spell of a threatened state of mind, we remember all the other moments when we have felt similarly, and our perceptions are in lockstep with our feelings. Our strong tendency is to protect our interests at all costs. That is why partner skill is so very important. A partner, upon recognizing the other's state shift into unsafety or insecurity, must return their threatened partner to safety and security before doing anything else. We call that *leading with relief*, which is another way of saying, return your partner to a felt sense of safety and security or suffer the consequences of an altered mind that is prepared to fight or flee.

The best protection partners have against this typical human phenomenon is to orient as a two-person psychological system of taking care of self and other at (relatively) the same time. This means, I have to consider your interests, your fears and concerns, your experience of me, and your wants and needs before or close to considering my own. I have to express that I know you, I know myself and my behavioral effect on you, I know both what you fear and want, and I let you know that I do as I make my complaint, my request, or my point.

This idea of taking care of oneself and the other at the same time is nothing new. It's an essential tactic in all successful negotiations. If partners are to influence each other, persuade each other, understand each other, and then bargain or negotiate to get something accomplished, win-win orientation is the only path to success. Win-lose will never work in the long run. It's too unfair and therefore will result in the winner ultimately losing. A typical couple's road is littered with memories and resentment over unfairness. One-person orientations lead to unfairness, injustice, and insensitivity too much of the time. The couple eventually becomes burdened with attempts to square an unleveled field, a result that leads to frequent litigation and relitigation and a worsening safety and security system.

Remember, in order to win, you have to think of your partner and your partner has to think of you—always—when communicating, when reacting, and when interacting, or you both will end up losing.

Keep Your Eyes Where They Belong

Partners sometimes complain when I have them maintain continuous eye contact when interacting under stress. They have a tendency to interpret doing so as other than self-protective. Yet, maintenance of eye contact during stress or distress is vital to coregulation (a.k.a. interactive regulation) between two nervous systems. If you lose each other's eye contact, you will miss significant shifts in your partner's state of mind.

Every thought, feeling, sensation, fantasy, image, or impulse shows somewhere in the face or eyes. Interaction, particularly when stressed, is a fast-moving process. Drop the eyes and misattunement can quickly follow. Misattuned or mismatched moments commonly occur even when you're feeling good. These moments increase radically when you're not feeling good.

Like the rest of us, you make more errors in communication, perception, memory, and appraisal without realization. You can make more errors if you eliminate the visual field. Maintaining eye contact doesn't prevent errors, it just reduces them. Your eyes will quickly scan the mouth and the other's left eye automatically, checking words with other sensory inputs.

Because humans are primarily visually centered animals, we envision our partner even when not looking at them. Lower your eyes for too long and what are you looking at? Firstly, you're solely in your own heads and using areas of the brain for memory, imaging, anticipation, planning your next move, and interpreting. If you're angry, you're remembering similar moments of feeling angry, helpless, or threatened. The picture of your partner is static, fixed, and congruent with your current state of mind. But that's only on the inside. You and your partner are now cut off from the actual flow of data coming toward each other in the present moment. Think about the disrepair that has already happened in your relationship and what could happen in some future rapid, heated moment. Can we agree right here and now that neither of you needs or wants that—or any more of that?

As an observer of couples, I have used digital video frame analysis to study partners' macro- and microinteractions, and I now know how these mistakes occur and how common they are. Most people do not know this and therefore fight for their lives unnecessarily. During times of stress, people are fully automatic, reflexive, fast, and unaware of the real intentions of others. Nuances are nonexistent as are possible interpretations differentiated from one's instant appraisals based on immediate threat.

Keeping your eyes on each other just makes tactical sense. Dropping your eyes, gaze averting to think, or eye blocking (closing your eyes) simply puts you at a disadvantage. You're out of real-time tracking, and you're going to make errors.

I remember a regretful moment in my life when I was embattled with someone I loved. All I felt was anger, and I thought only anger was coming at me until I looked up to see only genuine sadness. But it was too late to shift. I'll never forget that moment. It taught me something about taking my eyes away.

Slow Down

The ambassadors, the expensive areas of our brain that error-correct sensory-emotional information, are slow and dependent on plentiful oxygen and glucose to run. If we get too excited or too sleepy, these areas become compromised. The neurobiology of fight-flight changes our brain and body chemistry along with where blood flows. Under conditions of threat, the ambassadors are starved of sufficient oxygen and glucose to run properly as energy shifts to striated muscles in the body to ready it for action. Makes sense, right? Time for action, not for thinking. However, even if we are not in a full fight-flight neuroendocrine state of being, simply going too fast will also compromise ambassador function. These areas are not nearly as fast as primitive brain areas. The faster we talk, move, act, or respond, the more automatic and reflexive we become. Our error rates begin to soar.

When interacting with each other under stressful conditions, going too fast can be disastrous. I see and hear it all the time. Some partners are really fast naturally. Some enjoy being fast and nimble. Like fast or not, fast equals high error rate. That means lots of misunderstanding, miscommunication, rising heart beats, rising blood pressure, and fights.

While it is true that partners should move quickly in their back-and-forths while under stress, that does not mean talking fast or stepping on each other's lines or failing to hold and wait your turn. **Moving quickly means to stay on message, be concise and to the point, take care of yourself and your partner, and aim for mutual relief as quickly as possible—for now.** Fast may feel good, but it will mostly likely end badly.

Make Amends, Amends, Amends

Many a war, lawsuit, and divorce could have been avoided had folks just made amends—apologized for their part and demonstrated restitution or reparation. Families could still be intact, friends could still be friends, and partners could restore faith and trust in each other. Yet, when I interview most people, they are hard-pressed to remember either parent fully repairing with them before the age of twelve. There were a lot of things wrong with my immediate family—in my opinion—but lack of repair was never one of them. In our family, if a beloved relationship was breached in some way, that rupture caused personal anguish, which led to making some kind of amends.

There are no perfect people, no perfect relationships—only perfectly imperfect people and relationships. Repairing, making amends, and making things right *is* love! Perfect is *not* love. Relationship-oriented people put relationship before self and thus bow to the gods that make human relationships possible. In other words, we strive to make things right between us, not to make ourselves right. **Of all the human relational mistakes, the refusal to put our relationships first above ourselves is one of our greatest failings.** To win the battle of righteousness is to lose so much more. When I see this happening with others, it breaks my heart. Of course, when I'm in the middle of my own righteousness . . . well . . . that's quite another thing. I'm as stubborn and prideful as most others. Nonetheless, that pridefulness is short-lived for me. Painful as it can be, I am willing to sacrifice my notion of truth and fact to hold on to my precious relationships. Pick your poison, I suppose.

One thing is for certain, individuals who fail to quickly repair misunderstandings, injuries, or perceptions of insensitivity with their partners will gradually pay the price. Relationship repair begins in infancy, with the infant caregiver continually going through moments of attunement, misattunement, and reattunement. This error-correction faculty initiated by the adult caregiver becomes the nascent properties that evolve into repair, relief, restoration of safety and security, and a reassurance of love and care. This mistake-driven process of restoration is essential for that felt sense of safety and security that pervades my writing.

If you do nothing else with the recommendations in this book, repair your mistakes, make amends for what *you* did (not why) and if necessary (as is often the case), offer a behavioral assurance (a guardrail) against future similar mishaps and proof of understanding ("I'll show you I get it"). Do this quickly and save all other matters for after you complete this task. How will you know if you've completed the task of repair? By observing visible relief on your partner's face. The softening of your partner's face, voice, and body are your most reliable indicators. If you care about your relationships, repair first, complain later.

Before moving on, just one other important point. The person receiving an effective repair *must* show some sign of gratitude. If you want your partner to fall on their sword for the relationship, the least you can do, before uttering or doing anything, is say thank you.

Understand Proper Management of Thirds

As an infant coming into this world, existence includes only the one: me. The one encompasses all that is inside and outside of me. As my brain develops, I begin to notice objects around me, including objects on my caregiver and parts of my primary caregiver's body. As I develop further, I notice I have a body, and my body is separate from my primary caregiver's body. Now we are two. As my brain further develops, I begin to notice the difference between me and not me, caregiver and not caregiver. Others exist outside of my tight orbit with my primary caregiver. As my brain continues to get upgrades, I begin to notice that these others, perhaps my other caregiver(s), threaten my exclusive relationship with my primary attachment figure—my primary caregiver. I do not like that. Yet, I grow accustomed to sharing my primary caregiver and enjoy spending time with others. Now we are three.

As we go from dyads (twos) to triads (threes), we grow into groups of fours, fives, sixes, and upward. Some of us, however, were repeatedly injured at earlier stages when we were just one (me) or when we were two (me and the primary caregiver). For us, we have not yet progressed from dyads to triads because of unmet infancy needs as yet ungrieved. For us, threes are a definite crowd.

Those of us who did progress from dyads to triads have found ourselves in an exclusive adult romantic partnership. That partnership becomes a primary-attachment system for both partners and therefore, we are back to an exclusive orbit of twos. Here, threes, fours, or more do not necessarily pose a problem except under certain circumstances.

I will argue that primary-attachment partnerships and their tendency to be exclusive are both normal and psychobiologically universal among human primates. Yes, there are polyamorous and polygamous systems and societies. However, a closer look at these alternative lifestyles shows evidence of primary dyadic formations within the group and that there often exists a primary partnership within polyamorous-, polygamous-, and open-relationship configurations.

The point I am making is this: within the primary attachment dyadic system is a psychobiological expectation, going all the way back to infant-caregiver times, to remain in primary status and not be relegated to secondary, tertiary, or anything lower than top dog. Primaries, no matter where they are on the planet, are less than neutral when consigned to being a third wheel, downgraded to a lesser station, or thrown under the bus by their primary partner.

This has less to do with maturity and more to do with our attachment system. Envy is a dyadic concern. You have something I want. I envy you. In some cases, that envy inspires me to be like you. In other cases, envy makes me despise and want to destroy you. "Mirror, mirror on the wall, who's the fairest of them all?" If it is not me, the other must perish. Jealousy, on the other hand, is a triadic concern. I have something I do not want to lose, and someone or something is threatening to take it from me.

In a primary attachment system, jealousy can be a lot of things, but it certainly falls under the category of security. We can say someone is immature if they believe they can covet a person and have that person all to themselves as a kind of entitlement. We might say someone is paranoid when they project their own wishes onto a partner or obsess over a fantasy of their partner being taken by someone else. Or, we could say that, in many cases, the jealous partner's sense of security is being threatened by some behavior, perhaps nuanced, exhibited by their partner. And finally, the jealous partner has real hard evidence that would threaten anyone's sense of security.

A *third* is any object, task, or preoccupation that threatens the primacy of the dyadic experience by either partner. **A third can be a person, an obsession, an addiction, a video game, a job, a pet, or anything that is felt to steal resources or primacy from the relationship.** Thirds exist. They are not the actual problem, but they become so when they are mismanaged by one of the partners.

Mismanagement of thirds is in the top tier of threatening behavior that plagues romantic partnerships. It seems innocent enough: a friend, an ex, a parent, a child, a boss, or a business partner. Yet, the opposing partner experiences a threat, not really from the third, but from their partner's management of that third in their relationship. Something in the couple system is promoting insecurity in one of the partners. The doubting partner would best be advised to take this very seriously and work quickly to reduce or eliminate the threat of the third. Blaming the threatened partner will not work.

Goodwill: The Essential Factor

We just finished talking about threat. If either of you experience a threat that remains unmanaged, your unrepaired goodwill is definitely going to suffer. That just makes sense. Without consistent demonstration of goodwill, trust will erode, and relationship management will become very difficult if not impossible.

Most people I see in clinic operate with goodwill. Most people are doing what they do out of automation, memory, and reflex, not out of evil or bad intention. Most of what happens between partners feels personal, yet much of what goes on during periods of stress invokes primitive survival systems that mistake many environmental signals as threat cues, particularly when the environment involves people interacting. Perhaps a trained observer, knowledgeable about human behavior, might recognize many relationship tribulations as simply mirroring the human condition, but most people involve themselves in the drama of who's right and who's wrong, who's good and who's bad, who's the victim and who's the perpetrator. We all identify with our personal experiences.

In my work with couples, there are no angels and no devils, just people protecting their interests. Of course, there are the occasional devils—those who are antisocial, malicious, morally and ethically corrupt, and sadistic. Thankfully, people who enjoy abusing power are in the minority.

And then there are those folks who, in order to protect their interests, are corruptible, act in bad faith, and do terrible things in order to escape consequences for their actions. Sadly, their behavior still falls into the normal, albeit primitive, low-level human potential for selfishness, opportunism, deception, aggression, impulsivity, and all-around thoughtlessness.

Their bad-faith actions cannot and should not be excused, however, as the social justice world of adult attachment relationships cannot square betrayal, injustice, and unfairness with simple reasoning or understanding. In this world, as in the larger world, there are harsh consequences for misbehavior, deception, and bad-faith actors. And there is redemption. The alchemy of forgiveness is powerful stuff. More on that later.

Goodwill and good faith between you and your partner are essential to trust, safety, and security. Cultivate them daily.

Personal Will: The Unknown Factor

People come to me claiming they want this or that for themselves or their relationship, but the personal will to achieve something, even something we say we want, is an unpredictable factor. Wanting something is no assurance that I will get what I want. For one thing, I may not be willing to expend the effort necessary to acquire or achieve my target wants. For another thing, I may not even know if I understand what I am wanting. And lastly, since many of my wants depend on factors outside of my control, I may be unable to get what I want if, say, my partner doesn't want the same thing or doesn't want to endure the challenges to achieve it.

So when I hear, "I want a secure-functioning relationship," I take it with a huge grain of salt, because in the next breath, that person will often fight mightily against behaving in a secure-functioning manner. "I would do it if my partner would do it" just doesn't cut it. "I want to, but I can't get over what my partner did to me over the years" misses the point as well.

For me, "I want" falls into the same worthless category as "I'm trying" or "I'm working on it." These phrases mean nothing to anyone other than the person saying them. If you take a photo of someone *wanting*, or *trying*, or *working on* a behavior, an internal psychological or emotional matter, what will the photo show? Anything substantial? No. We either do things, or we don't do things, period. In the world of secure-functioning relationships where shared power, authority, fairness, justice, and sensitivity are central to peace and harmony, such things as intention, motivation, emotional challenges, and past history don't count. The only thing that really counts is doing or not doing the right thing for a two-person system.

The personal will to achieve anything is the pivotal factor in change of any kind. It will be tested by all who attempt secure functioning as an actionable reality and not simply an idea or ideal. Secure functioning, becoming a full-fledged adult, operating interdependently in a two-person psychological system of full mutuality is not easy. It requires discipline, character, will, and faith that doing the right thing when it's the hardest to do, in our closest relationships, only makes us better people (I talk to myself when saying this).

Blending versus Congealing

One last point about threat reduction: it's each partner's responsibility to maintain the sense of safety and security that their partner feels, not just how they alone feel. Partners who maintain a continuous *felt sense* (in the other partner) of safety and security will influence each other, and their differences—to a large extent—will begin to dissolve. Each will become more like the other as time progresses. The opposite will be true for insecure-functioning partners who do not maintain a continuous felt sense of safety and security for each other. Those partners will congeal, harden, calcify, and strengthen in their resolve that their differences are irreconcilable. This is true of all unions where threat is allowed to run wild without quick repair.

I cannot say this enough: If at any time your partner is feeling unsafe or insecure in the relationship, you will not be able to influence, convince, or persuade them on any matter. Case closed. This is not your partner's fault, it is yours. **You both have a responsibility to maintain each other's felt sense of safety and security at all times or you will be at war.** You will find yourselves further divided, adversarial, and deeply unhappy. Root out threat wherever and whenever it arises in your partner. View threat perception as a virus that can take hold, a weed that can overgrow, or a fire that can consume the two of you. Remember, you are in each other's care, *not* simply your own. In other words, worry more about your partner's perception of unfriendliness and threat than your own. If you both do that, you will be fine.

Chapter 3

Reading Your Partner

Because this book is filled with common complaints, it's important to remember that everyone's complaints about their environment include other people. When we are unhappy, we don't necessarily think about what's wrong with us or maybe that we're part of the problem. We mostly think to ourselves, *I'm unhappy. Why is that? Oh yeah! It's you.*

Although the complaints here are directed externally, I hope you will come to understand that in couples rarely are there angels or devils. Usually where there's one, there's the other. And since partners pick each other based on recognition and familiarity, it is highly unlikely that you are not equally guilty of the same complaints that are in this book; the very ones that you think are about your partner.

Secure-functioning partners remain humble. They realize that they are likely doing the same things to their partner that they complain about. **One important rule about being human is that while we usually know that we don't like what is being done to us, we're not very good at knowing that we're doing the same damn thing to the other person.**

Recommendations for Dealing with Each Other When Under Stress

The real problems for couples come when either or both partners are under stress or are in distress. Good times don't count. When we feel good, we're sailing along, still making lots of errors in communication, still creating misattuned moments—but largely unaware as our good feelings allow for larger margins for slipups. This margin narrows considerably with stress. Our tolerance for misattunement, mismatching, and misappraisal of meaning and intent becomes an increasingly serious matter that ends up, like a memory loop, in a repetitive sequence of threat perception, narrative certainty, and defensive action.

Most of us focus on the subject or topic of stress. Yet the real problem lies in the interactions themselves. *How* we interact during stressful moments is the culprit, and it repeats no matter the subject.

Due to our brain's rapid memory recognition systems, we identify threat signals through a variety of sensory inputs: visual, auditory, gustatory, olfactory, visceral, and tactile. Our survival instincts override all other impulses, and we *act*. The thing is, our threat detection abilities connect to action motor areas of the brain and body, not areas concerned with love, friendliness, consideration, or thoughtfulness.

Our threat detection equipment is hooked up to our fight, flight, freeze, or collapse response—all of which are considerably faster than thought. We become more animal, and not the conscious kind. Consciousness, or cognition, is a higher-level function that requires slower, more energy-consuming brain areas. Consider those more human areas as *ambassadors* in that they are more attuned to the complexities of the moment and can make decisions based on current contingencies, possibilities, and probable outcomes if action were to take place.

Unfortunately, our ambassadors are not entrusted by nature to make life or death decisions when time is of the essence. No, nature entrusts quick survival decisions to less fancy, less discriminant, cheaper, faster brain areas that initiate our "act now, think later" impulses. We can call those brain areas our *primitives*. God love them because we'd literally be dead without them. As for love, well, hopefully that's intact after the dust settles.

For humans, apologizing, making amends, providing relief, and offering restitution are the actions that save the day—and the relationship. And unfortunately, a great many humans don't do any of that repair work and, therefore, the love light will eventually go out.

Understanding Clues and Cues

Before we continue our journey on managing stressful interactions, I want to set the stage for a very important social skill. You're going to develop a talent—called Sherlocking—for sizing up your partner and tracking them closely when you are either in, or believe you are about to be in, conflict with them.

Sherlocking refers to the skill of reading a person's face and body as they go in and out of stress. Our arousal level can be measured by heart rate, blood pressure, skin color or blood flow, muscle tension, breathing, vocal pitch and volume, gestures, posture, pupil size, and movement. This is all reflected in the body. We don't need fancy measuring equipment if we know what to look for and where.

In order to manage each other's stress or distress, we need to find these cues in our partner's body when we are engaging with them. It's very important that as you sit across from your partner, face to face and eye to eye, you pay close attention to certain occurrences. Get to know the unique look of your partner, and with practice you will be able to make note of certain changes in them, even when they are subtle. Let me explain what happens in the body when arousal goes up.

Facial cues. In general, when a person, your partner, becomes more excited, the muscles in their face begin to tighten, and blood flow increases, reddening their face. Their eyes may appear to glare as pupils dilate. Breathing from the chest grows faster and is more pronounced. Their jaw often gets tight, juts outward, or moves slightly to either side. Their lips might press together, pull inward, or push outward. Their eyebrows may pull together, and if angry, pull downward as well. In anger, some people bare their teeth.

Early signs of sadness include swallowing, nose reddening, eyes dimming, face elongating, mouth corners turning downward, and chin quivering and moving upward. Fear will appear as a radical raising of their upper eyelids, showing the whites above the iris, and a horizontal stretching of the mouth muscles.

When arousal goes down and your partner starts to relax, the striated muscles in their body and face will loosen. You'll notice a slackening and a lengthening of their face, especially if arousal goes down too far. Smile lines will fade around their eyes, thanks to the orbicularis oculi muscles, and that has a warmer look. Also worth noting as arousal goes down, especially way down, is that their face will begin to blanch and lose color.

Optical cues. The eyes often reflect the real state a person is in. When our arousal goes up, our eyes brighten and sometimes widen. When a person is excited, their pupils might dilate. This can happen when we're flirting or turned on and also when we are feeling angry or frightened. When arousal goes down, the pupils constrict. People with light skin and eyes are light sensitive, so their pupils may chronically constrict—and in that case it doesn't mean anything. So, get to know your partner.

Vocal cues. The voice is another powerful indicator of how a person is doing. When arousal goes up, we start to raise our pitch. Our speech begins to get a little more staccato, and our voice a little more plaintive. When arousal goes down, our speech begins to slow, and we lower our pitch. When our voice gets very low, we sound resigned. If it's too low, we start to sound a little drunk even, and that's because the vagus nerve—the tenth and longest cranial nerve running from the brainstem down the entire spine—is interfering with our vocal cords.

The function of the vagus is fascinating. Its main branch is reptilian, unmyelinated, and crude. It is deeply paired with the parasympathetic nervous system to act as a braking mechanism for slowing our heart rate, lowering our blood pressure, and helping our digestion and immune system.

So, if the sympathetic system is like a helium balloon ready to rise up unrestrained, the crude, reptilian vagal branch is the rock holding the balloon down. **If we believe we cannot fight or flee a dangerous situation, this vagal branch will shut down our entire system, and we'll collapse, faint, play dead, stay still, or otherwise go into life** threat (**Porges 2011**). Because the vagus enervates the vocal cords, on our way down toward the parasympathetic regions of arousal, our voice may begin to crack a little. This is a common early sign of sadness.

Body cues. When looking at the body as arousal goes up, the striated muscles in your partner's arms and legs begin to tighten, which may reflect a skin tightening as well. Their muscle features also grow more pronounced. You may notice increased scratching as skin cells contract and blood flow increases. Their spine elongates, and sometimes their chin will rise. You'll start to see a lot more jerky movement, not just in the head and neck but in the hands and the arms as well. When arousal is going down, far less movement happens, but the head drops, the eyes dim, and the voice lowers. If the head and/or eyes drop, it can be a sign of shame. If arousal is going up, many times the opposite happens: the neck lengthens and sometimes the person will raise their chin.

Lead with Relief

If you read your partner and see that they are in distress or under stress, soften them. Say something kind. Say something loving, friendly. Direct a sincere smile close to their face. Do whatever you can to give them some relief from that stress and change that face, because until that face changes you won't have an audience for the issue you are actively working to resolve.

As you read your partner, you are also staying present with yourself. Remind yourself to relax your muscles. Scan your body as frequently as you can for any big muscle tension, and if you can, drop it. It only takes a second, and it doesn't require you to take your eyes away from your partner.

Keep your eyes on each other, because you have to be in real time during a conflict or when talking about areas of importance where there's likely to be a lot of stress. You are both responsible for guiding this system, and if it goes off the rails, it's on you both. This is a coregulatory system where you're watching each other and holding each other as best you can in your window of tolerance[2] (Siegel 1999).

2　*Window of tolerance* is a term used to mean relaxed *and* alert.

You can think of it as a meditation. In meditation we follow what's going on inside of us moment by moment: our breathing, our body sensations, our thoughts. In Sherlocking, your object of meditation is your partner's face.

Let's say you are with your partner, and you want to get something from them. You want to convince your partner, persuade them about something. You have to know what they need, what they want, what their fears are, what they worry about. You have to express their needs and your understanding of those needs before you argue for yourself. Basically, you need to lead with relief. That is step one.

Leading with relief will disarm your partner's primitives, so that your partner feels safe, feels understood, and trusts that their needs will be met too. And, of course, at the same time you are Sherlocking—taking care to notice how your partner is feeling via their face, tone, and body language.

Chapter 4

Structural Issues

Structural issues, for the purposes of this book, are those circumstances that the partners themselves create. These include some conditions that seem outside of the couple's control but are not. I bring them up here because no one outside of the couple can solve structural issues, including me or any therapist. A therapist can help partners understand the situation, but the situation likely cannot be changed because the *structure itself* is the problem. As such, the following are examples of conditions and situations that the two of you may not be able to fix.

Many of the following examples represent what may, in fact, be deal breakers for going forward. Deal breakers usually involve two people pointing in different directions in areas significant to each of them. Despite the presence of flat-out deal breakers—where one person desperately wants something the other does not—partners will often go forward, kicking the can down the road. It's a dangerous decision, yet people will do this anyway.

The real reason isn't love, though that's what people will say it is. It's about *attachment*, which is a human biological mandate to remain bonded despite better judgment. We get stuck to each other, just as we do with our children and pets. For some, quitting another person is pretty easy. For most, ending a relationship is incredibly painful. For some, breaking up is absolutely Herculean if not impossible.

"Conditions Out of Our Control Keep Us Physically Separated"

When partners are unable to be together in the same place because of conditions out of their control, such as military tours of duty, oil rig assignments, entertainer and crew tours, or jobs and situations that demand separate living conditions, one or both partners are likely to complain about the distance, and this can become a chronic problem that leads to dissatisfaction.

Some of these conditions come about later in the relationship and cannot be vetted in the beginning. Some conditions exist at the beginning and get kicked down the road as partners hope conditions will eventually change. Some partners believe they can handle the distance only to find out it's intolerable. Still others will start families under these conditions and find they've added another structural problem that cannot be solved.

"One of Us Wants a Child, the Other Doesn't"

The problem of having one partner who wants a child and another who doesn't falls into the structural category because "don't want" and "can't live with" might carry the same weight. If "I can't live without having a child" meets "I can't live with having a child," that's called a *deal breaker* and is thus structural. Neither is right or wrong—but structurally, they can't live together, at least not in harmony.

More than one couple has come into my clinic with this deal breaker of an issue. Yet they go forward with at least one partner believing the other will change their mind. As I said above, human beings are driven by a biological mandate called attachment, meaning, "I just can't quit you."

"One of Us Is Monogamous, the Other Isn't"

Human beings are, by nature, nonmonogamous. We may choose monogamy, but we'd better have a good reason for doing so. Like so many other human drives, libido waxes and wanes throughout life. A certain number of neuropeptides and hormones lead to a more natural ease with regard to monogamy while others may drive us to seek more than one partner. I won't get into biochemistry here. Personality issues as well as attachment issues are more predictive than others when it comes to monogamy as opposed to any other preference.

Regardless of these factors, there are no right or wrong, good or bad choices. However, if partners disagree on this level, we consider that a deal breaker. All this means is the partners must take this deal breaker off the table or they cannot be together without risking problems downstream.

The most difficult thing for partners and for clinicians working with couples who face deal breakers, such as this one, is getting both partners to be completely honest and declarative with one another. There can be no equivocation, at least at the very beginning. Both must be very clear as to where they stand and why. I may ask each partner, "Why be monogamous? Why is that a good idea for you personally, and why is that a good idea for your partner?" I will then ask the other partner, "Why be polyamorous or swingers or have an open relationship? Why is that a good idea for you personally, and why would that be a good idea for your partner?"

The clinician pays close attention to how partners answer and how well they're able to defend challenges to their position. Then partners must challenge each other and do their best to convince the other as to why it would be in their best interest to adopt this or that orientation. What we don't want is for people to fold their cards and give in because they don't want to lose the relationship. We don't want people to pretend they are something they are not. This is assessed by how people defend their arguments. A good clinician can tell when someone is bending reality in order to avoid loss. Partners by themselves may not be so good at this. No matter which partner is less than 100 percent on board, if the couple goes forward, both partners are making a very bad deal. Therefore, this deal-breaking issue must be addressed from the very beginning and taken off the table.

Is it possible for people to change their attitudes as they move through life? The answer is, of course. That is different, however, than partners pointing in different directions from the very beginning. Anything and everything can be renegotiated along the way. Even then, partners must get each other fully on board before they do anything to get full agreement.

"We Both Cheated on Our Exes, and Now We Don't Trust Each Other"

Partners who have cheated on each other have provided proof that they are cheaters. You cannot deny or dismiss proof. If they also lied to their ex-partners, and they both have that information, that also creates evidence neither can dismiss. Despite all this evidence, couples will come to therapy complaining that they have a trust problem when in fact this is a structural problem that they created.

There is a big difference between suspicion and evidence. Without evidence, a person's suspicions should be investigated with caution. Chronic suspiciousness can seriously degrade the couple's safety and security experience—in both directions. Some people maintain suspicions due to other factors present in the relationship—such as lack of transparency, lack of knowledge or understanding of the other, or subtle, nuanced threats emanating from the suspected partner. If the suspected partner is unaware of their implicitly signaled threats to the other's felt sense of security, they will naturally feel persecuted and unfairly accused. The suspicious partner may also carry memories of earlier betrayals, either experienced personally or observed between their parents. And there is the classic projection situation whereby the suspicious partner is themselves guilty of betrayal or thoughts thereof.

Evidence, however, is everything. **Once someone is caught lying, withholding important information, or cheating, all suspiciousness is now and forever justified because they have evidence to the fact of lying and cheating.**

Partner A, while dating Partner B, was once caught grabbing their own phone away in a panic. They quickly deleted a message from a previous lover, which they later admitted to when pressed by Partner B.

Flash forward ten years. They are now married. Partner A once again wrestles their device away from Partner B in a panic to which Partner B responds by accusing them of deleting a message.

Partner A How dare you accuse me of lying to you. I didn't delete anything!

Partner B You've done it before, so you proved you could do it again.

Partner A That was ages ago! We were just dating. You can't let anything go.

Unfortunately, Partner A must lose this one because evidence doesn't go away. If it happened, it's in memory and therefore, Partner A doesn't get a pass. *They must take responsibility for creating the evidence in the first place.*

"My Partner Had Me Sign a Prenuptial Agreement"

I understand the need for prenups. They make sense to me. Having said that, in my work as a couple therapist, I find that some prenups can greatly unlevel the field for a couple. For example, one partner comes into the marriage with a lot of money, the other with very little or none. The prenup protects the partner with money from ever sharing their funds with the other. There's no shared couple fund and so no shared equity and leverage in managing money.

In my opinion, that complicates governance. The couple cannot claim equality and authority. What often happens is that the party with money calls the shots. Now, if two people agree to such a prenup, that's a structural issue that cannot be resolved through couple work as no one should sign a prenup that they believe is unfair or won't work.

Yet, I continue to see couples who, post-marriage, hold grudges against the partner who required the prenup. I've worked premarital cases where a prenup put one of the partners in a bad financial situation.

Despite looking at the matter quite clearly, they went through with the marriage. In one particular case, the inequity would span over financial, sexual, and living situation areas. Again, despite a thorough forward-looking examination, the partners went to the altar. These people have yet to return to my practice, so I don't know if my concerns played out, but I do see plenty of people who made these agreements and later came in to complain about them.

Let me remind you, secure-functioning partners are fully autonomous adults, coming together to form a conditional union based on specific terms, which therefore make them interdependent. These relationships ought not to be based on love, sexual attraction, attachment bonds, or anything other than purposeful, actionable terms that suit both partners.

Secure-functioning relationships are pay to play. They're expensive in that partners are expected to be doing things for each other that nobody would want to do unless they were paid a lot of money. Partners are equal burdens and that levels the field. Adult romantic partners are not children. They cannot expect unconditional love. They cannot claim entitlements the other cannot claim for themselves. This should be a relationship of equals. How they deal from there is their business.

For some partners, the field is level if the partner with money provides them with what they materially want. For others, prenups are less a problem when both partners have money and careers that provide them income. And there are those who come to the table agreeing to keep their belongings separate and do so without incident.

When partners sign a pre- or post-nuptial document, they make an agreement. If either has a complaint, that issue now becomes a structural matter that's tough (but not impossible) to renegotiate. I'm purposely skipping how that could work out because the couple agreed to self-impose a problem from the start.

Serious Attachment Breaches

Certain situations and events weigh heavily in the attachment world. Normally, this subject would not be in the structural issues category.

However, I'm putting it here to warn readers that failures in certain circumstances can prove fatal in primary attachment relationships.

Certainly, chronic mismanagement of thirds and chronic lying, cheating, and withholding of vital information become structural problems that will tank any relationship because either rules don't exist or they do and are ignored. Yet other misdeeds in the attachment value system may occur without realization that they are indeed breaches.

Sickness

When a partner is ill, attachment values suggest the other partner is present for them in all ways possible. No matter if this partner is from the distancing group and protests their need to be left alone, the effort is nonetheless there to care for the other. Distancing people eventually come around to this. Human beings do less well alone or in solitude when in distress; that is, if the conditions are correct. While in distress, no one likes being pestered or forced to deal with someone else's distress or demands or expectations. If the conditions are supportive, relaxed, and comforting, we all do better.

Failure to attend to a partner who is sick, unwell, injured, or scared is tantamount to neglect and abandonment in the attachment-aware world. Failure to go with a partner to a doctor or procedure that induces fear can be equally remembered as a breach in the attachment system.

Amends

Failure to admit wrongdoing, to apologize, and to make amends are other violations of attachment values. It is oh-so-common and oh-so-wrong to withhold an admission of harm done to another person. People have fought duels to the death, sued, taken vengeful actions, and lost love over such arrogant behavior. Our failure to make swift amends whenever a breach occurs is perhaps the most threat-inducing message we can send to our important others—that we care more for being right than we do for our relationship. This, to be sure, is a structural issue of unfairness and injustice and, as such, will always lead to relationship failure.

Celebrations

Missing a partner's (or child's) celebration is an attachment no-no. Again, celebrations fall under a memorable category, and your unavailability will be remembered. Of course, mitigating circumstances of all kinds happen that would or could prevent someone from attending their partner's celebration, for which they may be forgiven. Like it or not, it matters little what your celebratory partner says on the matter; make certain you and your partner are good with the arrangements.

Funerals

Going to a funeral of your partner's family member, best friend, or someone else extremely important to them is another memorable event that requires presence and support. As with celebrations, your partner may insist you do your work, stay at home with the kids, or tend to some other function other than partner in chief. However, as with all similar matters, be very clear that you are willing and able to attend if your partner should wish.

Crises

If your partner is going through a crisis of any sort, what you do will loom large in the recounted annals of your relationship. Many a partner hath ignored or dismissed the distress of their mate, failed to respond to their crises, or misattuned to the moment they could have demonstrated their care, interest, and attention. These opportunities are sometimes one in a hundred, and therefore a partner cannot easily repair the disappointment.

All breaches of attachment values amount to a structural flaw that, if not repaired and fixed, can eventually cascade toward union dissolution.

Chapter 5

Fighting Dos and Don'ts

L et's face it, your relationship should be easy because you both decide it to be. That means you work together to allow for quick and easy means to both push and limit each other as needed to get things accomplished. That includes solving each other's annoyances.

People make their relationship difficult when they do not orient toward a two-person psychological system of full collaboration and cooperation. That lack of two-person orientation is at the center of all difficulty in couple unions. One-person thinking automatically leads to adversarial actions and reactions. In my one-person moments, I am only thinking of myself, my needs, my concerns, my interests, my fears—you are nowhere in that configuration except maybe as the target of my complaint. Talking this way may make me feel good, but it will be at your cost—and then I will pay for thinking only of myself. I guarantee you this is what will happen every time.

To feel better, I may have to make my point and discharge all my bad thoughts and feelings, but nothing good will happen as a result because in my original one-person moment, you didn't matter to me. Message received. Countermeasure coming next.

Making Our Relationship Easy

Our relationship becomes easier when we work together to solve problems and avoid attempts to solve the other person. Our relationship becomes easier when we are free to be ourselves while being mindful of the other. In our families of origin, many of us existed in what we thought was an atmosphere of unconditional love and acceptance. We could be rude, inconsiderate, selfish, unfair, impulsive, opportunistic, and expressive. We may have been punished, but we expected to be forgiven.

Now, that is *not at all* the experience for a great many of us, I know. Yet, even for those of us who were severely neglected, abused, or abandoned, we often went through life either entitled or unentitled because of mistreatment in childhood. Why? Because those systems were too one-person oriented, too unfair, too unjust, and too insensitive too much of the time. Consciously or unconsciously, we will all set out to settle these scores as we hold others accountable for the sins of our caregivers. Entitlement and unentitlement, by the way, include any number of lived experiences, not only growing up rich or poor. They also surface as "I'm entitled to act badly because of what happened to me;" "I'm entitled to punish Dad for divorcing Mom;" "I'm entitled to still come home unannounced because I once lived here."

Adult attachment relationships are *conditional* and should be two-person oriented, yet most people do not hold this in mind. We mistake partnership for family and, in many families of origin, relationship was or was not the center of the universe.

If you can remember to take care of yourself and your partner at the same time—at all times—you will have all you need to make your relationship easy. You must think win-win—I want what's good for me and good for you—at all times, even when under the greatest amount of stress. This simple principle is very, very hard to do. The reason is equally simple: **we will all be inclined to revert to a one-person orientation when under stress or distress.** So it's a practice and, if you believe as I do that only a two-person system of full collaboration and cooperation can work long term, the effort will be worth it.

Putting the Relationship First

This simple agreement to put the couple relationship at the top of all other priorities will make your relationship easier. Think about it. If you both represent the very top of the food chain—in other words, in charge of your shared environment and the people in it—your well-being is essential to your availability to everyone and everything around you. If the two of you are not okay, how will that affect your health, your work, your creativity, your vitality, and your other relationships? Putting the relationship first allows you to fashion other rules and principles that cohere with that top idea.

Full Transparency

If the relationship comes first and the two of you are in charge, it makes sense to share all information in a timely fashion. Information therefore becomes a vital currency between partners. Information includes what others say, internal thoughts and feelings, plans, scheduling, knowledge about each other's comings and goings, affiliations, and so on. Actually, the two of you decide what transparency means and its limits, but it's a real discussion so there is no confusion or misunderstanding. Always think about the downstream effects of nontransparency. If my partner learns of this, will they be unhappy? If so, that should be a cue to tell them right now. Never wait for your partner to discover what you believe they should know now.

Proper Comanagement of Thirds

As mentioned in chapter 2, any and all thirds that threaten the safety and security of the couple system should be comanaged by partners in a timely fashion so as not to disturb the peace. Thirds can be alcohol, drugs, people, tasks, work, porn, parents, children, friends, exes, pets, or electronics. If one primary partner experiences jealousy, that is certainly a sign of mismanagement by the other. The proper use of a third is to work with it—on it, for it, or against it—together and not separately. We'll revisit this topic in chapter 9.

Work the Problem, Not Each Other

Learn to focus together on the task at hand whether it is a problem, a decision, a desire, a conundrum, or a plan. The issue between you is a third that must be managed together if you are to be an alliance and a team. Any other approach will not work as you will likely be working on each other—and that is war! Yes, there are times to express your feelings to your partner or to settle past hurts. Until you both understand how to do this, however, I'd avoid those typical talks you have that strive to repair past ills and stick with a more focused, limited, and task-oriented structure of repair and fixing things for the next encounter. That will take discipline, purpose, and intention—not feelings.

If you find yourselves focusing on each other—what the other did or did not do—stop and refocus on what *you* did or did not do that contributed to the problem. That will encourage the other to do the same (if they know what's good for them). It's easy to point fingers, but the truth is that you both represent a system that is reacting to itself. If I point my finger at you, you are compelled to protect yourself and point back. That's all we are going to do for the next . . . however long. Nothing, and I mean NOTHING, will get accomplished, and you both will walk away empty-handed and angry. It's stupid.

Understand again that all people are inherently annoying, disappointing, contradictory, self-serving, and generally irritating. That includes you.

Take Care of Yourself and Your Partner at the Same Time

If you can both take care of yourselves and each other at the same time, all the time—regardless of stress or distress level—you will never need this or any other book on relationships! It is the magic formula of secure functioning. So simple yet so very hard to do under stress. Here's why:

The very moment I take care of myself—my needs, my interests, my concerns, my points, my wants—and drop you, we square off and become adversaries. When that happens, and it will, we will both walk away with nothing, except perhaps more threat, memory, and resentment. In order to show you (not tell you) that I am a friend and ally, that I have you in mind as I have myself, I must prove this fact to you at all times lest you doubt my intentions. This continuous condition in human interaction is necessary to maintain a sense of friendliness, mutuality, collaboration, cooperation, and fairness. In order to influence you and keep you as my audience, I must anticipate your concerns about me, your memories of my past behavior, your fears and wants, and all that pertains to my in-depth knowledge of you. Any other approach will alert you to possible threat.

Remember, human beings are threat animals, meaning we have a highly sensitive threat detection system capable of lightning-fast recognition of threat cues—faces, gestures, postures, sounds, movements, voices, words, and phrases. **Always remember to whom you are speaking—your audience—before you speak and act. Take your eye off the ball, and get hit in the head you will.**

Lead with Relief Whenever Possible

Stress and threat reduction can and should be accomplished quickly and as soon as discovered in *your partner* (not you). Words are slow; gestures, facial expressions, vocal modulation, and tone are fast. Learn how to quickly recognize and reduce your partner's threat and stress level. Never lead with an explanation, description, excuse, motive, or intention. Always lead with acknowledgement of your partner's grievance in a manner that does not dismiss their complaint. Apologize immediately with a recognition of the behavior that caused the breach, irrespective of your own perception or belief in the matter. That is a conversation for another time. Give thanks if appropriate without pause or qualification. Learn graciousness in the brief.

Only when perceiving evidence of your partner's return to safety and security do you proceed with any further business. Remember this principle—leading with relief—before attempting any other response, and you'll do better than most.

Consider the following scenario: I step hard on your toe in a room full of people.

Now consider the things I could say to you immediately afterward:

1. "I didn't see your foot."

2. "It wasn't my fault; someone pushed me."

3. "Watch where you're going."

4. "Your foot is too big."

5. "Oh no! I am so very sorry. Are you okay?"

Which one *would you* prefer to hear from someone who stepped on your toe?

Now consider this scenario: I tell you how sorry I am for leaving this morning without saying goodbye to you. I admit that it was rude and inconsiderate, despite the reason for doing so.

Your response options might be:

1. "Why did you do that?"

2. "Yes, it was rude, and you do it all the time."

3. "And you want me to be loving to you, but you do this."

4. "I'm angry for a whole lot of reasons, and that's just one. . ."

5. "Thank you."

Which response would you prefer to hear before any other business?

"I'm sorry" and "Thank you" are simple but smart relief responses that lower stress in the other person. Relief can be offered through one's facial expressions, vocal utterances, and gestures even while a partner complains. Nodding the head in agreement and saying "Uh-huh," "Right," "Of course," "You're right," "I agree," all go a long way to signal relief and friendliness to your partner prior to your verbal reply. Conflict-avoidant partners may fail to signal enough while their partner complains. Keep in mind that the human brain with its negative bias will fill in blanks with negative ideas of attribution. Leave those blanks in there and guess what will happen?

If your partner likes physical touch, use it! If your partner responds well to you staying put and keeping your hands to yourself, use it. If your partner responds well to you lowering yourself physically or just tilting your head in friendliness, use it.

Change Position, Change State of Mind

Since state of mind is the main concern when in stressful situations, it is best to know how to shift your own state and that of your others. One such technique is to change your position and, if possible, change your partner's as well. Moving to another nearby location can make a big difference. Moving from standing to sitting or from sitting in one area to sitting in another area will help shift states. Moving to the floor, the couch, the bed, the porch, or someplace more relaxing can be a very good idea. How you accomplish this is equally important.

"Come over here and tell me more," is usually a winner. Notice that I am not just suggesting another seating location but inviting more discussion from my partner—even if it's a complaint. Doing so disarms threat. As with all suggestions, your mileage will vary depending on a lot of variables—your attitude, your partner, the environment, the context, and dozens of other factors.

Put the Kibosh on Negativism: It Destroys Morale

When team members make negativistic comments, such as "We're going to lose" or "I can't do this" or "You'll never come through," the result is crushed morale. That team member will likely be excoriated or kicked off the team. Negativism is a well-known defense against disappointment, often employed by folks who are allergic to hope and positive envisioning of success. Negativism is the opposite of collaboration. It suggests that either a partner will never come through, or the relationship will fail. It's a self-protective, predictive vote of no confidence that puts the kibosh on forward motion, future planning, and constructive teamwork. It's akin to saying, "I'm going to lose anyway so what's the point of doing anything?" and then kicking the sandcastle. It is annoying, self-defeating, and insecure functioning. Only folks operating as a one-person system behave in such a manner.

Negativism must be called out and squelched whenever it arises as it is anticollaborative, antirelationship, and destructive to morale for both partners. Always remember the following statement: **The relationship is exactly what you both say it is—nothing more, nothing less.**

Relationship does not actually exist except in our own heads. If either of you say it is frail, then it is. If either of you say it won't work, then it won't. If either of you say it is not strong enough to handle who you both are, then it must be so. Be careful how you address your relationship with your partner. If it is actually true that your relationship won't work, or your partner will not cooperate or collaborate, or your partner will "never" come through—you'd better be ready to exit the relationship, otherwise your negativism is the problem.

Scurry Toward Mutual Relief

Stressful moments require swift action that reduces stress. Human beings talk way too much, and talk can raise stress fast. Focus on your purpose, which is to get to mutual relief as quickly as possible, and then strike the issue off the table—for now. Always go for win-win or at least for the promise of win-win if you are not able to accomplish this goal in this sitting. Time is of the essence, as time spent during stress is far from neutral. More time, more opportunities to fight; more words, more opportunities for threat.

Keep yourself on message, on topic, and don't hog the stage. Watch your partner for signs of increased stress or distress. This may mean you are talking too much or for too long. It may mean you just said a threatening word or phrase or that your face or voice expressed something threatening to your partner. No matter, stop and yield the floor. The more you talk, the more trouble you are causing yourself. Check with your partner by taking a calculated guess as to what you did or said. Making this guess takes the pressure off your threatened partner to explain themselves.

Anything in the following list is a good idea to say:

- "Did I go on too long?"

- "Was I talking too loud?"

- "Was I lecturing again?"

It is *not* a good idea to say any of the following:

- "What? What did I do?"

- "Why are you making that face?"

- "Stop looking at me like that."

Always Move Forward

Keep the ball moving forward, never backward. This is a decision you both make before getting into stressful situations. Decide together that the only way forward is to keep your attention on the present and the future and resist going into the past. As already discussed, memories, even those from last night, are highly unreliable. If you bring up the past you both will be in the tar pit and likely to stay there. Here's an example:

Partner A Last night you said, "Take care of this yourself" in the meanest way possible.

Partner B I didn't say to take care of it yourself. I said you are perfectly capable of handling this in case I'm unavailable, and I wasn't mean.

The next ten or more minutes *for sure* will be about memory. So . . . just . . . don't. Learn to take care of messes as they happen, not afterward. If you understand what is happening here, you'll quickly take care of messes, glitches, missteps, and mishaps effectively without having to process the whole mess later.

Know the difference between what's done and predicting, planning, and preparing for what's next.

When It Is Time to Take a Stand

There comes a time for some partners when fighting and arguing becomes defeating, ineffective, and a sign of helplessness. Usually, partners end up here because they believe they have no other alternative but to either give up or continue to complain angrily about the same issue. Their mate just will not cooperate or behave fairly or collaboratively or is simply acting in bad faith by breaking agreements.

People, whether you like it or not, will generally act badly because they believe they can. Anger and punishment do little because the uncooperative mate can acclimate to negative reactions and simply continue to do what they want. What stops us from destructive behavior in relationships is action that proves the behavior is unacceptable.

Let me explain my reasoning here. A partner who takes a stand for a principle that protects the fidelity of the union stands on strong ground as long as it is a principle that benefits both partners, not simply the one. Standing for a principle that is just and fair forces the other partner to similarly take a stand to either fall in line or be expelled from the union.

Taking a stand for a principle that is secure functioning takes courage, conviction, and faith in the relationship and in the partner to do the right thing or lose the relationship. It is a nonviolent response to an intractable resistance to secure-functioning behavior.

Where there is one partner chronically misbehaving, breaking agreements, or acting badly, there is an enabling other partner. Anger, threats, and punishment do not represent boundaries or limits. They are received as signs of powerlessness and helplessness—signals received by both children and adults as tacit permission to continue bad behavior, as the consequences for doing so are too weak. Powerlessness telegraphs fear of loss, not of taking a stand.

The stand one takes in this instance is binary: this behavior stops (or starts), or I am out. This is not a threat. In fact, one way to keep it from being a threat is to actually leave for a period of time. The least threatening is to leave before a partner returns. There is no rapprochement until terms are fully met with plenty of proof before returning.

This is a very powerful, nonviolent, nonaggressive act of strength and conviction and requires commitment. Most people recoil at the thought of taking such a stand, most often due to fear of loss, abandonment, and other consequences involving children, finances, reputation, and general disruption. Still, adult unions are pay to play, and sometimes taking a stand is the only remedy and hopeful risk to get a partner on board. The alternative is a life of resentment, surrender, fighting, and defeat, with nothing ever changing.

Taking a stand should never be frivolous or threatening. It is drawing a line in the sand with seriousness and resolve, with preparation to act decisively. To do so otherwise would be to court disaster providing evidence of all bark and no bite. Throwing down for a principle is not a decision to quit or leave the relationship. It is a counter move to an unserious other who believes insecure functioning or one-person governance is just fine.

Section Two

The Complaints

Chapter 6

Safety and Security

People are more divided on issues related to safety and security than ever before—a worldwide pandemic, countries at war with each other, media outlets protecting their biases rather than the good of all, individuals waging and witnessing the mass shootings in their communities, people taking marketed pills, products, and advice based on internet reviews instead of seeking professional medical counsel. The list of threats to our safety and security is astonishing, and many of them find their way into the complaints issued in my couple clinics.

"My Partner Won't Protect Our Child from Illness"

The matter of safety versus beliefs about illness, vaccines, the government, the science, the medical community, and the media have fragmented society to a frightening degree. Conspiracy theories abound, leading people to distrust one another and turn to tribalism as a way to feel safe. This issue emerged with the COVID pandemic in 2020 but continues to rage on as one of the most challenging couple issues.

The current societal mayhem, seemingly growing exponentially in recent years, has culminated in families bitterly splitting apart over politics, race, culture, sex, gender, freedoms, and patriotism. The societal macrocosm and couple microcosm mirror each other in ways unfamiliar until recent times. And so, many partners may begin to square off with each other in their own home, with one partner believing that vaccines are a necessary societal duty to protect children and others from exposure to deadly viruses, and the other believing vaccines will lead to autism, cancer, or other future problems.

With the expansion of internet information, a great many people are getting their medical and research information from sources that reinforce their own concerns. This has put a great burden on the medical community who now must battle misinformation and various opinions and theories influencing their patients' choices and directives.

When one partner has a compromised immune system or a child or parent who is vulnerable, and the other partner opposes medical or psychiatric intervention, the result can be explosive.

The Complaint in Action

This particular couple has a newborn. One partner believes in early vaccinations against polio and other known infectious diseases, and the other feels strongly that all vaccinations for the child must be avoided. This partner has collected evidence that proves their concern that vaccines cause more problems than they solve. The couple is at a stalemate.

> **Partner A**   I can't believe you would take such a risk! Vaccines have been around for centuries and have prevented major transmittable diseases like smallpox, black plague, and German measles. Why wouldn't you want to protect our child from that?

Partner B I keep telling you and sending you articles to read—vaccines are not what you think. There's a ton of data around vaccines causing autism and infant immune systems to become overloaded and containing huge amounts of toxin, most of which we don't even know about. Infections are lower today than ever before, and it's not because of vaccines. It's because we take better care of ourselves. Our child's natural immune system will take care of itself.

Partner A You don't know what you're talking about. Those are myths, and they've been debunked by the government and everyone in the scientific community.

Partner B Right, and you believe everything you read about what the government says, what the pharmaceuticals say. You're so naïve. Wake up! Expand your reading. Here, take a look at this article.

Partner A No! I already recognize the source, and I don't trust it.

Partner B And you don't trust me, your partner. This is also my child we're talking about. You don't think I care about my child's health and well-being? How dare you!

Partner A Of course you care. I never said you didn't.

Partner B Remember what you did when you kept telling me that your other child, my stepchild, needed medication for ADHD, and I kept telling you that they needed to get off sugar? You scoffed. You completely dismissed me until you found I was right. We avoided the medication, we took them off sugar, and what happened?

Partner A They got better. Right, but that was a while ago, and they're back to having problems again.

Partner B That's probably because your ex is allowing them to eat sugar again.

Partner A Will you at least come with me to the pediatrician's office and be open to what they say?

Partner B No! I already know what they'll say. Will you at least read some of these articles and be open to what they say?

Partner A I already have and no, I think it's all conspiracy crap.

And scene.

Neither seem to be able to be moved or influenced on this matter. I've seen a good many couples in this deadlock, even to the point where partners will not return to the clinic. I should say that I do not take a particular stand on this matter, at least not professionally. It is not my place to take sides when it comes to strong beliefs and values held by one or both partners.

The problem is not about who is right or wrong. The problem is that they cannot agree on something of equal importance to them.

Why Does This Keep Happening?

This split in partner beliefs and values has existed since the beginning of partnership so there's nothing really new here. We can't say that the stakes are particularly higher today than at any other time (feelings aside). Yet when an interdependent couple disagrees on the level of belief and values, we get into deal-breaker territory. This, of course, is messier when the care of a child may split and not just the relationship between partners. The problem cannot be solved by partners simply going their separate ways—not that a breakup is simple by any means. I'm not a lawyer, but I would imagine that parental disputes like the one above could end up in the courts if the safety and security of their beliefs become more important than the safety and security of their relationship.

The Central Culprit—the Interaction

This section dissects the initial couple interaction from a secure-functioning perspective. Let's begin with Partner A's first statement.

> **Partner A** I can't believe you would take such a risk! Vaccines have been around for centuries and have prevented major transmittable diseases like smallpox, black plague, and German measles. Why wouldn't you want to protect our child from that?

These are fighting words and a stance that conveys helplessness. "I can't believe you would" is an admonishing, degrading, and contemptuous sentence. Not a good way to start. This is topped off with a guilt-inducing rhetorical question meant to shame the other. It is much better to start with the second sentence, "Vaccines have been around for years . . ." and finish with, "What are your thoughts about that?" That's a bid for collaborative interaction.

> **Partner B** I keep telling you and sending you articles to read— vaccines are not what you think. There's a ton of data around vaccines causing autism and infant immune systems to become overloaded and containing huge amounts of toxin, most of which we don't even know about. Infections are lower today than ever before, and it's not because of vaccines. It's because we take better care of ourselves. Our child's natural immune system will take care of itself.

Had Partner A reconstructed their message as suggested above, the conversation would've been different at this point. No telling how different, of course. But the tailing bid for collaborative interaction would also be a place to maintain the focus of the discussion: "Should we consider the historical benefit vaccines have had on the world population?"

Partner B responds less defensively than Partner A deserves at this point—and also changes the subject matter enough to degrade the orderliness of the discussion. While their point is important, a question emerges as to what the partners are attempting to accomplish, other than to be right. Either partner at this point could say, "Let's come back to that and just stick to this first idea until we're done with it."

Partner A You don't know what you're talking about. Those are myths, and they've been debunked by the government and everyone in the scientific community.

Partner A's hostile, attacking manner will surely fail to work with anyone. The bullying approach of "You don't know what you're talking about" as a way to work things out conveys Partner A's weakness and lack of skill to be persuasive in any other way.

Partner B Right, and you believe everything you read about what the government says, what the pharmaceuticals say. You're so naïve. Wake up! Expand your reading. Here, take a look at this article.

Partner B now defaults to attacking and devaluing statements, and it's beginning to sound more and more like war. Both partners are so sure they are going to lose, they've given up any curiosity, flexibility, or openness to anything other than their position.

Partner A No! I already recognize the source, and I don't trust it.

Partner A will not be influenced; they've already decided that Partner B is wrong.

Partner B And you don't trust me, your partner. This is also my child we're talking about. You don't think I care about my child's health and well-being? How dare you!

Neither trusts the other, which makes sense. Neither partner talks like an ally, neither partner respects the other's view as possibly legitimate, and neither affords the other a chance to be right.

Partner A Of course you care. I never said you didn't.

That's the first repair attempt, but it doesn't go far enough to return Partner B to safety.

Partner B   Remember what you did when you kept telling me that your other child, my stepchild, needed medication for ADHD, and I kept telling you that they needed to get off sugar? You scoffed. You completely dismissed me until you found I was right. We avoided the medication, we took them off sugar, and what happened?

Partner B again takes the focus off-course by bringing in a third—a child—as an example of Partner B having been right about something. The tailing sentence is a question, which is ill-advised when either partner is under stress. A question requires resources that are low during stressful conversations—particularly a question that sounds like the partner is on the witness stand.

Partner A   They got better. Right, but that was a while ago, and they're back to having problems again.

Touché, I suppose, despite Partner A joining in on the change-of-topics bandwagon.

Partner B   That's probably because your ex is allowing them to eat sugar again.

Partner A   Will you at least come with me to the pediatrician's office and be open to what they say?

Partner B   No! I already know what they'll say. Will you at least read some of these articles and be open to what they say?

Partner A   I already have and no, I think it's all conspiracy crap.

A heated battle of bidding to consult each other's third-party experts ensues. At this point, however, nobody's listening. Both have lost their audience.

Corrections

The matter of safety and security is foremost in the minds of all who form unions with others. Safety and security are foundational reasons *to* unionize; human primates have long formed alliances for no other purpose than to remain safe and secure. If we accept that as true, it follows that partners who consciously elevate safety and security to the very top of their priority list reduce, if not eliminate, the number and frequency of complaints. However, both partners are concerned with the safety and security issues of vaccinating or not vaccinating their child.

I generally tell partners who argue about medical treatment, financial planning, religion, and politics to soften their positions enough to seek—together—third-party professional advice, classes, research, and other methods for gathering more information, separate from what either of them has already done. I advise partners against doing their own research—that only furthers their tendency to prove themselves right and the other wrong.

Secure-functioning partners are intent on being more collaborative, cooperative, gracious, friendly, patient, orderly. The way they communicate and negotiate allows for a differing of opinions, ideas, and attitudes. As a result, they influence each other more readily than insecure-functioning partners.

Each partner's task here is to "sell" each other on their ideas and sway the other, influence the other, and find places where they will agree. The problem both face is fear of loss. When we disagree on something important, we may fear ourselves defeated before we begin the work. We may anticipate losing our position and what we want. Our memory and predictive minds conjure feelings of helplessness and hopelessness, which give rise to aggression or giving up. **When partners behave as one-person entities in a two-person system, each congeals, hardens, tightens, and conveys an adversarial attitude.** This attitude is highly compelling and difficult to change in the moment. And so, partners will fight as they do in the above example.

Variations of This Complaint

"My Partner Won't Get Vaccinated"

As soon as vaccines became available, people divided themselves into camps of those anxious and eager to get vaccinated and those anxious about the vaccine. Media misinformation, conspiracy theories, and political opposition to vaccine mandates served to consolidate antivaccination sentiments among a great many folks, leading partners to take opposing sides.

Several of the partners I see in clinic broke apart while others continue to fight over this debate. Safety, masks, social distancing, and vaccines take the fight to existential levels of anger and despair.

While I will not weigh in on the merits of one's personal beliefs and sense of safety, I do view these opposing views between partners as deal breakers. A deal breaker is something that points partners in opposite directions and cannot be solved without resulting in resentment and unhappiness. We will delve much deeper into this subject later in the book.

"My Partner Drives Like a Maniac"

I often joke with partners that complaints about driving likely go all the way back to horse-driven carriages. There's something about being a passenger—the one who is not in control—that makes us feel vulnerable. The driver may find a passenger-partner's anxiety grating, distrusting, or controlling. Yet, a partner's sense of safety should take precedence above all other complaints.

The Complaint in Action

The couple is in a car, driving through a rainstorm.

Partner A Please, please put the windshield wipers on high speed. I can't see what's in front of us.
Partner B I can see, and that's all that matters.
Partner A (*Huffs*) You're going too fast. What if a car is stopped ahead?
Partner B I have the automatic system set. It will detect an object that approaches.

Partner A   What? What do you mean by automatic system? This is not the time to use that. That's for good weather and good vision. Please don't do that.

Partner B   It's alright. You're going to have to trust me. I know how to drive.

Partner A   Babe, you're driving too fast, and you've put the automatic thing on, and we're in a rainstorm. And please! Put the faster wipers on!

Partner B   (*Silent*)

Partner A   I'm really uncomfortable. Would you please slow down and put the wipers on faster so I can see better? And please don't leave the car to do its automatic thing. Please, honey. I'm begging you.

Partner B   You're distracting me right now. That's more dangerous. Will you please just let me drive? I know what I'm doing. STOP! You're upsetting me.

Partner A   Don't yell. I'm scared, and you're not . . . you don't even. . . .

Partner B   (*Turns on the radio*) Here. Listen to something. Get your mind off my driving.

Partner A   (*Silent*)

Partner B   Look, do you want to drive? If you think you can do better, drive. I'll pull over.

Partner A   DON'T pull over. I'm not talking to you.

And scene.

Why Does This Keep Happening?

For some, driving is a control issue. Those behind the steering wheel often don't like their driving critiqued. The old saying "Don't be a backseat driver" sticks in their head. "Leave the driving to me" is another well-worn aphorism. While these stances are annoying, irritated driver-partners might be just as annoyed by the criticism they continuously face from their passenger-partners.

This fight will repeat ad infinitum because the couple architecture is all wrong, or not coconstructed. The mistake is organizational. Either these partners know what they're doing—in most cases they don't—or they do but are not enforcing their agreed-upon principles. Both can be true, yet the former is the likely culprit since the majority of couples never cocreate their own culture and guardrails against misbehavior. So the same or similar fights repeat over and over again.

The Central Culprit: The Interaction

The above interaction is appalling because of Partner B. However, if you've sat in Partner B's seat and don't see their behavior as faulty, let's pick some of it apart to understand why I say that.

Partner A Please, please put the windshield wipers on high speed. I can't see what's in front of us.

Partner B I can see, and that's all that matters.

That's only true if the driver is alone, but they are not. Therefore, seeing the road may be equally important to the passenger-partner in the front seat. Partners keep each other safe by having two different brains, two sets of eyes, ears, and . . . you get the idea. The addition of another person, therefore, should be a feature and not a bug.[3]

Partner A (*Huffs*) You're going too fast. What if a car is stopped ahead?

Partner B I have the automatic system set. It will detect an object that approaches.

Partner A What? What do you mean by automatic system? This is not the time to use that. That's for good weather and good vision. Please don't do that.

Partner B It's alright. You're going to have to trust me. I know how to drive.

---

3   The term *bug* refers to a computer software metaphor that differentiates something that is intended to benefit from something unintended that is a flaw.

Once again, Partner B makes clear that they are in charge, and Partner A is not. Their response is neither settling, cooperative, nor fair (unless a prior agreement was in place).

Partner A Babe, you're driving too fast, and you've put the automatic thing on, and we're in a rainstorm. And please! Put the faster wipers on!

Partner B (*Silent*)

Most people by far consider nonresponses negative, hostile, and even aggressive. A nonresponse leaves the negatively biased human brain to conjure the worst possible meaning to the blank space. It is never in a person's best interest to leave blank spaces for the other to fill in. It may seem like a good idea for some, but it is really, really a mistake. At least grunt, hiss, huff, sigh, nod, or shake your head. But it is far better to relieve your partner so relief can come back to you. **Like it or not, you and your partner are emotionally tied together. Where one goes, so goes the other.** Partner B could show leadership here but instead demonstrates dominance and stubbornness, neither of which is secure functioning.

Partner A I'm really uncomfortable. Would you please slow down and put the wipers on faster so I can see better? And please don't leave the car to do its automatic thing. Please, honey. I'm begging you.

There is *nothing* in Partner A's narrative that is threatening. In fact, it is exactly what Partner A should say in this instance.

Partner B You're distracting me right now. That's more dangerous. Will you please just let me drive? I know what I'm doing. STOP! You're upsetting me.

Ugh, so painful. Partner B's narrative is entirely dismissive, distancing, unfair, insensitive, noncollaborative, and uncooperative.

Partner A Don't yell. I'm scared, and you're not . . . you don't even. . . .

Partner B (*Turns on the radio*) Here. Listen to something. Get your mind off my driving.

And, Partner B doubles down, treating Partner A like a prisoner. It is abusive and violates a primary purpose of partnership, which is to protect each other from harm. Inexcusable.

This is different from road rage, something I'll get into a little bit next. However, many of you armchair psychologists might peg Partner B for a narcissistic personality disorder. While this book does not get into the *Diagnostic and Statistical Manual of Mental Disorders* (DSM-5), Partner B's behavior may seem in line with a narcissistic defense against feeling small, but the behavior is nevertheless common in nondisordered individuals, regardless of gender.

You may have noticed this book is purposely written as gender neutral, but many readers will still attempt to genderize examples portrayed here. I won't argue with that tendency. Yet, please keep in mind that our tendancy to genderize folks is similar to our labeling and categorizing people in all forms. That is the brain's energy conservation in action—to think quickly and not critically.

The point of this example is not about who or what Partner B is, but what Partner B is doing.

Partner A (*Silent*)

Partner B Look, do you want to drive? If you think you can do better, drive. I'll pull over.

This is a deflection tactic that closely resembles *gaslighting*, which is an attempt to shift blame, shift focus, or make crazy the one who catches the liar in the act of lying. Another blight on Partner B's record of deception and bullying.

This whole scene demands a serious sit-down around agreements, particularly regarding safety and security. These fights are quite common, but they have serious consequences. If partners do not honor the first rule of an alliance, which is to protect each other's interests at all times, the relationship will fail sooner or later. Moments such as these remain in memory, particularly in the threatened partner's mind. To disregard a child's or partner's fear, despair, pain, or lack of safety or security is tantamount to killing the relationship on an attachment level.

Corrections

Secure-functioning partners are collaborative and cooperative with each other. They put their relationship first before other concerns, including being right, feeling justified, doing only what they want when they want, and refusing to share control. Despite the above example being a safety issue as perceived by at least one partner, the lack of collaboration or cooperation automatically demonstrates insecure functioning. Partner B is choosing their own desire for control, to be right, to be the driver in this instance. They are orienting to one-person thinking: it has to be good for me, and if it's not for you, sorry.

If you, the reader, put aside your personal opinions about drivers and passengers and instead think of two commanders, then you know that Partner B is behaving inappropriately. Having a steering wheel doesn't necessarily equal being in charge. Driving is a responsibility, to be sure, and the responsibility is also to passengers. In the above case, Partner B is acting irresponsibly both with their driving and their partner.

Secure functioning means that as partners you always do your part in good faith to remain fair, just, and sensitive. It's foundational to thriving relationships, not a corrective tool you pull out to repair a little damage here and there. Secure functioning serves a purpose. Feelings do not play a role in the creation of your shared vision, purpose, or principles (see the introduction). In secure functioning, you *do* what is right, not what *feels* good or right for yourself. Secure functioning, as a measure of right or wrong, is easier to determine objectively than your personal feeling about your own behavior.

Variations of This Complaint

Complaints I hear generally involve safety, but I also hear things like, "Your choice of music bothers me," "Your car smells," "Your car is always dirty," "You don't talk to me when we're on a long drive," or, and this is more about safety, "You're always checking your phone when you drive."

Checking the phone while driving may make your passenger-partner nervous, and for good reason. Plenty of research indicates that texting while driving causes accidents. So, there you go.

The following is an important variation of the previous complaint.

"My Partner Reacts with Road Rage"

Road rage puts others at risk for injury or death. The human primate threat system reacts instantly to either fight, flee, freeze, or collapse. It's a very primitive response that some people can be trained to control (fighter pilots, for example) but, in most cases, it is overridden by ambassador brain areas that inhibit or push against an impulse to do the right thing in the moment. Some people have impulse control issues that get them into trouble. Such is the case with road rage.

Fear is the initial motivating factor that kindles rage. "Someone is trying to harm me," says the brain. And, if the fight response is easily kindled, wham—it's to the death. For others, fear triggers a flight or withdrawal response, and thus anger may be felt but is inhibited, and the person backs away.

If someone jokingly frightened you, you probably feel anger immediately following the startle. Perhaps you hit them and say, "That wasn't funny." Or, someone takes your parking space, and you feel like confronting them. Stealing your space feels like an act of aggression. What are you going to do about it? Perhaps you'll just mutter something nasty to yourself and find another space. You might give them a nasty gesture to register your disapproval. Or, you might be someone who gets out of your car and gives them a piece of your mind.

Whether you fight (charge forward), flee (run away), freeze (do nothing), or collapse (play dead) under threat, your response—depending on the circumstances—could cause you harm. That is where critical thinking comes into play. Additionally, PePPeR (see chapter 1) is extremely useful for predicting, planning, and preparing for such threatening encounters in advance. It is also a good idea to know your general tendency to respond when threatened so that you can better predict yourself.

Road rage is a choice. In some rare cases, certain individuals are unable to control their rage impulses and require medication or other intervention. But in most instances, people act out their rage, particularly at strangers, because they believe they can do so without consequence.

If you or your partner acts out road rage, safety becomes the major issue and something must be done. If children are involved, road rage is child abuse and must be handled immediately. I've interviewed far too many adult children of road-rage parents who can attest to the trauma all but the driver experience under such frighteningly helpless circumstances.

DOMESTIC VIOLENCE IS A SERIOUS MATTER. IT SHOULD IMMEDIATELY BE TAKEN UP WITH AUTHORITIES, AND STEPS SHOULD BE TAKEN TO PROTECT THREATENED PARTNERS, CHILDREN, AND ANYONE WHO CANNOT FEND FOR THEMSELVES.

IF YOU BELIEVE YOU ARE IN AN ABUSIVE RELATIONSHIP, SEEK HELP IMMEDIATELY. THIS BOOK WILL NOT HELP YOU.

"My Partner Bullies Me"

Let me start off by saying there is no place in relationships for any kind of physical abuse. Full stop. This section on bullying has nothing to do with physicality. Rather, it refers to a partner's emotional sense of being bullied.

I have seen bullies of all kinds. Some of them have been victims of trauma. Most have been fearful, acting out of helplessness. Helpless people become aggressive and can bully others. Insecure-functioning partners often resort to using fear, threat, guilt, or shame to get what they want. Or, they leverage fear as a way to control the other person.

Human beings are memory animals. As mentioned earlier, all people rely on what they know, and what they know is what they've experienced or have seen or heard, especially in their families of origin. If partners have witnessed a parent or sibling being a bully, that experience is in them and is likely to rise up under times of stress. In some instances, a child feels that they are able to bully a parent. For whatever reason, that parent shied away from setting limits or had trouble enforcing them. Either way, this behavior comes from somewhere and usually has a history beyond the experience of helplessness.

When I meet with couples, one of whom relates as a bullied partner, I also tend to find a history somewhere that matches that experience. In other words, partners tend to have the bite that fits the other's wound. As I say, where there is one, there is the other. That's nature at its best, repeating itself through recognition systems in the pair-bonding process. You can argue with our natural repetition compulsion when under stress, although it would be far better to understand it and see it for what it is—a threat response and our automatic brain.

The Complaint in Action

These partners are arguing at a sporting event. One partner complains that the other is being inconsiderate.

Partner A I can't believe that you once again walked ahead of me as if I didn't even exist. How humiliating. Then you went to the concession stand and didn't get me anything. You didn't even ask me if I wanted anything.

Partner B I did not walk ahead of you on purpose. I was trying to get us to our seats, and you were distracted. I didn't get anything for you because every time I ask, you tell me to stay with you and watch the game. Can we just have a good time for once?

Partner A (*Silent with arms folded*)

Partner B So now you're not going to talk to me?

Partner A (*Silent*)

Partner B Great.

Partner A (*Muttering*) I can't . . . anymore.

Partner B What?

Partner A Forget it.

Partner B What?

Partner A I said I can't do this anymore.

Partner B Okay. Do what?

Partner A This! I can't do THIS. I'm done.

Partner B What are you talking about? Why are you doing this again?

Partner A Nothing's going to change. I'm trapped in a loveless relationship. I'm done.

Partner B Because I walked ahead of you? You're overreacting. You keep doing this to me. You get angry and you just . . . threaten the relationship. Every time. You do this.

Partner A (*Silent*)

Partner B (*Staring at their partner*) Do you want to leave?

Partner A I want to leave you. I don't want someone who treats me this way.

Partner B What *way*?

Partner A You know I have abandonment issues. You know I don't like it when you walk ahead of me. And I don't like your attitude right now, and I don't like the way you're talking to me.

Partner B Look, I'm sorry. I'm sorry I walked ahead of you, and I'm sorry I didn't ask if you wanted any food.

Partner A I'm done. I don't believe you're sorry. You're insensitive. You clearly couldn't care less about my history. If you did, you wouldn't treat me like this. But you're incapable of empathy. It's always about you. And you're abusive. I don't deserve to be abused.

Partner B Sweetheart, what—did—I—do? I am sorry. Why do we always have to go through this? You make me out to be a terrible person.

Partner A If the shoe fits. . . . (*Pause*) I've got the car keys, so I'm leaving if you want to come (*Stays seated*).

Partner B Really? Come on. Let me get you something to eat.

Partner A Too late. You should've thought about that earlier. I'm not hungry now. (*Long pause*) My therapist says you're a narcissist. Okay. Enough. Stop talking. I want to watch the game.

And scene.

Why Does This Keep Happening?

Many types of bullies live among us. Some bully by playing the victim. Some bullies use their trauma histories as a platform for tyranny. In the above case, Partner A uses their vulnerability of abandonment as a rationale to threaten abandonment. They view it as leverage to punish or to frighten their partner into submission of some kind.

Threatening the relationship is a verboten no-go in secure-functioning unions. The primary partnership is based on a biological survival imperative, and threats to the relationship amount to an existential concern. A threat should not be thrown around as a strategy to manage a partner's behavior, particularly while under stress or distress. The only circumstance that a threat may be warranted is in the case of a deal breaker (see introduction and chapter 2 on mismanagement of thirds) and, of course, violations to safety and security.

In the above vignette, the only person directly affecting the couple's safety and security system is Partner A. Please do not read further into the example by imagining some justification for their behavior in that snippet. The human mind will do that as we all identify with these small scenarios differently.

Yes, Partner B bears responsibility for lack of consideration, and the implications that follow this behavior are multifaceted and perhaps even ubiquitous. It bears repeating that in couples, there are (mostly) no devils and no angels—where there is one, there is almost always the other. Undeniably, there *are* devils in the world and true victims of those devils. I consider devils to be those who are bad-faith actors—corrupt, truly antisocial, sadistic, intentionally and routinely cruel. Yet, in the majority of my cases, most are people of good faith (meaning, of good moral character) doing bad things.

The Central Culprit: The Interaction

Let's take a quick look at how this couple talked to each other in the above scenario.

Partner A I can't believe that you once again walked ahead of me as if I didn't even exist. How humiliating. Then you went to the concession stand

and didn't get me anything. You didn't even ask me
if I wanted anything.

Partner B I did not walk ahead of you on purpose. I was trying
to get us to our seats, and you were distracted. I
didn't get anything for you because every time I ask,
you tell me to stay with you and watch the game.
Can we just have a good time for once?

Partner A's use of "I can't believe you . . ." (as in a previous example
with a different couple) is going to fire up anyone's threat system. That
start is sure to catch the brain's attention and nothing else that follows.
It may be unfortunate, but it's likely true. The rest is going to be blah,
blah, blah to the other person, even though the rest contains important
information, such as "humiliating" and "ask me if I want anything." The
phrase "How humiliating" is less an expression of how Partner A felt as
it is admonishing Partner B for their act of humiliating them.

Partner B's response isn't great either. They could have easily just
apologized for rudely walking ahead and forgetting to ask their partner if they wanted anything at the concession stand. To make matters
worse, the following beat is a full dismissal.

Partner A (*Silent with arms folded*)
Partner B So now you're not going to talk to me?
Partner A (*Silent*)
Partner B Great.

Silence or nonresponsiveness is never neutral in the human world.
Nonresponsiveness is perceived as negative. Because the human brain
is preloaded for negativity as a survival mechanism, it always fills in
blanks and does so with a negative bias. So, when partners fail to signal
through words, sounds, or gestures, the other person will fill in the
blanks with negative thoughts, feelings, and fantasies. Therefore, nonresponsiveness or what one might think of as being neutral is actually
perceived as aggressive and hostile by most people. This was clearly
Partner A's intent.

Partner A (*Muttering*) I can't . . . anymore.
Partner B What?

Partner A Forget it.

Partner B What?

Partner A I said I can't do this anymore.

Partner B Okay. Do what?

Partner A This! I can't do THIS. I'm done.

Partner B What are you talking about? Why are you doing
this again?

Partner A mutters "I can't . . . anymore" and though Partner B says, "What?" Partner B already gets where this is going, particularly as Partner A's tone has already implied it. This interaction clearly repeats often. Partner A is threatening Partner B.

Partner A Nothing's going to change. I'm trapped in a
loveless relationship. I'm done.

Partner B Because I walked ahead of you? You're overreacting.
You keep doing this to me. You get angry and you
just . . . threaten the relationship. Every time. You
do this.

This disconnect is a *loop*. This couple, and others as well, fall into loops; the system reacts to itself and becomes circular. Loops repeat because of memory and state interacting with each other. Partner A acts out negativism—a defense against helplessness—and threatens the alliance rather than protecting it.

Partner A (*Silent*)

Partner B (*Staring at their partner*) Do you want to leave?

Partner A I want to leave you. I don't want someone who
treats me this way.

Partner B What *way*?

Partner A You know I have abandonment issues. You know
I don't like it when you walk ahead of me. And I
don't like your attitude right now, and I don't like
the way you're talking to me.

It is highly likely that Partner A is reenacting either what happened to them with a caregiver or witnessed this kind of interaction between their caregivers. No matter what it was, the behavior is self-harming and bullying. There is no way out of this predicament for either partner because Partner A is set upon destroying the relationship. Why? Partly due to rage over the injustices of others in their past. Here, the victim is the perpetrator with little or no awareness of having made the switch. The expectation and experience of disappointment is so painful they act out their rage rather than talk about it in a collaborative, nonthreatening way.

Partner B   Look, I'm sorry. I'm sorry I walked ahead of you, and I'm sorry I didn't ask if you wanted any food.

Partner A   I'm done. I don't believe you're sorry. You're insensitive. You clearly couldn't care less about my history. If you did, you wouldn't treat me like this. But you're incapable of empathy. It's always about you. And you're abusive. I don't deserve to be abused.

Partner B finally attempts to make amends, but it fails to quell Partner A's punishing rage, increasing rather than decreasing their threatening narrative, which now includes a declaration of abuse. Taking just this piece of interaction between the two, it would appear that Partner B is behaving abusively in this instance.

Partner B   Sweetheart, what—did—I—do? I am sorry. Why do we always have to go through this? You make me out to be a terrible person.

Partner A   If the shoe fits. . . . (*Pause*) I've got the car keys, so I'm leaving if you want to come. (*Partner A doesn't move.*)

Partner A doubles down, threatening to leave the venue and their partner.

Partner B   Really? Come on. Let me get you something to eat.

Partner A   Too late. You should've thought about that earlier. I'm not hungry now. (*Long pause*) My therapist says you're a narcissist. Okay. Enough. Stop talking. I want to watch the game.

Once more I will leave diagnosis out of this book. It should be clear, however, that Partner A is projecting throughout this interaction and doesn't appear to accurately appraise their partner or situation.

Corrections

Let's try to improve the above dialogue:

Partner A I can't believe that you once again walked ahead of me as if I didn't even exist. How humiliating. Then you went to the concession stand and didn't get me anything You didn't even ask me if I wanted anything.

Partner B I'm sorry. I know my walking ahead is annoying. You keep telling me that, but when I get excited and directed I just move. I'm sorry. If we walk arm and arm or hold hands, that will remind me. What would you like to eat or drink?

Partner A (*Silent with arms folded for a brief moment*) Sorry. I'm still mad but I'm thinking . . .

Partner B Okay. Take your time.

Partner A Hmm. For now let's just share.

Partner B Great.

Partner A (*Grunts*)

Partner B Hey, look at me for a sec. (*Looks at their mate with a friendly smile*)

Partner A (*Returns the gaze*)

Partner B I love you, and I'm sorry for dropping you.

Partner A I love you, too. (*Smiles back*) I'm okay now. (*They kiss.*)

In order for the above to work, one partner, the accused, must be the anchor in the moment. Repair, make right, don't argue, don't explain, don't qualify, just provide full relief to the injured or misunderstood partner. Still, this wouldn't work without the other partner's cooperation and wish for mutual relief, not simply their own.

Collaboration and cooperation are two different behaviors and intentions. Both are necessary to secure functioning. Both are required to quickly put out fires. Both partners must scurry to mutual relief and get there as quickly as possible—then move forward. Delaying, pointing fingers, defending, excusing, dismissing, or anything other than relieving each other quickly simply prolongs interpersonal stress and distress, which leads to increased threat memory, rancor, and ill-health.

Secure-functioning partners never threaten the relationship as a ploy to get what they want. Threatening the relationship to punish or bully a partner is manipulative and dishonest. Moreover, it's dangerous to both individuals. It's a sign of helplessness and weakness because that partner has no other way to engage, set limits, or otherwise enforce fairness and justice that should go in both directions. It is a unilateral strategy to frighten the other into submission and, therefore, it's bullying.

Helpless people often default to aggressiveness as a primitive means to defend their interests. The driving force is commonly fear. However, fear, as with all feelings, can lead people to do very bad things. Fear is no excuse for noncollaborative or destructive behavior in partnership.

 ### Variations of This Complaint

Negativism, the act of kicking one's own sandcastle, is an act of bullying that destroys relationship spirit and morale. Negativistic partners become so preoccupied with past injustices and unfairness that they perpetrate injustice and unfairness on others. They commonly anticipate the worst without contributing to solutions. Negativism is neither collaborative nor cooperative. It is as self-centered and one-person oriented as extreme narcissism. It exists as a protection of self but manifests as a destruction of union and alliance. There is no place for negativism in teamwork. Imagine a troupe of actors just before the start of a play, and one of them says, "We're just going to flop tonight." Thank you.

"My Partner Always Wants Me to Join in What They Want, with Whom They Want, When They Want"

All examples in this chapter highlight unfairness, inequity, and lack of shared power and authority. Partners can want or not want. There's never a problem with that. Secure-functioning partners know they must get each other on board with wants and don't-wants. A two-person psychological system represents a fair and just union of equals and, accordingly, partners have to work together, not separately, unless they otherwise agree to do so.

Some negotiations and agreements can happen quickly. In fact, the more you practice, the faster you both will become. But first, you both must understand that without mutual agreements, enforcement is impossible, and problems will simply repeat. The same with getting each other on board completely with win-win solutions. If you know nothing else will work without creating bad downstream effects, if you know there is no other way to "do business" with each other, then you will both learn to get faster and faster at accomplishing this task each time.

This particular complaint suggests that one partner leads and the other follows. We can be angry at the driver-partner, but what of the passenger-partner? When and why did that passenger-partner surrender their rights and authority? Perhaps one makes and distributes all the money and goods, and the other has "no choice"? Perhaps one—due to sex assignment or gender identification—is given natural rights and power over the other? In secure functioning, both partners are responsible for power imbalances.

"We Never Make Decisions Together"

One of the principles of secure functioning is that partners get each other fully on board before making decisions. Partners must resolve the specifics in advance, such as which decisions must be fully mutual. If partners share ultimate power and authority, it follows that both share accountability for their decisions.

The Complaint in Action

Partner A You went ahead and made the decision to make that investment, didn't you?

Partner B I did.

Partner A And you didn't think to ask me or consult with me first?

Partner B That investment is part of my business. That's *my* domain. You don't know anything about my business. You're just going to have to trust me.

Partner A Like before? When you lost all that money? Trust you?

Partner B I had no control over that. I told you.

Partner A You told me, but how do I know what really happened? You tell me things after the fact. I'm not an idiot. I understand investments. This is *our* money.

Partner B No, it's not. It's my company's money. You don't know investments in my business. I don't interfere with your business at home.

Partner A You mean, our kids? That's not simply *my* domain, my friend. Remember, I left my business for you, and we switched places. Remember that. This isn't the first time you've made decisions without me. You decided on our vacation, on our holiday plans this year, on the garage . . . shall I continue?

Partner B Wait a second, you decided to put our kids in private school. I didn't make that decision. You did.

Partner A That's because you said you didn't care to get involved. We're not working together at all!

And scene.

Why Does This Keep Happening?

Structure, folks. If you build a shoddy structure, don't be surprised if walls collapse and ceilings fall. No structure, no plan, no collaboration? It's going to be pandemonium. Operate as separate agents doing your own thing when both of you are stakeholders, and the results will be disappointing and substandard.

Partners, like the ones in this example, err by operating independently in this fashion. Why do they do it? Because that is likely what they saw and experienced in their families of origin. "It's how business was done in our family. You did your thing, I did mine." This is not thought through; it's memory, it's experience, it's the way things were done.

And this is *most* people. Few people create innovative relationship principles and constitution. That takes too much energy expenditure, time, and maturity. Most rely on what they already know.

The Central Culprit: The Interaction

This couple's main problem is their lack of shared purpose and vision. Once again, they believe they are family and not strangers establishing a union that requires continuous shaping and reshaping to suit both partners' needs and wants.

Partner A You went ahead and made the decision to make that investment, didn't you?

Partner B I did.

A curt response, signaling hostility to the question. Partner A's question wasn't formulated to be friendly and so got a defiant response. The fight begins with the first shot across the bow.

Partner A And you didn't think to ask me or consult with me first?

Was there an agreement to do so? If so, then this should be a statement focused on that agreement being broken, not a question which, in this case, sounds inflammatory.

Partner B That investment is part of my business. That's *my* domain. You don't know anything about my business. You're just going to have to trust me.

Never a good idea to tell someone, "You're just going to have to trust me." It's obviously noncollaborative and threatening. In fact, Partner B's response is aggressive, devaluing, and dictatorial. Their unapologetic "I did" implies they have had no other kind of arrangement. Partner A's complaint about not having been consulted first is toothless if no previous agreement exists. Without agreements and policies, partners will fight needlessly.

Partner A Like before? When you lost all that money? Trust you?

Partner A's questioning approach is passively hostile and baiting, when it should be declarative. Partners are fighting *around* a problem without addressing it head on. Should we inform each other and get each other fully on board with important decisions? **If the answer is yes for one partner and no for the other, we then have a deal breaker to settle. That's the elephant in the room no one is addressing.** These two are firmly planted in a one-person system and expect peace, well-being, and productivity. This is a losing team.

Your own partner fights are symptoms of your central problems. Those problems are *not* each of your psychological histories, parents, exes, or other deeper issues many couples use to distract from the obvious. Where will you agree, where will you disagree, and is there no way to find accord? If the latter, then, deal breaker. Yet even with deal breakers, if you take the time, you often discover misunderstanding and rigidity. Once the two of you understand what's happening, rigid silos collapse. You can start repairing and making more things happen for both of you. You must work to find ways to satisfy each other's needs and wants and settle each other's concerns, fears, and anxieties. No other path will work in a two-person system.

Partner B I had no control over that. I told you.

Not a great statement to go along with "You're just going to have to trust me." When two people fully agree to do or not do something, both share in that gambit's wins and losses.

Partner A You told me, but how do I know what really
happened? You tell me things after the fact. I'm not
an idiot. I understand investments. This is *our* money.

Partner B No, it's not. It's my company's money. You don't
know investments in my business. I don't interfere
with your business at home.

Another huge flaw in the relationship structure. Who owns what? Is everything shared? If not, what isn't shared, and why isn't it? This epiphany—"My company's money isn't yours"—is either a new idea or a misunderstanding from the very start of their relationship. However, Partner B's implication doesn't appear to be a misunderstanding.

Partner A You mean, our kids? That's not simply *my* domain,
my friend. Remember, I left my business for you,
and we switched places. Remember that. This
isn't the first time you've made decisions without
me. You decided on our vacation, on our holidays
plans this year, on the garage . . . shall I continue?

Partner A has their guns out now with "my friend" and "remember that" and "shall I continue." This is an escalation despite the seemingly innocent wording.

Partner B Wait a second, you decided to put our kids in private school. I didn't make that decision. You did.

Partner A That's because you said you didn't care to get involved. We're not working together at all!

True, they are not working together at all, and yet Partner A is a coconspirator nonetheless. Their interaction is a lot of blah, blah, blah. A pox on both their houses, as neither plays by rules of mutual decision-making. It's the "I know you are, but what am I" circular accusation. This is in no way made up. We—all of us—will do and talk like this when we exist without purpose, principles, or guardrails.

If you and your partner recognize that you have similarly established separate domains where the other may not intrude, look for drift (see below). Time to take steps to repair it and tend to what matters most to you both. Allow section 1 of this book to be your instructional guide. There I explain how to establish a purpose, a vision, and shared principles of governance (SPGs). Establish your own and allow yourselves to practice thriving in each other's care.

Corrections

This fight is unnecessary from a structural perspective. In general, when partners do their ground work and first cocreate a real sense of purpose and vision for doing business as a couple, this fight will not occur. Perhaps there will be other fights, but not this one.

Disputes of this type recur because neither partner will bother to set up shop properly, by consensus, which first requires getting each other on board. These partners tend to bifurcate their roles and responsibilities. They mostly become siloed and solo players.

This practice almost always leads to relationship *drift*—a trajectory launched by distancing and avoidance that points toward eventual dissolution. Drift is a pernicious course of action spurred by a continuous choice to avoid and distance. You and your partner will naturally find your own interests, but watch for signs of drift. Discuss it as soon as you see yourselves growing apart. Correct drift by actively doing the opposite by spending more time together each day and not simply by planning a date night. Find new things to do together—projects, travel, adventure, learning something entirely new, and sharing your separate friendships. More on correcting drift in chapter 9.

Variations of This Complaint

The following grievances have similar things in common, and they each involve two people operating as one-person systems:

"I can't get a word in edgewise."

"I have no power."

"I have no say."

One sounds like they want parity, but wanting is never enough. Trying is insufficient. Working on it means not yet. Only expectation of and insistence on parity, equity, and teamwork do the trick. Adult love relationships, as with all adult interdependent relationships, rely on fully formed individuals who are willing to stand for principles, not wishes or promises. Principles require action, otherwise they are merely words, and words only do not a pact make.

Human beings are, by nature, self-centered, opportunistic, moody, fickle, impulsive, aggressive, stubborn, and self-righteous; they are also wonderfully willing to love, sacrifice, serve, join, commune, cooperate, and collaborate. These are basic qualities (see chapter 14 for a full list) common to us all. This is neither a positive nor negative view of human primates. We would be naïve to believe in or to count on human nature to be in consistent harmony with a selfless affinity for true mutuality. The only thing that prevents us from being at our worst is knowing we can't do our worst and also get along well with others.

If your partner is being unfair, it's because they can. Yelling at them doesn't translate to "they can't." Punishing or threatening doesn't work either. Plenty of kids and adults learn to tolerate threats and punishment in order to do what they want. Only when faced with the prospect of breaking the fidelity of the relationship will the message get across. It's a show, not a tell, that I will not stand for that deal. It's a bad deal for me, and if I give it even more thought, probably bad for you, too. So no, we agreed not to make unilateral decisions. I can't, you can't.

When you and your partner orient yourselves as a two-person psychological system, what you can and cannot do becomes extremely clear because each of you is affected by the other, and there's no getting away from that. You're in each other's care.

If your partner interrupts you or takes all the space, learn to graciously expand without harming your obnoxious partner. Take your place, your space. Power is taken, not given. When power is shared, it's not useful as a tool for domination. Shared power and authority lead partners to only use tools of persuasion, influence, seduction, bargaining, negotiation, and consensus creation. Failing to use these tools merely leads to war. Make no mistake, two people make these choices, never just one.

Chapter 7

Messiness and Timeliness

With this chapter, we explore two of the most common complaints heard from couples in my clinic: messiness and timeliness. Fights over messiness include everything from leaving clothes on the floor, dishes in the sink, clutter in rooms and overstuffed closets, dust or dirt on surfaces, pet and children's items around the house, and old food in the refrigerator. You may have your own list. It is important to note that one person's idea of messiness is another person's notion of tidiness.

Similar complaints surround collections and projects. Some partners love sparsity while others love collectibles—tchotchkes, trinkets, and souvenirs. Other partners complain of crafts, hobbies, and home projects overrunning the living space—too many objects in a room, collections of unused objects, abandoned projects—the list goes on, and most households seem to have at least one of these issues.

Timeliness complaints include being late, being early, completing tasks on time, forgetting tasks, missing important dates or events, and poor preplanning (e.g., weather, traffic). Being on time is more important to some than others. For instance, timeliness in various cultures can refer to clock time or acceptable time.

Again, as partners, sit down together. Address your need for a simple policy to govern the messes and schedules you make. Instead of fighting unnecessarily over something that you can settle in advance, it's possible for you both to establish a guiding principle that serves each of you, your hobbies and interests, and the time you're willing to take to care for your things and each other's complaints.

"My Partner Is Messy"

The complaint here is that one or both partners are messy. I include the possibility of both because often one partner will complain of messiness while the other has evidence of equal or similar messiness. Look around you. If that is the case for you and your partner, stop pointing fingers and start figuring out a solution, which may include getting a housekeeper if you are financially able and if you agree that getting help in the house is important to your mutual happiness.

The more common grievance in this category of complaints is one fastidious partner complaining about a specific issue they want their sloppier companion to address.

The Complaint in Action

Partner A You're always leaving your clothes on the bedroom floor. You're worse than the kids. Why do I always have to pick up after you?

Partner B You don't have to pick up anything. Just tell me, and I'll pick them up.

Partner A Why should I have to tell you? You're an adult. You should know when you leave things around. You pick them up and put them where they should be. It's simple.

Partner B If it's that simple, you can pick them up yourself. I've picked up your things before.

Partner A What? When do I leave things around for you to pick up?

Partner B In the kitchen. You'll leave your coffee cup on the counter. I put it in the dishwasher. You've left your towel on my side, and I've put it back. I haven't complained about that.

Partner A It's not the same. I'm talking about things you leave on the floor of the bedroom every day. I don't leave things around on the floor or in the kitchen every day, now do I?

Partner B All I'm saying is that I don't get any credit for picking up your stuff, and I don't complain. I'm busy in the morning. I'm running out the door after I shower, and you know that.

Partner A I'm done talking to you. This is impossible!

And scene.

Why Does This Keep Happening?

Things repeat when partners fail to create policies based on fairness and cooperation. They also get into power struggles that reach back into early experiences with authority figures and forget that they are both authority figures who agree to collaborate and share power. Making more work for one partner creates a problem for the other partner down the line.

In this case, Partner B is creating a problem with fairness by resisting relief to Partner A, a problem that will accrue memory and lead to content spread (complaints about other areas of unfairness) and amplification (increased inflammation and intensity). This is unwise. Still, the larger problem is a lack of policy that allows for equal enforcement of principles of governance.

These partners could wait until things cool down and then talk briefly about managing household tasks and shared responsibilities, including any perception of unfairness and inequality of workload. Should partners get each other fully on board with such a policy, enforcement becomes much easier.

The Central Culprit: The Interaction

Now, to give you a chance to absorb an improved version of the same complaint, let's do a deeper dive into specific parts of the original interaction. Examining these errors and missteps may give you insight into how to improve your approach as well as the twists and turns of phrase—the small culprits—that cause these loops to repeat in the first place.

> **Partner A** You're always leaving your clothes on the bedroom floor. You're worse than the kids. Why do I always have to pick up after you?

A problem with the first sentence is the word *always*. Though the sentiment is perfectly understandable, words like *always* and *never* can be heard as threatening by your audience. People usually object to accusations that dismiss any possibility of variation. The reason people use these terms is because something is happening too much or too little.

It's better to say something like, "I'm getting tired of your clothes on the floor," or "The clothes on the floor are really getting to me," or "Pick up your clothes, or I'm going to pile them on your bed for later." The last comment is less a threat than a consequence, which is fair.

The last sentence, "Why do I always have to pick up after you?" is problematic because it implies that Partner B told Partner A to pick up after them. Unless this was actually said by Partner B, it's not directly Partner B's problem. Also, it's a question masked as a complaint. To certain partners, this question can be interpreted as an attack. The implied pressure to answer a question that's really a complaint will likely lead to a return attack.

It might be better to say, "If you persist in leaving a mess, we're going to have a talk later about how we want our bedroom and home to look and feel," and finish there for now. The time to talk policy is when both partners are fully calm and relaxed. In this case, make your point and exit. Otherwise the interaction itself will become the problem.

Partner B You don't have to pick up anything. Just tell me, and I'll pick them up.

While this response implies something annoying—that this person has to be told to do something obvious—it isn't entirely unfair if it's true. Human beings are almost totally automatic, reflexive, and oblivious. Partners must be willing to train each other and be trained. That actually works! People quickly lose their visual, auditory, and olfactory awareness if accustomed to an environmental signal. A cluttered home can become normal to folks until a photo is taken and then they experience a sudden, rude awakening. We can easily get used to environmental messes, dust, wall cracks, and warping floor boards and fail to see these things with fresh eyes.

The same is true for remaining aware of our surroundings, of our partner's face and body, of our children's constant changes—the people and things that matter to us. We can get angry with each other for failing to see, hear, smell, or notice, but that doesn't help anyone or anything.

Partner A says, "Pick up your socks," and Partner B balks. Partner A's command would be a problem if Partner B's "Just tell me, and I'll pick them up" were true. If true, then telling Partner B in the moment to pick up after themselves should lead to them remembering the next time.

"Pick up your things, please" and then "Thank you" when it's done is the training. However, two conditions must be in place: Partner A must be willing to issue a friendly command to pick up enough times to get this going, and Partner B must be willing to respond to a friendly command. Partner A must also stay present while Partner B completes the task, say, "Thank you," and exit without remark (perhaps other than a kiss). This will work as remembering becomes a natural outcome—sooner than later—if the correction is made in the moment and not later or too early.

Partner B If it's that simple, you can pick them up yourself. I've picked up your things before.

Big mistake! Not only is that first comment dismissive, but it's also begging for a fight. The other partner is now challenged to fight back, and that's a foolhardy tactic.

The second comment is pure deflection as it evades the complaint. Deflection is a common deceptive strategy. Use it at your own peril. **Deflection makes others angry because it distracts from the topic, and it demonstrates a refusal to cooperate. It also deprives both partners of timely relief, which means heart rates and blood pressures will continue to rise, making war more likely.**

> **Partner B** All I'm saying is that I don't get any credit for picking up your stuff, and I don't complain. I'm busy in the morning. I'm running out the door after I shower, and you know that.

Another deflective tactic that will surely lead to a fight. It does, in fact, lead Partner A to give up and leave the room. Nonetheless, this is a fight that will continue with no relief in sight. Perpetual fights take a toll. Not only does the repetition add to inflammation of threat anticipation and response, it also becomes a health problem if distress periods become more sustained. Better—when both partners are calm—to put a policy or a guardrail in position for the next time. This requires that partners predict each other and use the prompting method, as described in chapter 1, that reminds the errant partner to either yield or get moving.

Corrections

If one partner starts off poorly; that is, speaks in a manner that considers the self only and not the other, the burden falls on the other partner to respond properly as a team member protecting the relationship rather than simply the self. This may not seem fair, as the other partner may feel something like, *You just punched me. I* must *punch back.* Or, *You just impugned my reputation. I* must *protect myself.* Or, *You just accused me of something. I* must *set the record straight.*

While any of these impulses are completely natural, they're not collaborative or friendly or helpful. They just contribute to the fire that will quickly consume both of you. This will be self-evident if it already hasn't occurred to you. Remember, there are just two of you (unless you're in a polyamory situation) holding up the union. Therefore, what you do as individuals counts in every moment.

Blaming each other, though enticing, is simply contributing to the problem. If you both go up in flames, it's on both of you. Either of you could have done something to change the trajectory of the interaction and therefore changed the outcome.

Better to focus on *what you did or didn't do* that contributed to the quarrel. If you both do that, you will be well on your way to secure functioning. But focus on the other, and you'll fall into a loop that forces both of you to protect your own interests, and fighting will repeat. Justice and fairness work differently in a two-person system. In a scrap, partners can easily declare the other one as unfair and, in doing so, act unfairly. **Remember, the relationship comes before having to be right.** I truly acknowledge how difficult this is; I can attest to it myself. And yet, this book is about doing the right (or best) thing when the right (or best) thing is the hardest to do.

Let's see a do-over with the above dialogue and start with a better way to approach a difficult topic.

Partner A Okay. Let's talk about this problem we keep having. I hate that you leave your clothes on the bedroom floor. You hate that I nag and complain about this. Right?

Partner B Right.

Partner A Should we allow each other to leave things around on the floor, or the kitchen table, or the bathroom, or anywhere? Keep in mind, if you or I don't pick up after each other, the stuff just gets left there, and we end up with a messy house—again. Is that a good idea as a policy? We leave whatever we feel on the floor or wherever and neither of us picks up. Do we want that?

Partner B (*Thinks a bit*) What if we pick things up eventually but not right away?

Partner A Okay. What should "eventually" be? How long can I leave things around, like on your side of the bathroom or in the kitchen?

Partner B A reasonable amount of time.

Partner A   Okay, but what's "a reasonable amount of time"?
An hour, five hours, a day, two days? What?
Consider also, do we want the kids to do the same
thing, because they will if they see us doing it.

Partner B   Can't our housekeeper clean up?

Partner A   Yes, but that's every two weeks. Should we have
a messy home for two weeks while we wait? Also,
the kids are going to say the same thing. What are
we teaching them?

Partner B   Okay. I see your point. How about if either of us
sees something lying around, we just take care of it?

Partner A   But that's not fair because I don't leave nearly the
same amount around the house. Do you agree?
I mean, think about it. And do you want that
same policy with the kids? You're angry with them
already for not cleaning up after themselves.

Partner B   Alright, it's probably best that we all are
responsible for picking up our things and cleaning
up our own messes.

Partner A   Probably? Or is that what you really want as a policy?
I want that. I want the kids to do that. But we have
to do it first. Are you really on board with this idea?

Partner B   Yes. I'm on board.

Partner A   Here's the thing. Does that mean that I don't have
to ask you and . . . hold on . . . if I do, you agree to
do it without giving me a hard time?

Partner B   Yes. I'm sorry for doing that. Yes, I'll pick up without
you reminding me and, if I forget and you say
something, I promise I won't give you a hard time.

Partner A   Deal! [They kiss and problem is solved for now.]

Variations of This Complaint

"My Partner's Car Is a Mess"

Some people complain that their partner's car or other belongings are messy or disorganized (such as one's purse, shoulder bag, personal area, or other nonshared space). The question here is why it matters to the complaining partner.

Partner A It just drives me crazy that you'd keep your car like that. It looks like you live in it. How could you be so, I don't know, teenager-like?

Partner B What's it to you? It's my car. It doesn't affect you.

Partner A What if I'm driving with you?

Partner B We never go anywhere in my car.

Partner A It's just emblematic of how you take care of your things.

This complaint has to do with another person's care of their personal items or space. It's not about being a team, at least as expressed in this scene. It's more of an annoyance to the partner who doesn't like to see messiness. If the complaint relates to a larger, communal issue of messiness, one that actually affects the partner, then the complaint becomes more reasonable. Though I would suggest the argument remain about shared interests and avoid making personal comparisons. That's a good way to get into a needless fight.

In this particular case, Partner A would likely lose each time because the complaint doesn't involve a shared interest. It's simply irritating. But many of my clients and readers have heard me say that people are annoying, irritating, disappointing, and burdensome in love relationships. So what else is new? Adult partners aren't children; therefore Partner B has the right to treat their own car as they wish.

However, if Partner A has a good argument for why their partner's messy car directly affects them, okay. For instance, "Your messy car is a terrible example to our young kids of how they should care for their things." Or, "Your mess is a real driving hazard, and here's why." Or, "When we have to drive in your car, I hate sitting in trash, and it smells." These, perhaps, are better arguments. If it's, "It reflects badly on me," well, that might not go so well. You're individual adults, accepting each other as is. You're both free to do as you please if it doesn't actually affect the relationship safety and security system, mutual protection, fealty, or shared values.

Messiness comes in different varieties: tech, makeup, or gaming equipment scattered about; clothes and shoes in every room; hair on the floors or in the shower. Pick your complaint and tackle it in the same way we did in any of the vignettes in this chapter.

"My Partner Is a Hoarder"

Collecting, minor hoarding, and holding on to things are actions that are often, though not always, familial in origin, with at least one parental figure or caregiver passing this characteristic on to their offspring. On the other hand, it may be that a partner's caregivers threw everything away, and now it's very important for that partner to hold on to things, particularly items that have sentimental value. Other people are simply so busy that they never get around to looking at what they already have and continue to accrue the same objects.

It's important to distinguish between two variations of hoarding. The first is the most common: partners holding on to things, forgetting to sort them, give them away, sell them, or throw them out, or holding on to memorabilia that is just too painful to lose.

Many people tend to collect papers, files, art work, magazines, books, electronic accessories, and knickknacks. Other people like to keep their possessions lean. For them, if it isn't being used, they donate it, gift it, sell it, recycle it, or throw it away. Arguments about keeping versus throwing away are about as common as any complaints I hear in my clinic. I'm sure these complaints go all the way back to some of the earliest civilizations and pair-bonding unions.

The second variation is related strongly to anxiety and obsessive-compulsive disorders. These hoarders often become worse with time. Their hoarding can be one of the most difficult challenges to overcome and to treat psychologically. There is some evidence that genetics plays a role in this type of hoarding (Ivanov et al. 2017). Nonetheless, a partner who is in this category will fill up whole rooms, garages, storage areas, and even several houses. Obvious health and safety problems—rodents, spoilage, and combustibles, to name a few—accompany this type of hoarding.

For relationships, however, this type of hoarding is often disastrous. The hoarding partner cannot keep from allowing their purchases, papers, souvenirs, and other objects to stack up. They usually won't allow their partner or an organizer to help them reorganize or declutter. At the same time, they will make countless promises to get the task done, but time keeps slipping away, leaving their partner in despair.

In this chapter, I focus on the most common type of hoarding and collecting. My one word of caution is that this problem may indeed become a deal breaker for the partners. Of course, personal therapy and psychopharmacological remedies are available for such individuals, but in my clinical experience, these individuals tend to refuse these interventions. Sadly, there are a good many severe hoarders in the total population that cross all socioeconomic, ethnic, racial, gender, and sexual-orientation strata.

The Complaint in Action

Partner A I just found two more of those cords you keep buying. How many do you need? I mean, I keep finding them, and you keep saying you can't find them.

Partner B Stop. They're not a big deal. Those cords are inexpensive.

Partner A That's not the point. Listen, I keep finding piles of your things stacking up all over the place. That's not fair to me.

Partner B What stacking? Where?

Partner A In the living room, the kitchen area where we sit and eat, our shared office area. Come on. You know what I'm talking about. It's not fair that our shared space is filling up.

Partner B I just haven't had time to sort through everything. When can I? We're both working all the time.

Partner A I have time this weekend. Can I go through and throw things out?

Partner B No! Don't do that. You don't know what I need.

Partner A Well then, help me out here. Let's do it together.

Partner B No, because you'll bug me about every little thing.

Partner A This is making me incredibly angry.

And scene.

 ### Why Does This Keep Happening?

Once again, we must look at the couple's policy on maintaining their living space. Like so many people, these partners keep leaving things for later, including policymaking. Without policies or principles, partners leave each other to do as they please, as they are accustomed, and as they were raised.

We are energy-conserving animals. Most every task is accomplished through memory and habit. We take all kinds of shortcuts—in our verbal and nonverbal communication, in our appraisal of people and situations, and in our interpretations of the purpose and intent of others, particularly of our partners. We forget that we have separate minds that only approximate each other at any given time. Our processing of social-emotional information is variable, as are our states of mind and body. Our histories and family cultures are different. Our tastes, ideas, emotions, thoughts, perception, personality—all different. This is not a problem unless one expects otherwise.

Mutually created, shared principles based on what partners deem is the best policy for the best outcome for both will win the day—and the argument. **All principles or policies must be win-win or they're no-goes. In order to achieve mutually created principles of governance, partners must remain committed to working on the problem and not on each other. It's a puzzle to be solved, not a finger to be pointed.**

The Central Culprit: The Interaction

Now for the original dialogue from the problem in action. Let's take a deep dive into their actual interaction.

Partner A I just found two more of those cords you keep buying. How many do you need? I mean, I keep finding them and you keep saying you can't find them.

Partner B Stop. They're not a big deal. Those cords are inexpensive.

This isn't a terrible response, but it's not very good either. It's dismissive and that will cause blowback and a longer back-and-forth, as in the following reaction.

Partner A That's not the point. Listen, I keep finding piles of your things stacking up all over the place. That's not fair to me.

Partner B What stacking? Where?

Again, this response requires more time and more stress. It's possible, though unlikely, that Partner B knows nothing of this. "Show me" might be a shorter route.

Partner A In the living room, the kitchen area where we sit and eat, our shared office area. Come on. You know what I'm talking about. It's not fair that our shared space is filling up.

Partner B I just haven't had time to sort through everything. When can I? We're both working all the time.

So Partner B just tacitly admitted they knew about what and where. The problem is that Partner B is building frustration in Partner A, which will turn out badly for both. Additionally, Partner B's next statement is a deflection, which can be taken as a deceptive move. The problem here is that Partner B is risking their own credibility when responding in this way. It doesn't sound honest, cooperative, or collaborative.

Partner A I have time this weekend. Can I go through and throw things out?

Partner B No! Don't do that. You don't know what I need.

Answering yes or no to a question like, "Is it raining outside?" is fine because no other answer and no further response is expected. However, when asked, "Is dinner at 6:00 p.m. tonight?" and the answer is no without further information, that's frustrating. Something more like, "No, it's at 7:00" is expected. When a partner is asked a question, as in the above example, "Can I go through and throw things out?" answering no without anything further will likely be interpreted as noncollaborative. "No! Don't do that. You don't know what I need," should be followed by an offer of some kind. "How about I go through it first and then you can throw things out?"

Collaborative partners bargain and negotiate. Take a penny, give a penny. Just saying no leaves the other partner holding the bag and the burden. Partners must always work toward mutual relief of some kind and do it quickly so as to avoid remaining in stress or distress.

Partner A Well then, help me out here. Let's do it together.

Partner B No, because you'll bug me about every little thing.

Partner A This is making me incredibly angry.

This is the logical outcome with such an interactive segment. There is no shared burden to solve the problem, which is one partner seeking relief that isn't available. These sequences add up and become larger issues for the future. Additionally, these smallish arguments become sorted into each partner's childhood history narratives. Partner A may have witnessed one parent behaving this way toward the other parent. Memories of their parents' arguments might cause Partner A to maintain a childhood narrative of never being respected, attended to, or treated equally or a narrative of being neglected or used. Conversely, Partner B may experience recognizable feelings of being accused unfairly, criticized, or told what to do and may have witnessed this behavior in their parents or siblings.

Either way, when couples complain that these small issues aren't important because there are bigger issues underneath it all, they usually have it backward. The small back-and-forths they get into while under stress that fail to get repaired are actually the causes of what *appear* to be larger issues!

The couple's failure to deal with distress quickly with an eye toward relief and repair is amplifying deeper, more troubling memories of trauma, unfairness, and insensitivity. Our narratives are always formed through our memory system and our confirmation bias through sensory perception and appraisal. Our narratives, under stress, are always self-serving.

Corrections

How might this couple work the problem? Let's see how calm civility works.

Partner A Do we want shared spaces that feel comforting, organized, clean, and attractive?

Partner B Yes, but we have to define *comforting* and *attractive* and, for that matter, what is *good enough*.

Partner A You mean good enough for both of us, not just one of us?

Partner B Yes, of course. I know these things are more important to you than they are to me.

Partner A (*Sigh*) Okay, but work with me on this, please. I don't think either one of us wants to have this same fight over and over again.

Partner B Agreed. Okay, how about this? I do want our space to be nice, and I want you to be happy. How about we make time each weekend, say an hour or two, going through all of our stuff together. We can decide what to keep and where to keep it. If it's not being used, we can talk about throwing it out or giving it away. If we do it together and schedule a weekly time, it will get done. How's that?

Partner A Really? I like that idea. And then we can schedule something fun to do together right after, like go out for food or something like that.

Partner B Sure.

Partner A Do you really want this? I mean, please don't just do it for me. I want us both to want organization. And it will save us money. We don't need to keep buying things that we have already. Let's figure out what we have and where to put things for easy access.

Partner B   If this ends these arguments, it's a win for me. You are more detailed than I am, and that's a good thing even though it annoys me sometimes. I know I'm disorganized. I'm on board.

Partner A   (*Big sigh*) Well, that didn't take long. Thank you.

Partner B   I love you.

For you and your partner—or any two (or more) people—to get along, you must continually show demonstrations of goodwill and a willingness to find mutual ground. Only individuals stuck in a one-person oriented mindset will act in a manner that suits their interests only. Secure functioning means relationship before self. Insecure functioning is the reverse: self before relationship. If both partners are in service to one another, the self is served.

Variations of This Complaint

As mentioned earlier, variations on hoarding range from a small but consistent collection of newspapers, magazines, knickknacks, photographs, and keepsakes to ever-increasing stacks of objects. The best thing is to take photographs of clutter so that both partners can get some distance from the daily eyeballing of the environment. The only problem in doing so may be the shame and avoidance of the cluttering partner. Hoarding, when it becomes pathological, can become a shaming experience for the hoarder. Complicating factors, such as complex grief, personality disorders, obsessive-compulsive disorder, and even dementia and Alzheimer's, often contribute to hoarding.

For the most part, however, hoarding and cluttering range from "normal" (a common or average amount) to "enough is enough," according to a partner. Variations include children amassing clutter or collections. My daughter still has her collection of Beanie Babies from her childhood in our attic along with her large collection of books, which for her would be a sin to part with. Will they ever leave the attic?

In our garage, we have collected family photo books, memorabilia, and other items belonging to various family members who are now spread across the globe. We're still waiting for everyone (anyone?) to claim their items.

I personally have collected electronic items, parts, and software that are considered Stone Age now. Tracey, my partner, keeps stacks of magazines that seem too dated to be relevant, and yet she wants to go through them first before giving them away.

We joke with many of our friends who, like us, thought the COVID period would finally allow us time to clear out stuff, and we found other things to do instead. So there you go. Still, we don't fight about this. We're on the same page: we want an organized, comfortable living space without clutter. We remain busy, perhaps overly so, and we intend, someday, to get rid of our stuff.

"My Partner Is Always Late"

Time is yet another common complaint I hear in my clinic. Why is one person loose with time and another so very tight? Time isn't subjective if a clock is involved. In a clocked reality, time is an objectively agreed-upon measurement of temporal experience. However, time *is* subjective without awareness of a clock. We sit in a movie theater where time either slows or speeds up, depending upon our engagement in the movie. The same with engaged conversation or engaged sex or engaged anything. Time becomes relative, depending on our state of mind. If we are on certain drugs, time can either speed up or slow down, sometimes in rapid alternation. If we are depressed, time seems to slow. If we are excited and moving, time seems to speed up.

People who are focused on a task often lose track of time. They may think only a few minutes have passed when it's been thirty minutes or more. Others may want to remain focused because they can't let go of the moment. Still others continually avoid the next thing in favor of what they are doing (or not doing). And of course, there are those who are loath to move forward with anything. They linger and lounge until it's too late.

Some people are never on time to anything. They have their reasons, hopefully, because nobody appreciates "I don't know" as an answer for rude or insensitive behavior. On the other end of the spectrum, some people are never late, don't tolerate being late, and don't tolerate others being late. They may get labeled as having harsh and punishing standards. Still others believe that "on time" is equal to being late, so they prefer to be early. This can be annoying to those hosting a party and having to deal with unexpectedly early arrivals.

Time can be a sticking point for a great many individuals, and so it counts as one of the most common areas of conflict between partners.

The Complaint in Action

Partner A I waited for you, again, for over thirty minutes and, again, you're late! No call, no text, no nothing. I don't know what to do with you. Do you know how rude this is? Is this how you show your love for me?

Partner B If you'll just calm down for a minute, I have an explanation.

Partner A Of course you have an explanation, you always have an explanation. I don't need an explanation, I need you to be on time!

Partner B Are you going to calm down for a second so I can talk to you, or are you going to just lay into me?

Partner A I'm going to lay into you. I'm going to make you as miserable as you make me. Deal with it! I had to deal with waiting. You deal with my anger. Argh!

(*Silence for a few beats*)

Partner A Argh! Why do I let you do this to me? I must be an idiot. I am! I'm the stupid idiot that falls for this again and again.

(*Partner B just stands there, staring away.*)

Partner A Okay . . . what's your explanation this time?

Partner B There was a Sigalert on the 405. Check it out on your phone. You'll see.

Partner A I'm not going to bother.

Partner B Suit yourself.

Partner A What time did you leave?

Partner B In time.

Partner A *What* time?

Partner B I don't know. But I left to give myself enough time to get here.

Partner A So it must be true.

Partner B Look, nothing I can say is going to get you to calm down. Now, do you want me to stay and have lunch with you, or should I just go back to work? Your choice.
(*Partner A stares off into the distance.*)
The maître d' comes to seat them, and they follow.

And scene.

Why Does This Keep Happening?

This scene could've taken place anywhere, at any time, and under any circumstance. It doesn't matter one bit. The fact that it repeats is the primary issue and, like other repeating conflicts, there's a solution. However, a solution only exists if both partners are willing to be cooperative, collaborative, and fair.

Though time, as I have explained, can be a sticking point between partners, the real problem exists in the experience of unfairness and insensitivity. Chronic lateness is also experienced—rightly or wrongly—as unloving. For instance, childhood experiences of parents being late when picking their kids up from school is long remembered as an unloving act. The same is true when children find a parent late or missing from a school play performance or one of their sporting events. It's felt as uncaring. Chronic lateness is difficult to repair as it is a repeated, felt threat to the security of the relationship. Partners who argue against this perception only make matters worse. Lateness can cost money and time. For example, folks who are chronically late for planes miss their flights. That costs time and money for both partners. It also raises the stress level for both.

The Central Culprit: The Interaction

Let's now go back to the beginning of their initial interaction and see what might've been done better.

Partner A I waited for you, again, for over thirty minutes and, again, you're late! No call, no text, no nothing. I don't know what to do with you. Do you know how rude this is? Is this how you show your love for me?

The only other way for Partner A to have dealt with Partner B is to have left the meeting place when Partner B failed to appear at the appointed time.

Partner B If you'll just calm down for a minute, I have an explanation.

As this is a repeated problem, Partner B should know better than to even think of explaining. Partner B has no grand gesture to distract Partner A from their outrage, let alone an acceptable explanation. Even an "I'm so sorry" would've been better than "If you'll calm down for a minute, I have an explanation." Just lame.

Partner B Are you going to calm down for a second so I can talk to you, or are you going to just lay into me?

And that's called doubling down on a bad idea. Here, Partner B has the audacity to blame Partner A for ranting. No offer of anything that could come close to relieving for Partner A. The last thing any recipient of wrongdoing wants to hear is an excuse, a defense, or anything other than a full-throated apology and something that will prevent future injury.

Partner A I'm going to lay into you. I'm going to make you as miserable as you make me. Deal with it! I had to deal with waiting. You deal with my anger. Argh!

Fun, perhaps, and maybe justified, but still a waste of time and energy.

Partner B There was a Sigalert on the 405. Check it out on your phone. You'll see.

Same problem as above. An excuse may be warranted the first time, but subsequent infractions? Ill advised.

Partner B Suit yourself.

Remember that sledgehammer of justice and fairness I mentioned earlier? If partners have declared equal power and authority over one another to legislate and enforce their SPGs, they each have a sledge-hammer behind them that says, "No, you can't do that. I can't, you can't. We agreed on this."

Partner B Look, nothing I can say is going to get you to calm
down. Now, do you want me to stay and have
lunch with you, or should I just go back to work?
Your choice.

That first part is true. Nothing can be said. The only method for repair at this point is a future grand gesture by the wrongdoer. But they are currently unrepentant because while Partner A is showing their displeasure at Partner B's behavior, they are not really doing their job. They have not brought out the sledgehammer! Without Partner A truly making a stand for what's fair and just, they relinquish their power and leverage to insist on the right thing—something that is supposed to go in both directions.

If Partner B is unimpressed with fairness and justice, Partner A has a bigger choice to make. If Partner A steps up and reminds Partner B of their "constitutional" obligations (that is, if they have a constitution), then Partner B has only one way out of trouble—a grand gesture, a demonstration, proof that Partner B gets that they have created an injustice for which they must make right, and then keep proving they understand by being on time.

Corrections

Partners should discuss this in terms of the relationship's safety and security system rather than pointing fingers at each other, labeling one overly rigid and the other flakey. That will go nowhere pleasant. The issue centers around consideration, concern for the other partner's well-being, fairness, sensitivity, and . . . wait for it . . . threat reduction. Any other argument is a waste of time and energy.

As I said above, one move Partner A didn't exercise was to leave when Partner B was late. If it's already understood that Partner B is chronically late, and they've been forewarned, the appropriate thing to do is simply leave at the appointed time. That's not a punishment; it's a consequence. The next time this happens, Partner A can predict Partner B's behavior and make alternate plans beforehand in the event that Partner B does what is predicted. This shouldn't take too many times for Partner A to get the point across.

If the late partner is doing the airport thing, the on-time partner must think ahead. First, by giving a heads-up to their late partner that, if late, the on-time partner will board the plane as planned. I realize that's a lot of inconvenience and money, but the alternative is to be overly stressed and fight.

Now you might ask, What if Partner B doesn't care for this new way of managing the problem? Then we move up a level and have a sit-down when calm and come up with a better policy that works for them both.

Partner A We have a serious matter here. It appears we don't see eye to eye on the matter of caring for each other since nothing works except you doing things your way. I think it's time we discuss if we're compatible. I'm not going to discuss this in terms of being late or on time. That's not why we're discussing this. I'm talking about whether or not we're going to put this relationship first, ahead of our own wants, needs, and desires alone.

It's very important that Partner A is (1) willing and able to have this bottom-line talk about what's important and (2) willing and able to keep the discussion away from time and squarely focused on the topic at hand, which is, "Are we both committed to each other's happiness, well-being, safety, and security?" Full stop.

This speaks to an especially important point: if you are secure-functioning partners, then you are truly committed to a genuine, freely chosen relationship of mutual terms with shared power and authority, making each of you joint stakeholders in both surviving and thriving.

If this is true, then does it not follow that you each have a figurative sledgehammer behind you? Mind you, I'm not talking about threatening the relationship or hammering anyone. The metaphorical sledgehammer I'm talking about is one of fairness and justice. "We hold each other to our mutually agreed upon principles of governance or we cannot survive or thrive." I certainly do not support threats to any relationship, but I do support clear, concise terms that are fair and just.

If you declare the fact that you each have equal power and authority over the other with shared interests, than you both have that sledgehammer, if needed, to hold the other to account. "This is what we agreed *we do*, and this is what we agreed *we don't do* under any and all circumstances." Only in relationship dissolution do these principles dissolve. Is that not power? Is that not full agency? Is that not what will ensure safety and security for both of you? If you disagree, what other structure do you have in mind?

If you and your partner agree that the union foundationally relies upon mutuality, fairness, and justice, then trust, which is all two people really have, has a chance to repair and strengthen. You both must be able to trust and remind each other of these bottom-line conditions: *We either both abide by the utterly unimpeachable reality we have agreed upon, or our partnership cannot possibly survive.*

Remember, the couple relationship exists in each partner's head. It's a cocreated mythology of meaning and purpose. It's a two-person psychological system of two separate, autonomous individuals voluntarily joined together by shared purpose and vision for the future and therefore, interdependent. You need, want, and strive for the same ends; both of you are looking to survive *and* thrive in ways you've clarified.

Variations of This Complaint

"My Partner Insists on Being Early"

When a partner cannot tolerate being late—or even on time—it could be an issue if that partner has children and can't tolerate the vicissitudes of managing children and adults to finish a task in time. That includes packing, dressing, eating, cleaning, gathering, herding, and getting out the door.

This couple not only needs to create policies that work for both partners, but in this case especially, they need to talk about cooperation and consideration. Then, in order to repair the damage of not following through on commitments, they need to create or revisit their SPGs as I discuss in the introduction of this book. This couple must choose their SPGs wisely because shared agreements are unbreakable. They are the foundation of a secure-functioning relationship. By committing to their agreement they can repair and, more importantly, trust again. The latter attribute is central for doing any business, getting anything done, and being able to influence others. Without trust, nobody is going anywhere or winning anything.

Any issue between partners that involves breach of trust will come down to a fundamental matter of safety and security. The reason we base secure functioning in justice, fairness, and sensitivity is that they directly affect the couple's safety and security system. If that system becomes damaged, the relationship's days are numbered. There can be no happiness, joy, love, romance, or true engagement. Trust is everything. Without trust, partners cannot influence one another, they cannot bargain or negotiate, they cannot be gracious or generous or allowing.

Trust is the holy grail of all relationships. Don't mess with it.

Chapter 8

Interests

This chapter explores some of the most common and often contentious arguments around interests. Interests include but are not limited to religion, politics, work, games, sports, children, neighborhood activities, school, spiritual advancement, socializing, drugs, alcohol, and sex.

When partners are secure-functioning, with trust intact, they are more likely to share many of the same interests. They tend to develop in a roughly parallel fashion, influence each other over time, and start to become more alike (see figure 2). Because their relationship is relatively free of acute or chronic interpersonal stress and there is low-threat reactivity, they share interest in projects and adventures and naturally influence one another. Conflict avoidance is relatively low, proximity seeking tends to be high, contact maintenance issues are mild, and teamwork is preferred.

Figure 2. Influencing partners

Unlike *fused partners*—those who remain undifferentiated, code-pendent, or lacking autonomy—*interdependent partners* merely move through time in a manner that is more shared than separate. They are a team, not solo players. They find ways to do things together, create interests together, invent objectives together, and support each other's aspirations. This tendency to merge interests and values is a natural outcome of how they work and play together, not some pathogenic process, although we might say that fully independent, autonomous adults *should* be able to merge at will when appropriate, such as during lovemaking, dancing, or other creative or sensual activities.

In contrast, when partners are insecure functioning, trust is low, threat is high, and systemic avoidance becomes part of the cascade toward distancing. Partners congeal into adversarial positions that separate them into their own pods or siloes. They do not influence each other, and they drift. This wandering away can be insidious in its origins and can manifest well before partners realize they've each set a course that points in different directions. It's like a Venn diagram where the two circles are *trending* apart (see figure 3).

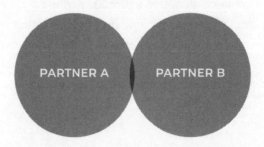

Figure 3. Congealing partners

Relationship drift is predictable with distancing-prone partners, who are commonly avoidant, one-person oriented, siloed, and quite happy to remain independent and separate. But they may find themselves too far from each other at some point and if that happens, then it is no wonder that one partner's zest for adventure, exploration, travel, education, or growth departs from the other partner's trajectory. Keep in mind, the problem is not simply divergent interests, it's a runaway threat response that pushes partners apart. When partners lose trust, safety, and security, they will actively resist the other's wishes, wants, and interests. **Partners might actually agree on which interests to pursue, but in their present state caused by insecure functioning they disagree because they have divided into one-person systems.** Their desires are polarized by their mutual unfriendliness.

Partners should be curious about strongly divergent interests, particularly when they appear later in the life of the union. Is it a function of drift? Is it a function of built-up threat perception and degradation of trust? Strongly divergent interests later in relationships usually reflect a larger problem.

Keep this idea in mind as we traverse this subject of interests and the complaints often voiced in couples' sessions.

"I Want Us to Grow and Become More, My Partner Doesn't"

Before we get into the specifics of this complaint, let's first talk about developmental stages. Every time we get a developmental "upgrade," through brain plasticity changes, societal comparisons and pressures, or just awareness of our mortality, we can become depressed and anxious and wish to go to back in time to a perceived better or simpler period. This is nostalgia and often an illusion, as the past, as lived, probably wasn't all that simpler, easier, or better. We also have developmental upgrades in which we change our perspectives, our outlooks, and our ideas of what's important.

No developmental period of our lives compares to midlife. Though midlife, as a perception, varies according to an individual's life circumstance, awareness of mortality, and culture, a biological midlife is.

fact, common to all humans. Evidence even shows that many primates go through midlife changes (de Jesús Rovirosa-Hernández et al. 2017).

The complaint about growth can come about at any time during one's relationship development, but in my experience, it appears most often during or around midlife, where one partner is or has been involved with individual psychotherapy, while the other partner has not. Or, in some cases, one partner has found a spiritual path, and the other hasn't or is resistant to doing so. Midlife brings about what the lyrics express in Peggy Lee's droll, depressing song, "Is That All There Is?"

- *Is this all there is? I'm sandwiched between raising children and aging, dying parents. I'm becoming my parents, and I can see I won't have everything I wanted in my life.*

- *What's it all about? What have I been doing all this time? Has it been worth it? What have I given up?*

- *What can I expect before I leave this earth? Is this what I had expected for myself?*

These are just some of the thoughts people say out loud as they lament midlife and review their existence in 360 degrees. We tend to review our lives in this manner every time we get a developmental upgrade. Often we reach backward for our lost talents, religious upbringing, forgotten friends and lovers, or our hometown. We may shift our views on politics, our views on relationship, or our views on ourselves. It can be a time of personal crisis, and it can become a crisis in our most committed relationships.

The Complaint in Action

Partner A I want to talk more deeply with you.
Partner B What do you mean?
Partner A I'm tired of talking about gossip, about the kids, about our work. I don't know. I want us to have exciting, stimulating things to talk about.
Partner B Okay. What do you want to talk about?

Partner A   Let's talk about diversity, like the lack of diversity in our country. It's really upsetting to me. I've been reading a lot on White privilege and issues like gender discrimination, and I wish I could talk to you about those things.

Partner B   Don't you have friends you can talk to about that?

Partner A   I don't want to talk to friends, I want to talk to you.

Partner B   I'm not really interested. I'll talk about other things, like what we're going to do for our son's upcoming wedding. I'll talk about that.

Partner A   I know! That's what I'm saying. That's the kind of thing we always talk about.

Partner B   Because that's the thing we *have* to talk about. What do you want from me?

Partner A   Don't you want to expand yourself, even just a little bit? Your interests are just centered around your small little world. There's a larger world out there. There's more to life than just planning our next event, you know.

Partner B   I'm not interested in the larger world. It's a mess. Who cares? We live in *this* world. We can't do anything about *that* world.

Partner A   That's not true. You tell me things that are so devaluing about some of your staff—racist, mean things. You are a part of my world, and you don't want to learn anything about yourself or your ideas.

Partner B   If you're just going to criticize me, I'm not interested. Racist? Me? How dare you!

Partner A   I'm sorry. I'm not trying to criticize you. I'm just saying that I live in the larger world, and it affects me—*you* affect me. Don't you want to talk about these things?
(*Silence*)

Partner B Talk to your friends.

And scene.

Why Does This Keep Happening?

These partners lack a shared purpose or vision around such questions as learning new things together, expanding shared interests, and willingness to interact over a variety of subjects. As partners, this couple must start talking to address the gap in their interests and interactions. The following are a couple of examples for good starter questions to get a new discussion going. Replace "kids" with a familiar topic of your own.

- "Should we be able to talk about matters outside of our kids? Would that be a good idea for both of us?"

- "What shouldn't we be able to talk about and why?"

Let's imagine partners will likely agree they should be able to talk about anything and everything. No constraints on subject matter. Now this does *not* include the manner in which partners speak, nor does it include the right to be insensitive or threatening. That should be established.

Now, what could go wrong?

One partner says, "I'm not interested in talking about that," or "I won't talk about that subject," or "I don't know anything about that subject, and I don't want to talk about something I know nothing about," or "I'm not interested in anything outside of my world."

This is where your social-emotional skill comes into play. How will you as partners remain engaged without becoming threatening? How will you as partners be curious rather than furious?

Attacking and withdrawing is easy. Everyone can do either. Remaining engaged, curious, and friendly is much harder, and yet, that's the skill everyone in an adult romantic relationship must achieve. No other viable option ends well.

And, no giving up. Giving up on your partner is tantamount to giving up on yourself. It's self-harming. You can't give up unless you leave the relationship.

This couple will repeat this issue until they find a different way to interact. Let's see how they (and you) can make strides toward repair. I will elaborate in the following section.

The Central Culprit: The Interaction

Let's break down their convo so we can recognize how it goes awry—and how you can prepare for a better outcome in your own version of this interaction.

Partner A I want to talk more deeply with you.
Partner B What do you mean?

Good question. Partner A could save significant time and effort and the aggravation that is about to ensue by having a topic or two in mind and by elaborating before handing it off to Partner B. If you are the partner who similarly wants to talk more deeply, understand that you're responsible to lead with suggestions. If you are the partner who doesn't want to talk about any of those suggested ideas, have the grace to say so kindly and then stay open-minded. Take time to think about a sphere of broader topics that interest you. Endeavor to connect. Bring a topic or two of your own lovingly back to your partner as an olive branch of sorts to see if you both can find common ground for future conversation.

Partner A I'm tired of talking about gossip, about the kids, about our work. I don't know. I want us to have more exciting, stimulating things to talk about.
Partner B Okay. What do you want to talk about?
Partner A Let's talk about diversity, like the lack of diversity in our country. It's really upsetting to me. I've been reading a lot on White privilege and issues like gender discrimination, and I wish I could talk to you about those things.
Partner B Don't you have friends you can talk to about that?

Okay, now that was just uncalled for. That's not just dismissive, it's rejecting and rude. It's war, baby!

Partner A I don't want to talk to friends, I want to talk to you.

That was a lot better than I would have been.

Partner B　I'm not really interested. I'll talk about other
things, like what we're going to do for our son's
upcoming wedding. I'll talk about that.

At least they offered something after saying no.

Partner A　I know! That's what I'm saying. That's the kind of
thing we always talk about.

Not skillful. Better to say, "Other than our son, what can we talk
about?" This would also be a good time for Partner A to share a few
ideas of interest to avoid escalation.

Partner B　Because that's the thing we have to talk about.
What do you want from me?

This person is really pushing for a fight. They're off topic. Remember,
Partner A is tired of talking about the kids; they want more exciting,
stimulating things and an agreement to talk together.

Partner A　Don't you want to expand yourself, even just a
little bit? Your interests are just centered around
your small little world. There's a larger world out
there. There's more to life than just planning our
next event, you know.

Now we're heading down the wrong road. Those are fighting words.
There's nothing attracting Partner B to engage.

Partner B　I'm not interested in the larger world. It's a mess.
Who cares? We live in this world. We can't do
anything about that world.

If Partner A were skillful and sincere about talking about something different, they could say, "Okay, let's talk about that. Why do
you feel hopeless?"

Partner A　That's not true. You tell me things that are so
devaluing about some of your staff—racist,
mean things. You are a part of my world, and
you don't want to learn anything about yourself
or your ideas.

These two partners are not coming back anytime soon. It's as good as over at this point. Both walk away with nothing except more aggravation.

Corrections

The correction needs to be in the communication—intention, facial and physical expression, words, tone of voice. One of these partners may sound collaborative, but we'll see that they're not if we look closely at their dialogue. Neither is using attraction to get the other on board, and so there's no cooperation. Partner A doesn't make "talking more deeply" attractive to Partner B. Rather, their choice of words could be taken as an attack, implying the other engages only in superficial conversation. Of course, the other doesn't have to take it this way. Still, it requires some extra work as that partner would have to figure out what "talking more deeply" means and override any tendency to interpret the comment as critical.

Partner A   I want to talk more deeply with you.

Partner B   What do you mean?

Partner A   Good question. I want to know what your most embarrassing moment was as a kid. And then I'll tell you mine.

Partner B   Why do you want to know that?

Partner A   Because I want to know more about you. So first, your most embarrassing memory from childhood.

Partner B   I guess it was when I froze in front of my classmates. I was giving an oral report on something. I just froze. My jaw wouldn't move. I could feel my face get hot. I heard laughing. I wanted to just die.

Partner A   Oh, I know what that's like. It's horrible. I felt that recently when I gave that lecture. I started to freeze, and realized I was freezing, which made it worse. Okay, my turn. I had a crush on this kid. I got my signals mixed up and thought they liked me only to find out . . . nope. I felt humiliated because it felt like everyone knew I liked them, and they didn't like me back. Awful. May I ask another question?

Partner B Sure.

Partner A Who broke your heart? Someone I don't know about?

Partner B Actually, my uncle on my father's side. I never told you about them. . . .

It's less about the actual questions or topics and more about Partner A leading when they realize they want something that is missing from the relationship. The rule should be: The one who wants something different must lead the way, and the other must follow or offer some other win for their partner.

Folks in the clinging group tend to do the opposite; they act out the wish for their partner to take the lead. But that's not collaborative. Both partners are expected to lead but often don't maintain that awareness. When one partner is made aware of the other partner's wish at the moment, they should be cooperative and respond appropriately. If one partner feels distant from the other, the best course of action is to *do* something that brings the two of you closer. Just making a statement can actually cause more problems because of the *amplification effect* between human beings. The amplification effect cuts both ways—positive or negative mutual experience. For instance, one partner looking into the other's eyes and saying, "I love being here with you" should lead to a positive mutual amplification effect of connection, comfort, and safety. In contrast, saying, "I'm afraid to tell you what I'm thinking" should lead to a negative mutual amplification of fear, trepidation, and threat. If I see you looking anxious, commenting on it will amplify your anxiety. Instead, I should simply *do or say* something to relax you.

Think before saying something. Ask yourself how your partner might take it. Consider your purpose. Is this the best way to achieve that purpose? Will your approach or response move you further toward or away from that purpose? If you don't know your purpose, perhaps wait until you do. Be mindful that everything you say and do has con-sequences in a two-person system.

Let's say I want to feel close to you physically right now. How do I achieve this?

- I can say, "I don't feel close to you." Though seemingly benign, it puts pressure on my partner to figure this out. It's a statement that throws them into the deep end of the pool. Perhaps this leads to unnecessary questions, which then turn into a stressful discussion, which leads to a fight.

- I can say, "How come you're never affectionate with me?" This question will put my partner on their heels and on the defensive.

- I can say, "Come here. I want you close to me right now." Or, "Come here and hold me, hug me, kiss me, and tell me that you love and adore me." This command—if performed with warmth and friendliness—is likely to work well because it puts the least amount of pressure on my partner. There's no guesswork involved. No implication that my partner is in trouble. It shows command and leadership in this moment.

Now, the success of this latter approach is predicated on the coop-eration of the other partner. If they refuse in a manner that results in dismissal or rejection, they are not operating as secure functioning and this then should become the subject of discussion either right away or soon. In this case, the problem shouldn't center on affection or close-ness but rather on the central purpose of the relationship as a unit.

Variations of This Complaint

"I Want Adventure, My Partner Doesn't"
Midlife can bring about many changes in attitude, inter-est, and drive. One such change is the wish for adventure. Whereas a couple may have once been matched in this area, midlife might bring about changes in energy, health,

and desire for or against adventure, particularly forms that involve physical exertion.

This specific form of mismatch often occurs with partners who are aged out of cohort, meaning, they are ten or more years apart in age. An aging partner may encourage a younger partner to "hurry up and live" because they're not ready to retire or become less active or be less adventurous. The mismatch in age, health, or energy becomes an existential matter for both partners. One can't bear the thought of muting their vitality while the other can't bear the thought of losing their partner to outside activities.

The challenges for partners who are out of cohort age range can be multiple. For one thing, they are generationally out of sync with regard to cultural markers, such as music, movies, popular figures, social politics, cultural attitudes, and language. For another, depending on age, they are at different stages of development. One partner may be ready to retire and focus on relationship, while the other may be ready to launch a career. One partner is beyond any midlife adjustment, while the other is just entering a midlife reassessment. One partner may have outlived their partying days, while the other is still going full bore.

So what to do about this mismatch? I'd like to say it could have been predicted, but that doesn't help anyone who finds themselves in this situation. For one thing, people age differently. For another, anything can happen to a partner's health that prevents them from engaging in activities. This matter becomes a structural issue that is baked in and cannot be changed (see chapter 4).

Assuming a disability of some sort either did not exist or was not known about at the start of the relationship, changes in brain and body can and eventually will take place in one or both partners. Most are age related, but some changes are due to unforeseen accidents or illnesses. Changes of these kinds happen—life throws us a curve ball and nature can be unkind. Secure-functioning partners are usually prepared for such occurrences in mind and spirit and therefore adapt and care for one another despite the change. Insecure-functioning partners may not. They may find these changes a deal breaker.

The latter is one of those situations I find most upsetting to me as a couple therapist. Equally as tragic is the situation whereby a partner remains unaware of a partner's disability until much later in the course of the relationship. Such can occur when partners reach various stages of adult development—such as midlife and older—where an emerging need by one partner exceeds the social-emotional capacities of the other to satisfy that need. Such is the case of a partner with a poor theory of mind, or little capacity to be curious about one's own mind or the other's. This particular disability may affect a person's capacity to put themselves in other people's shoes.

Before you take this ball and run with it, know that theory of mind cannot be assessed by laypeople. It is not something to throw around like I hear so many partners do with autism spectrum, narcissism, borderline, and ADHD. I have witnessed many people diagnose their partners with these disorders, only for many of them to find they have the problem, and their partner does not. I only bring up theory of mind because, as yet, there is no known treatment for it. People with this disability do not know they have it, tend to be unconcerned when they find out, and remain unmotivated to do anything about it. This and some other developmental disabilities only become problematic if and when a partner discovers it and finds it to be a deal breaker later in the union. That partner determines they want more in a specific area, and their mate simply cannot provide it. The same issue can arise with regard to sexual libido, energy level, lifestyle preference, and overall disposition. The central issue becomes less about your behavior and more about who you are.

When we get into things people can't change, everything becomes more difficult. The following are examples of things people can't change or where there is no easy fix:

- **Physical capacity.** This is an area that is unlikely to change. Someone with only one leg shouldn't be expected to run effectively alongside their two-legged partner. Granted, a good many disabled athletes can best nondisabled individuals. I'm not talking about them. Someone who is deemed disabled by a physical condition doesn't constitute a behavioral problem, nor should it represent a problem in a relationship. The only problem is that of perception by either or both partners.

The same goes for aging. Nobody can do anything about that. With aging comes varying alterations in energy, stamina, drive, and interests.

Acute or chronic physical illness is another reality that affects one's mood, energy, drive, and interest. The fact that many illnesses are aggravated by stress leads some to believe pain is a choice. I've witnessed several partners accuse an ailing companion of using their pain or illness as an excuse to avoid activity, such as travel, sex, socializing, and exercising. While depressed people might avoid activities, chronic pain or illness will also cause depression.

- **Mental capacity.** Depression, mood disorders, anxiety, panic disorder, and phobias can greatly limit one's mobility, positivity, motivation, and zest for life. Mental disorders are real and can be disabling for those experiencing them. For partners of sufferers, it may appear choiceful or as if their partner is malingering. This is understandable because from the outside, the constant fear, malaise, resistance, or avoidance can appear as an excuse for not following through, for not getting things done, or for not wanting to be with or do things with their partner.

- **Developmental capacity.** Some developmental issues are hardwired problems. These may be due to variations in brain structure and function from early childhood—autistic spectrum disorders, prosopagnosia (inability to recognize faces), prosody difficulties (vocal variability), and sensory integration challenges, whereby one is extraordinarily sensitive to touch, smell, or sound.

  Some people suffer from one or more software (social-emotional development) and hardware (brain function) challenges. These include personality disorders, massive early trauma, variations in theory of mind capacity, empathy, alexithymia (inability to recognize or give words to emotions), and affect blindness (inability to recognize specific emotions). Social-emotional acuity involves the ability to read one's own interoceptive cues or others' facial expressions, vocal expressions, and other social prompts.

This all may seem depressing, yet think again. None of us is without some manner of disability, be it with dyslexia, auditory/visual process, math, writing, foreign languages, eyesight, hearing, athletic ability, physical strength, small talk, public speaking—the list goes on and on. No brain or body can do everything well. We're also at the dawn of understanding and accepting the reality of neurodiversity. What may seem to be a disability in one area can be a special capacity in another. We should never underestimate our ability to expect others to be like us or be our fantasy of a perfect or even good-enough other. Our capacity for disappointment—our continuous awareness of what is missing—is legend and will cost us in our relationships if we miss the benefit of valuing what we have.

"I Need to Socialize, My Partner Doesn't"

One of the most common complaints I hear when it comes to interests refers to socializing. One person is highly social, the other one is not. Sometimes this is due to a partner's social anxiety. Other times it has to do with moving to another town or city, not liking the other partner's friends, or simply wanting to be home alone with their partner.

The problem may be present from the beginning, and it can change or develop over time if either partner becomes more or less socially motivated. Let me remind you, neither person *has* a problem. The problem is that the partners' interests have diverged, and the partners cannot find a middle ground that satisfies both.

The Complaint in Action

Partner A I want to invite people over next weekend. You don't have anything Saturday night. Neither do I. We don't have to make it a big deal— no dinner or anything. Just drinks and snacks. We can make it a post-dinner get-together.

Partner B Let me think about it.

Partner A I already invited them. They're your friends, too. We need to socialize more.

Partner B Why did you do that without asking me?

Partner A Because our dear, dear friends from church, you know, *our friends*, asked me about getting together. I've been putting both of them off for too long, and you always say no.

Partner B Now you put me in a bad position. If I say no to you, you'll tell everyone it's off because of me. Who else did you invite?

Partner A The other couples we know in our Mustard Seed group. You haven't talked to most of them in months.

Partner B Maybe 'cause I don't want to. Maybe 'cause they could contact me if they wanted to. Maybe 'cause we don't need you to be our social organizer. Damn!

Partner A You'll have a good time. And if you don't, you'll act like you're happy to see your friends.

Partner B Folks in Mustard Seed are *not* my friends, they're *your* friends. This is about you wanting to be with your friends, 'cause every time, you go off with your buddies and leave me to their partners. I'm not like you. I don't hang out. I don't do small talk. You know that.

Partner A You're an adult. You can handle yourself. I don't have any time for myself. I don't have any time to be with my friends.

Partner B Then take Saturday night and go out with your friends! Don't make me be with these people just because you want to be with your friends.

Partner A No. We're a couple. I want to be with other couples. I want you to have a social life beyond me. You don't go out with friends. You don't make friends. You could just be here all day and all night with just me, and I can't be your only friend. I'm sorry, baby, but it's true.

Partner B What do you care if I have friends? What's it to you?

Partner A Because . . . I don't know, it's not normal. It's not healthy for you to want to be with only me.

Partner B I'm happy that way. I'm not unhappy about that.

Partner A Well I am. Everyone asks about you all the time.

Partner B (*Muttering*) All the time, right.

Partner A They do. "Where's your partner? Don't they like us anymore? Clearly something is wrong if they're being this antisocial."

Partner B That's what they say?

Partner A That's what they say.

Partner B Well, now I'm really looking forward to seeing them. Thanks.

And scene.

Why Does This Keep Happening?

Variations of interest and desire are more common than not. Perhaps the illusion of greater similarity is present in the courtship period of a relationship. If so, we need to see the multiple reasons for that. Some partners will later complain of a bait and switch by the other, who misrepresented themselves at the beginning. While there may be *some* truth in the perception of misrepresentation, the reason for the change is likely reasonable and not at all pernicious.

During courtship, people want to put their best foot forward. They're auditioning for the partner position. They may even be thrilled to do most anything with the enthralling stranger, implying that they would continue similar activities in the future after partners automate each other (e.g., relegate to procedural memory) and return to their baseline. While deceivers who like to mislead others are out there, most people are not interested in doing so. They are simply wanting to win the other's interest and approval.

Still, the sense that one has been tricked, especially if it's backed by evidence, can be a compelling argument. If neither partner discloses their true nature with regard to socializing, that becomes their own fault. If, however, one does and the other either falsely claims an untruth or, just as troubling, doesn't disclose their true nature in this area, then resentment seems justified.

The Central Culprit: The Interaction

Asking a partner for permission *is not* the same as asking Mommy or Daddy. Only a child believes that. Among equals, getting consent is a sign of respect, an awareness of separateness and autonomy. You are not me. I am not alone. I impact you, and you impact me. Therefore, I check, I ask, I notify, and I get consent on anything that *could* affect you.

The same goes with "please" and "thank you" and "I'm sorry" and all the simple graces we (hopefully) learn in kindergarten. These formalities exist for a very, very good reason. Formalities protect us from violence, war, and lawsuits—and also preserve our relationships. Let's see where this one went wrong.

> **Partner A** I want to invite people over next weekend. You don't have anything Saturday night. Neither do I. We don't have to make it a big deal—no dinner or anything. Just drinks and snacks. We can make it a post-dinner get-together.
>
> **Partner B** Let me think about it.
>
> **Partner A** I already invited them. They're your friends, too. We need to socialize more.
>
> **Partner B** Why did you do that without asking me?

It makes sense that Partner B would respond this way unless they had previously agreed that Partner A makes all the social plans for both and, to make things easier, they agree to bypass permission. Formality exists for a reason. It prevents misunderstandings, demonstrates respect, and maintains civility and order. Yet primary attachment partners are the least formal. They deny their "strangerness" in favor of "familialarity," which can lead to recklessness, rudeness, and inconsiderateness.

Partner A errs when implying they know what's best for the other partner. What is best or right is a matter mutually decided upon—or it's simply one person's authority over another's. That will lead to a justifiable fight.

> **Partner A** Because our dear, dear friends from church, you know, *our friends*, asked me about getting together. I've been putting both of them off for too long, and you always say no.

Partner B Now you put me in a bad position because if I say no to you, you'll tell everyone it's off because of me. Who else did you invite?

Partner B's response is again justified; they've been boxed in. Also, if they are correct—that Partner A will throw Partner B under the bus by revealing they are the reason for not getting together—then Partner A is guilty of mismanaging thirds. Secure-functioning partners protect each other in public and in their outer social circles. Failing to do so poisons the well for both and makes further social engagement more threatening. Furthermore, it's tacky and unbecoming of an adult.

Partner A should immediately correct this mistake, first by reassuring Partner B that they will correct the matter with the friends and provide coverage for Partner B. That would be the right thing to do. Why? Because secure-functioning partners have each other's backs at all times. They are primaries. Others are thirds. Therefore, neither does or says anything to put the other in jeopardy. One's perception of jeopardy is what counts here. For instance, if Partner B believes they were put in jeopardy by Partner A, then it shall be true. Safety and security *first*.

IMPORTANT! IF YOU ARE IN AN ABUSIVE RELATIONSHIP WITH A DANGEROUS PARTNER AND FEAR FOR YOUR SAFETY, STOP READING RIGHT NOW. IF YOU BELIEVE YOU ARE BEING ABUSED BY YOUR PARTNER, SEEK LOCAL HELP RIGHT AWAY. NOTHING IN THIS BOOK IS APPROPRIATE FOR THAT LEVEL OF EMERGENCY.

In your couple system, throw yourself, not your partner, under the bus in public or with your peeps. That is more gracious. I am not talking about self-harm, self-degradation, masochism, or self-hatred. Just diplomacy and awareness of downstream effects on both you and your partner. If either of you find yourselves in a situation similar to Partner A, a soothing repair may simply be to turn to your partner, look them in the eye, and apologize. "Oh, that was *my* fault. I should have said something earlier. Sorry sweetheart. My bad."

When someone asks one of you to do something, let's say, in the near future, tell them you'll get back to them on that. If your partner says they don't want to go, your reply to those who asked can be equally as simple. "I'm so sorry, we have plans that evening. Can we take a rain check?" People understand. If you set up your partner—or your partner sets you up—to take the fall, it not only looks bad, but it damages mutual trust, unity, and safety in the partnership.

Partner B Folks in the Mustard Seed group are not my friends, they're your friends. This is about you wanting to be with your friends, 'cause every time, you go off with your buddies and leave me to their partners. I'm not like you. I don't hang out. I don't do small talk. You know that.

Partner A You're an adult. You can handle yourself. I don't have any time for myself. I don't have any time to be with my friends.

Okay, this is a legitimate dispute if the two have agreed to subgroup. By now you hopefully understand that the only *shoulds* in this book refer to what you and your partner have mutually agreed should happen in any subjectively important matter. I personally have no other stance here. This doesn't mean that partners should not have their own separate conversations or private meetings or move separately when engaging with others. However, if a partner is asking the other *not* to subgroup, they should have a discussion that makes it right for both.

Partner B What do you care if I have friends? What's it to you?

Partner A Because . . . I don't know, it's not normal. It's not healthy for you to want to be with only me.

The problem here is with the word *normal*. It's pejorative and suggests something is wrong with Partner B. The same with "It's not healthy." These are declarative statements that suggest Partner A knows what's normal and healthy, and Partner B doesn't. While those declarations may, in fact, have some truth in this or other situations, the use of these words will certainly be taken as threatening and will therefore lead to more fighting and less influencing.

Partner B I'm happy that way. I'm not unhappy about that.

Partner A Well I am. Everyone asks about you all the time.

Partner B (*Muttering*) All the time, right.

Partner A They do. "Where's your partner? Don't they like us anymore? Clearly something is wrong if they're being this antisocial."

Partner B That's what they say?

Partner A That's what they say.

Partner B Well, now I'm really looking forward to seeing them. Thanks.

The trouble with Partner A's tactics should be obvious to you by this point. They are using thirds inappropriately (see chapters 2, 5, and 9), sidelining the partnership in favor of what others say. Plus, the information poisons the well for Partner B. Understandably, the coming event is now less attractive for them.

Corrections

If all goes well during courtship, partners offer at least a few declarations like the following:

Partner A I gotta tell you, I'm a very social person. I love going out with friends, I love a good party, I love to entertain. Do you?

Partner B Well, I love doing anything with you, but honestly, I'm the type of person who likes one-on-one time with someone. I'm a homebody, and I'm not what you'd call highly sociable.

If something like this had been clearly stated, like a disclaimer, then their current arguments should be different. It's exasperating that many people are simply not disclosive enough during their courtship, a.k.a. vetting phase. Saying, "You never asked" is never a good excuse.

In the original scenario, several concerns appear to be present:

Concern 1: Partner A believes Partner B should socialize more and, because they don't, they're not normal. If either partner cannot sell the other on what should happen, then resentment will follow. In order for shoulds to work between adult partners, both have to agree.

Concern 2: Partner A doesn't initially get Partner B on board about having people over and then doesn't consult Partner B before inviting specific people over. No matter the issue, that kind of unilateral action, unless previously agreed upon, will also be trouble for both partners.

Concern 3: Partner B complains that Partner A abandons them during social engagements in favor of spending time alone with their friends. Unless both partners have agreed to that beforehand, it is reasonable that one partner would complain, particularly if the stated purpose of the event is to engage as a couple. However, while a couple's event doesn't mean partners must remain glued to one another, secure-functioning partners put the relationship first before other matters, which means that each partner's well-being, safety, and security is guaranteed by both partners. If one partner is especially shy, socially anxious, or a stranger among the other partner's friends or associates, the couple works the room together in whatever way makes it worthwhile for both of them.

Variations of This Complaint

"My Partner Won't Socialize on Their Own When We Go Out"

So many variables affect people's ability to socialize in groups. Do they know the people? Do they like the people? Are they shy? Introverted? Socially anxious? Some people have conditions that affect their willingness to be social, such as illness, pain, recent surgery, skin conditions, or general body dysphoria (they don't like how they look).

Other people become depressed or angsty when not socializing. Perhaps they grew up around lots of people or visitors. Perhaps they've been shut in for a while[4] or feel too bored (see next topic) being with just their partner or a few friends.

Keep in mind that partners, when reacting to each other, tend to amplify each other's predilections, making them appear more extreme. For instance, one person is craving social interaction outside of the home, and the other is happy staying at home together. If partners are insecure functioning, they will fail to bargain and negotiate to make things right for both and start to square off as adversaries. The oft-used solution to this standoff is to go it alone.

I would suggest that going it alone, while sensible at times, avoids (or sidesteps) a problem that's not going away and can have down-stream effects, such as drift. The easy one-person oriented way out is for each partner to do their own thing. Yet consider how this simple strategy can become a slippery slope, using, as a pretense, our independence as justification. I say *pretense* because my experience with most couples is that they use autonomy as a substitute for collaborating, cooperating, and cocreating win-win outcomes. Since most couples are insecure functioning, this would make sense.

Partners come to the table organized as one-person psychological systems, particularly when stakes become higher. If it's good for me and not for you, well, you do your thing, and I'll do mine. Why? Because in the minds of insecure people, the only other alternative is to impinge on each other's rights to do what they want. Therefore, their notion of autonomy while in a two-person system remains, in reality, one-person oriented.

Interdependence is *not* codependency, nor is it fusion or merging. It is a realization of autonomy, fairness, and choice with a willingness to cocreate new solutions to dilemmas that challenge either or both partners in a manner satisfying to both. The solutions do not simply affirm their autonomy while denying their interdependence which, among other things, is a shared stake in feeling wanted and in believing the union has real meaning.

---

4 The 2020–2021 pandemic led people to seek medication for anxiety, sleep, and depression. We experienced a suicide crisis among young and older people. The isolation most of us felt along with the inability to hug friends and family and meet and talk with people live and in person was traumatizing.

Partner A I know you don't want to go to this party, but I want to pitch this to you anyway. Okay?

Partner B Okay. What've you got?

Partner A What if you went with me, and we get there early so we can leave early and then come home and make love?

Partner B Hmm. That sounds . . . pretty good. Yet, what about the fact that I don't like anyone at that party?

Partner A Right. I took that into consideration.

Partner B Uh-huh.

Partner A So, how about this? I never leave your side while we're there. We'll meet and greet together. We'll treat it like our date—you know, hold hands, arms around each other, quickly move away from people you hate, maybe smoke a little pot before we go inside,[5] make people our own inside joke, and just look forward to leaving fairly soon, coming home, and making passionate love, just the way you like it? Better?

Partner B I love that you care this much that I go with you.

Partner A I do. I want to be with you, and I want to see some of those people. Together. But I want to make it good for you.

Partner B I want to leave no later than 9:00 p.m.

Partner A Done! You have my word.

Partner B Okay. Deal.

Partner A Deal after you agree that you cannot complain before, during, or afterward.

Partner B Deal.

I sit with couples who strain to come up with bargains and solutions. I often wonder why ideas flood my mind and partners will look blank. I believe the answer lies in orientation and attitude. It's certainly not about intelligence or not knowing how to work as a team. I believe that most partners think in particular ways that are inconsistent with teamwork.

---

5   Friendly reminder: this is not legal in all fifty states.

Bargaining is as old as human relations. Bargaining and negotiation, if done in the spirit of fair play, leads to mutual satisfaction and, therefore, peace. Whereas stealing, swindling, or otherwise manipulating others at *their cost* leads to resentment, revenge, and war. Unions forged in a free environment do not operate on any premise resembling "You do your thing, and I'll do mine"; that is, if they are to last.

Other Variations of the Interest Complaint

"I'm Bored with My Partner; We Don't Have Anything in Common"

I am of the belief that people who complain of boredom are, in fact, boring. What is boredom? Well, for one thing, it's an unpleasant emotional experience. But why? Though boredom is experienced by all and is normal, people who are easily bored are often prone to anxiety and depression and can exhibit what are called approach-avoidance behaviors (Martin, Sadlo, and Stew 2006; Perone, Weybright, and Anderson 2019).

When you are bored, novelty-focused areas of the brain are dormant. You're not engaged with the outside world in a manner that produces dopamine and norepinephrine, two major stimulatory neurotransmitters involved in attention and reward. When you're not engaged, a signal in the brain goes down and noise increases (Schore 2017). This is why some people become agitated when determined to sleep or meditate. Suddenly our mind and body experience sensations, emotions, and self-talk that make our skin crawl. Once we engage verbally with another person, these experiences seem to disappear.

If you are alert and not engaged with an interesting activity, you may experience a sudden urge to act or do something. You feel bored. But what if you're actually avoiding a particular state of mind? You may think you are bored, but what if you're actually experiencing depression, anxiety, sadness, grief, or dread (Havermans et al. 2015)? How do you figure out those feelings? Insight or mindfulness meditation can help answer that question. Frequent meditators will understand the phenomenon of a mind that won't quiet and a body that won't rest and be still.

One soon becomes aware of body pain, itches, urges, images, memories, and thoughts that won't go away. Is that boredom? It can feel that way. Or is the meditator simply aware of the constant ebb and flow of internal experiences without a method for managing those experiences?

Boredom is linked to inattentiveness. Inattentiveness is linked to automation. If partners rely on their automatic brains to get by in life, boredom will ensue. The automatic brain is a part of nature's energy conservation design. It allows us to be efficiently mindless. It dupes us into believing we know something that is familiar enough to ignore or to not give it our full attention.

Presence and attention are the only antidotes to the automatic brain and boredom. If I am not present and attentive with my partner, I may find them boring because I am not looking closely at them; I am not listening closely to them; I am not fully engaged with them. I might think my partner is boring—in their conversations, their interests, their activities or lack thereof. And as true as that might be, a counterpart to that calculation includes me and not simply them alone. Who then is actually boring?

"I Don't Like Our Home/I Don't Want to Live in This Location"

I hear partners complaining about their home quite often. Sometimes the complaint comes when one partner gives up their home to move into the other's house. This arrangement can be dicey as the place is not shared from the beginning. Even worse is when the original homeowner refuses or resists changes to the home. Worse still is when the home was also the residence of the previous relationship or family. It amazes me that some folks do not realize how this doesn't work. Of course, there are extenuating circumstances that might force this option, such as financial restrictions, real estate conditions, and other realities. Yet too often these conditions are not the issue. Instead, the homeowning partner may claim the property as *the family home* to accommodate existing children and grandchildren. In other instances, the homeowning partner has invested labor, money, heart, and soul into the property and is unwilling to part with it. Or perhaps the house is better than any others that can be found in the neighborhood.

This arrangement will not work for lots of reasons, but the big one comes down to this: the home belongs to one partner only. By "belong" I mean the partners did not start fresh and establish the property as shared from the beginning. Yes, there are quick deeds and other methods to make a previously lived-in home more shared, such as remodeling and redecorating, and depending on other factors affecting each partner's felt sense of safety and security, such makeovers could work. However, in so many of these instances, other relationship elements mirror this particular imbalance of shared investment and stake holding. For instance, the property-owning partner also has capital whereas the other partner has less, far less, or none. The more affluent partner may justify the imbalance as a matter of fairness measured by income and assets.

I can argue why this would be a poor measurement of investment and stake holding. The spirit underlying a union of equals is just that: we are equal from beginning to end. The measurement is *all in* with everything each has. I literally (and metaphorically) put all my money on you—and you put yours on me. I give you my full and complete trust—and you give me yours. We start as a *we*. *We* is a leap of faith, not a hedging of bets. Think about it. I only partially invest in you? I am not all the way in? What does that cynicism buy me? Another person who will do the same—whether or not they admit it. I have literally set the stage to be robbed, cheated, and ditched. Why? Because I have just communicated to my equal partner that they are, in fact, not equal, not full shareholders, and not worth my full investment. I will get exactly what I paid for—a bad deal.

Well, you might argue, love will make up the difference. And, I will say again, love is never enough. Neither is a business deal. We swear our allegiance to a shared purpose, a shared vision, and a shared destiny of mutual gain and mutual loss. We make a blood oath to real interdependency—even if that means mutually assured destruction or mutually assured survival and thriving.

I truly hope this rant helps you and your oath land upright. Creating a shared allegiance, even now in the midst of repair, is the big key to avoiding future hurt that will again need healing. Now, back to our regularly scheduled program, "I hate where I live."

Let's address other instances where the disenchanted partner wishes to remodel, redecorate, or simply upgrade to a nonstarter house. When one partner is resistant or downright unwilling to change anything, here again is an opportunity for secure-functioning partners to do right by each other and bargain or negotiate their way to a win-win solution of some kind. If partners are insecure functioning, this will be only one of their problems, as their lack of collaboration is likely repeating itself all over the place.

Partner A Look, I realize you don't want to move just yet, even though this house is just too small for the four of us. At least let me redecorate. Let me get rid of some of these ugly paintings and the 1950s furniture.

Partner B I like those paintings, and the furniture belonged to my parents.

Partner A Yes, but this is clearly *your* house when it should be *our* home. Nothing here reflects me or my taste. Do you agree this should be our home and not just yours?

Partner B Yes, of course.

Partner A Let's you and I go looking at what we could do together. We can preserve your family stuff and maybe put some of it in storage or in the garbage. Wait, did I say garbage? I meant garage. We have space there. Go with me to one or two furniture stores tomorrow morning, and right after I'll go work out with you at the gym. Deal?

Partner B (*Groans*) Uh . . .

Partner A Come on! What's it worth to you for me to stop complaining about the house? What's it worth for me not to show you new houses? It's a lot less expensive to fix this place up for now.

Partner B Alright. But if I don't like something, I want to have a say.

Partner A I want us both to have a say. I won't do anything without your okay. Okay?

Partner B Okay.

Now this brief conversation might seem unrealistic to you. Perhaps your partner is not on board with playing fair. If that is true, then the following approach may be more your cup of tea.

Partner A You and I have to talk.

Partner B About what?

Partner A About our relationship. We have to work something out because something's not right.

Partner B Oh.

Partner A Are we full and equal partners?

Partner B I believe we are.

Partner A Are we a team, you and I?

Partner B What are you getting at?

Partner A Answer the question.

Partner B Are we a team? If I understand what you mean, yes. We're a team.

Partner A I'm not feeling the team thing with the house. It's *your* house, not *ours*. We took this house after your parents died, and we agreed it was going to be temporary. Correct?

Partner B Well, yes.

Partner A It's been five years. We have two children. This house isn't big enough for us. I've been saying that for a while now, and you've been saying that I'm not appreciative of what we have. That's unfair. That sounds deaf to me as your partner.

Partner B (*Sighs*) I know, but I've told you, we don't have the funds right now for another house, and I'm just getting going with my career.

Partner A Okay, understood, but that doesn't make it right for you to prevent me from making this home yours *and* mine. Your family's furniture from the 1950s is in every room, your parents' paintings are still up on these walls, and your childhood stuff clutters up the place. It's time you let me fix this if we're to be here longer. Fair?

Partner B I don't see what's wrong with the way things are. It's a fine home, and it's furnished.

Partner A I'm not happy, and that should concern you. If we're a team, then be on my team, please. This has gone far enough. Work with me, or we have a big problem here. I expect us to be full partners. If we're not going to be, tell me now so I can make some decisions.

Partner B What do you mean by that, make some decisions?

Partner A If you and I are not really equal partners in your eyes, I may not want to accept that deal. Would you, in my place? Would you like me to call all the shots around here?

Partner B No. I don't call all the shots either . . . I . . . .

Partner A Good, then we're on the same page. I'll get started on the house tomorrow. You good with that?

Partner B I'd like to be involved.

Partner A And you will be because I want you to come with me to pick out a paint color for the living room and new carpets to replace the ones that have been here for at least a century.

Partners must work together as a crew of equals. Remember, in couples, where there's one, there's always the other. If someone is acting as the sole ruler, there's someone else enabling them. Be prepared to put your foot down for fairness, justice, and sensitivity and be equally ready to yield to your partner if they should do the same. Fairness, justice, and sensitivity are subjective, and you both will have to respect the other's claim of a transgression.

Sometimes, partners made a previous agreement to move elsewhere after a period of time. Or because an arrangement first suited only one partner, it is now time to balance the ledger. Or perhaps the family has expanded, and it's time to move. Other times, one partner is simply unhappy with the location because it is too far away from other loved ones, or they feel too isolated or unable to relate to the socio-political environment.

Despite the reason, one person's unhappiness is bound to affect the other. Therefore, both have a stake in making suitable arrangements if at all possible. Now, the word *possible* can become a problem if one partner views that word as simply convenient to the other.

Let us be clear, *fairness* is a quality both persons claim. As challenging as that might seem, possible/impossible is to be proven to both partners' satisfaction. If you believe you chose someone who does not live in reality, that is your mistake and your problem. Either quit or get your partner on board. Prepare to risk everything if you decide to be the sole arbiter of reality.

"I Hate My Partner's Politics"

Never in my lifetime have I witnessed such political divisiveness in coupledom as exists today. Now, granted, I'm not a political or romantic historian, but jeez! I first became aware of politics as a real threat to relationships during the run-up to the 2008 United States presidential election. Societal splits have always existed along political and generational lines, yet I had not experienced those splits as commonly occurring among married partners until recently.

And these splits have worsened over the years. Whole family and friendship pods have bifurcated and siloed off like the Hatfields and the McCoys (Jones 1948). Political beliefs have become grossly mismanaged thirds whereby relationship values are subjugated by different belief systems.

Consider Partner A and Partner B, both of whom are good, decent people in their golden years. Their political beliefs have taken on a deeply personal meaning that has split the two and pitted them against one another. Their goodness has shifted into mutual vilification as each sees the other's position as a personal indictment of who the other is.

They have no tolerance, curiosity, or real understanding of each other. Instead, they use their political views as cudgels with which to beat one another. Once in love, they now hate each other; once in the foxhole together, they are now enemies. They no longer see each other as real people, but as representations of or mere stand-ins for all those who hurt them in their childhood. Who they are is now defined by what they believe, and what they believe is now deeply dangerous to their existence as partners. They feel it's their relationship that sucks, not their beliefs.

How do couples with opposing political and religious beliefs and values maintain a solid partnership? They refuse to shred their relationship over their opposing beliefs. They don't mutually mistreat each other over politics. They respect, cooperate, and collaborate in their interactions with each other. They realize they could lose sight of what's important on a day-to-day basis—how they treat each other, regard each other, take care of each other, love each other. They lean on their common vision, common purpose, and common oath to bind them.

"My Partner Has Become Religious, and I Don't Like It"

Religion and politics: topics too dangerous to discuss in polite society? Some people believe this to be so and may include the topic of money to be equally taboo.

> "You cannot reason someone out of something
> he or she was not reasoned into."
>
> attributed to Jonathan Swift, 1721

Many of us become so sure of our beliefs and opinions that we remain closed to other possibilities. The more we challenge someone's beliefs, the more likely we will be to drive them further into feeling they are right. One's insecurity, as with one's beliefs or one's perceptions, cannot be altered by argument. That will simply drive the insecure partner into a deeper sense of insecurity and unsafety. The question is, Can we respect another person's beliefs and still get along?

Say your partner is religious and you are not, or you are religious and your partner is not, or you and your partner are of different religions. If your differences are an abomination to you, then why are you with this person? Hating their beliefs will be felt as hating them. Spare each other the misery and move on to someone who believes as you do. Or focus on how and where you see eye to eye. If religion is a deal breaker, so be it.

If your partner changed their beliefs after your relationship started, this may again be a deal breaker. But people change. Many people, especially in midlife, reach back for activities and passions they left behind in their youth. It might be an art form, an unfollowed dream, or a spiritual or religious practice. They may feel that something is missing in their lives, or they discover something that compels them to explore further. Here's an example:

Partner A I am really bothered by your affiliation with this guru person and that you spend all your time and money on their classes and retreats.

Partner B Their approach really helps me, grounds me.

Partner A But they're a charlatan. This is a money-making scheme. It's like a cult. What are you doing?

Partner B Why don't you come with me just one time and see for yourself.

Partner A No, I won't be a part of that. I've met people like that before. I've seen groups like that.

Partner B Well, if you won't go with me, get off my back and be happy that it makes me happy.

Partner A I just don't like you spending so much time away from me, going to this weekend retreat or that convention. It's just weird.

Partner B It's not weird. I'm not a cult person. This isn't a cult. It's a medical approach to my health problems. Yes, there's a spiritual component, but what's so bad about that?

Partner A I just don't want to see you get sucked into something and be fooled into believing this one approach is the answer to everything.

Partner B I never said it was the answer to everything. I said it makes me happy. It helps me feel better about my body and myself. I'm sorry you're too stubborn to see for yourself. Come with me and then complain, but you can't just sit there judging everyone the whole time. You have to come with an open mind for a change. Do that, at least one time, and then you can complain. Until then, stop dissing my interests.

A real problem can arise when beliefs, whether religious or political (see "I Hate My Partner's Politics" previously), become thirds that threaten the primacy of the attachment relationship. Meaning, one partner feels the other's beliefs are stealing center stage away from the relationship. Such can be gathered from the above argument. Partner A leaks their insecurity about Partner B's interest in their teacher and that approach. The leak is expressed in the complaint, "I just don't like you spending so much time away from me, going to this weekend retreat or that convention," which may mean one or more of the following:

- "It kind of feels like your religion has become 'the other person,' like I'm second in line."

- "It feels like your spiritual group is more important than our relationship. I'm an outsider unless I join it."

- "I feel like you see me as inferior because I don't believe the same as you."

When a third becomes mismanaged in such a way that it is perceived to be valued more than the relationship, a couple faces a problem of expectations. The expectation is that the primary attachment relationship *is* primary and will remain that way. Thus, this complaint becomes a secure-functioning problem *if* the agreed-upon understanding is that the relationship holds primacy, and one partner is jealous of the third stealing what is and should be theirs. This does not mean that the third should not exist, only that one partner—the nonjealous one—is using the third in some way unilaterally and without the other partner's go-ahead. Thirds are best managed by both primary partners and not by one partner alone.

If you and I have agreed that our relationship is at the top of the food chain, each partner has the responsibility to prove that statement is true and not simply expect it to be accepted as true. Fealty and fidelity in unions must continually be demonstrated—never assumed to be facts based on word alone. If that weren't true, I would be out of a job.

If partners have agreed their relationship *is not* primary or nonmonogamous, this would not be the case. Similarly, if partners agreed their spiritual practices and beliefs had primacy, or that their children, their families of origin, or their self-development had primacy over the relationship, then these thirds should not be considered mismanaged. The management of thirds is thoroughly discussed in the next chapter.

Chapter 9

Mismanaging Thirds

The mismanagement of thirds is perhaps one of the biggest issues facing all couples. As previously discussed, a third is anything or anyone who is not part of the couple unit. Primary attachment partners—most often a twosome—typically do not appreciate becoming secondary or tertiary to their primary partner. These partnerships generally expect exclusivity, or primacy, with regard to third objects, people, tasks, and interests. Of course, the matter of exclusivity is one that must be hammered out and made explicit to avoid mishaps and misunderstandings. However, beware of a basic belief in primacy involving a two-person system of interdependence. Partners enjoying a third or two may not be problematic; that is, unless you are the *other* partner.

Jealousy is the experience of perceiving that something is in danger of being taken away. Jealousy involves threes. I jealously guard my relationship with my child, and you threaten it. Or, I jealously protect my financial belongings for fear someone will cheat me out of what's mine.

In the case of primary relationships, partners are jealous of their relationship stations and entitlements. This is a matter of *security* within the system. We might blame a jealous partner for their immaturity, paranoia, or possessiveness—and we often do—but if partners understand attachment bonds and attitudes of primacy, blaming an insecure partner amounts to gaslighting.

"My Partner Cares More about Their Friends Than They Do about Me"

Partners may end up arguing repeatedly about friends when one partner feels the other's friends interfere with the primacy of the relationship. This happens most when partners do not merge their communities.

The Complaint in Action

Partner A I don't like that you are maintaining friendships with your exes. It makes me insecure.
Partner B I've told you, we're just friends. I'm not going to just cut off my friends because you feel insecure. You have to trust me, but you don't. That's the problem. Just because your partner in your last relationship cheated on you doesn't mean I'm going to do it. I thought you were more of an adult. Jealousy doesn't become you.

Partner A That's not helpful. I have stopped spending time with my exes out of consideration for you.

Partner B Don't do it for me. I'm not worried about you cheating. I *trust* you.

Partner A It's not just about trust. It's about respect for me. It's about caring about how it makes me feel.

Partner B No, it *is* about trust. You don't trust me to stay monogamous.

Partner A No, it's not that. I do trust you. But I know you talk to them about private things I would like you to talk to me about. You'll go off into another room to talk to them. I don't know what you're talking about. You meet with them for lunch and sometimes for dinner. You don't invite me.

Partner B I thought we were independent people. I don't complain when you get together with your friends, do I?

Partner A But I invite you. You won't come with me, but I always invite you or ask you if you're okay with me going out.

Partner B I don't want to go out with your friends. Besides, that's not the point. You don't want me to keep those friends I have because I dated or slept with some of them. That's the problem. You're jealous, and I'm not okay with that.

Partner A You'll never understand.

And scene.

Why Does This Keep Happening?

This type of scenario is a basic misunderstanding about the couple alliance. It keeps happening because the partners have no agreement to bring each other's friends together as joint friends. If they had originally agreed to have separate friends and keep them separate, okay. Clearly that is not the case here. The idea of having separate friends appears to threaten one of the partners.

The couple does not have a shared purpose or vision for mitigating security or safety issues. Partner B is operating from a one-person psychological vantage point, and Partner A signed on to this way of thinking. And so, in keeping with the maxim stated repeatedly throughout this book: where there is one, there's always the other. No angels or devils. One partner cannot get away with things unless the other allows it. If Partner A were truly oriented toward a two-person system, Partner B would certainly know it and act accordingly or be out on their butt.

Dovetailing on that point, Partner B may not be a good-faith actor as evidenced by the many signs of deception in their interaction, including deflection and gaslighting.

The Central Culprit: The Interaction

Many tactical problems are embedded within the above interaction. Let's take them apart and study them.

Partner A I don't like that you are maintaining friendships with your exes. It makes me insecure.
Partner B I've told you, we're just friends. I'm not going to just cut off my friends because you feel insecure. You have to trust me, but you don't. That's the problem. Just because your partner in your last relationship cheated on you doesn't mean I'm going to do it. I thought you were more of an adult. Jealousy doesn't become you.

Partner B is missing the point. Secure-functioning partners *are* obligated to ensure each other's sense of safety and security. Blaming someone for feeling insecure is self-harming because (1) it's dismissive and derogating of attachment values, (2) it will increase that person's insecurity and lack of safety, and (3) it will combine to blow back on the dismissive partner big-time. In fact, everything Partner B says here is inflammatory and guaranteed to make matters worse for the relationship. This entire narrative amounts to gaslighting, something Partner B will certainly pay for—eventually.

Partner A That's not helpful. I have stopped spending time with my exes out of consideration for you.

This is more common than keeping exes around when in a new union. Yet, as already mentioned, it is not always necessary.

Partner B Don't do it for me. I'm not worried about you cheating. I *trust* you.

I hear this often in my clinic. Partner B's behavior is threatening to Partner A, but Partner B *imagines* they *would not* be threatened if Partner A did the same. That is because Partner A has not yet given Partner B any cause for concern. If they were to do so, Partner B might very well respond differently. That is because Partner B feels secure. Partner A's behavior does not trigger insecurity for them. The same is not true in the reverse.

Partner A It's not just about trust. It's about respect for me. It's about caring about how it makes me feel.

Partner B No, it *is* about trust. You don't trust me to stay monogamous.

Partner B uses yet another gaslighting tactic here.

Partner A No, it's not that. I do trust you. But I know you talk to them about private things I would like you to talk to me about. You'll go off into another room to talk to them. I don't know what you're talking about. You meet with them for lunch and sometimes for dinner. You don't invite me.

Partner A just gave their mate a way out of this: invite your partner so they are not left out or with their imagination left to run amok.

Partner B I thought we were independent people. I don't complain when you get together with your friends, do I?

Gaslighting once again. Partner B is using a deflecting technique and is proving their untrustworthiness.

Partner A But I invite you. You won't come with me, but I always invite you or ask you if you're okay with me going out.

Partner B I don't want to go out with your friends. Besides, that's not the point. You don't want me to keep the friends I have because I dated or slept with some of them. That's the problem. You're jealous, and I'm not okay with that.

Partner A You'll never understand.

And Partner A may be correct. Actually, Partner B is proving themselves corrupt, which is a serious problem for both of them. Corruption is a clear demonstration of bad will and acting in bad faith. In cases where I find a corrupt partner, I am alarmed to the point of saying so and establishing the fact in session. This is where I draw a line. Most people act in good faith despite doing and saying stupid, self-centered things. Occasionally, I find bad-faith actors in my work with couples. These are folks who, if allowed, will get away with whatever serves their interests and will do so without guilt or remorse.

Corrections

You might be imagining this complaint is about exes remaining in a partner's orbit. It really isn't. Yes, one partner maintains relations with people with whom they were once romantically involved. That *could* be a central problem, given other factors. But the problem could also be solved by simply bringing the exes, who are now friends, out of hiding and into the shared partners' orbit.

The simplest solution to mismanaging friends as thirds is to bring them into the couple fold. If the ex poses no threat to the shared partners' relationship, why hide and make it something it's not? If Partner B's ex is partnered, then the shared partners' orbit could perhaps become a foursome, giving Partner A a chance to assuage their fear about Partner B's ex. If not, then a threesome. I am not talking sexually, by the way. I am talking about a new arrangement whereby partners create a shared community of friends and acquaintances. Proper management of thirds means that nothing and no one is hidden from the other's eyes or ears.

As with so many of the ideas in this book, one can view this as a restriction or an addition—a bug or a feature of a union. If partners in a secure-functioning relationship are to be in charge of everything and everyone as leaders, why would you do it any other way?

"My Partner Is a Drug Addict/Alcoholic"

When one partner is a drug addict or an alcoholic, it can be a dealbreaker issue. One person enjoys their alcohol, drugs, or other addictive behavior, and their partner does not like that behavior. The reasons for using alcohol or drugs and the reasons for objecting to their use are varied. One partner may complain that their addicted or alcoholic partner is behaving in a dangerous manner that could harm themselves, the children, or the safety and security of the relationship. This objecting partner might complain that the behavior—which involves thirds—takes time away from being close or effective. They might complain that these thirds alter their partner's personality, judgment, or behavior in a manner that feels alienating, and therefore they feel abandoned. Another argument may reflect the objecting partner's family history with drugs and alcohol, whereby they find all addictive behaviors aversive.

The using partner may argue that they do not affect anyone in the household, including the relationship, or that they have always used substances with the partner's knowledge and acceptance in the past. Or, they may claim their partner once used, or they both used as a couple.

Regardless of the reasons, this could turn into a situation in which the partners must make a decision to dissolve the deal breaker matter for good, or the problem could continue into the future and become increasingly embittering for both of them.

IF A THIRD, SUCH AS DRUGS OR ALCOHOL, ENDANGERS CHILDREN IN ANY WAY, THIS BECOMES A MATTER FOR CHILD PROTECTIVE SERVICES TO INTERVENE. THERE IS NO INSTANCE WHEREBY CHILD ENDANGERMENT CAN BE TOLERATED.

SIMILARLY, THERE IS NO PLACE FOR DRUG OR ALCOHOL-INDUCED VIOLENCE AGAINST A PARTNER.

The Complaint in Action

Partner A Last night you again stumbled around the bathroom, slurring your words and acting stupid.
Partner B No I didn't. I was perfectly fine last night.
Partner A Do you remember what show we watched?
Partner B Yes. A comedy.
Partner A Which one?
Partner B The one we always watch.
Partner A Honey, this has got to stop. You don't even know what we watched last night because we didn't

watch anything. We talked, and I know you don't remember that.

Partner B I know, I know. It's the only way I have to relax at night. I can't sleep without having something.

Partner A Let's find you some alternative. Please.

Partner B Okay.

Partner A Listen, I don't like the person you become when you drink. You're not you. You sound and act like someone with a lowered IQ of thirty points.

Partner B (*Laughs*)

Partner A No, really, it's not funny. Our kids notice it, too. They're worried about you. I'm telling you, it's not working for me. And you're not listening, but this is ruining our relationship. I can't stand the evenings with you anymore.

Partner B Okay, okay. I get it.

Partner A What do you get? And what are you going to do?

Partner B I'm overdoing the alcohol at night, and it's upsetting you. I'll . . . drink less.

Partner A No! I don't want you to drink every night . . . period! You never used to do that. I mean, you rarely ever drank alcohol before. You prided yourself on that. All your friends were lushes . . . *are* lushes. You were the key person. What happened to you?

Partner B COVID. Our lives. The stress.

Partner A Then go see a therapist. Get some help with stress and anxiety. Let's look at medication or some things you and I can do at night to relax.

Partner B Okay. That's a good idea. I'll make a call today. I promise.

In the ensuing weeks, Partner B has not followed up and continues to drink nightly, leading to more discussions at night and in the morning.

Partner A You haven't done anything to correct this problem, and I am becoming very angry. This is not fair. I can only talk to you about this in the morning. At night, you're impossible. You deny everything. You have no self-awareness when you drink. None.

Partner B I know. I'm sorry.

Partner A That's not working for me anymore. "I'm sorry" isn't making a difference. We're going to have to do something. I'd like to make an agreement that, if you drink more than I can take, I'm going to put you on the couch for the night. I don't want you in the bed with me.

Partner B That sounds reasonable. Okay.

Partner A Also, if I find that you're already showing signs of tipsiness, I want to be able to say "stop," and you'll stop without arguing with me.

Partner B Okay, deal.

Partner A You don't know when you're getting drunk. Let's see how that works.

And scene.

This strategy *does* work for them but not without glitches. Partner A has to face nights when they don't catch Partner B in time to stop them and when Partner A feels too badly about sending Partner B to the couch.

Why Does This Keep Happening?

I was an addictions specialist in my youth, so I realize for many readers the above example does not appear in line with conventional wisdom in the Alcoholics Anonymous and addiction medicine turfs.

Addictions are a difficult matter—whether they are to food, pornography, gambling, video games, work, or social media. All addictions, of course, have a neurobiological underpinning called the *reward circuit*—a neuropathway that hits both the feel-good excitatory dopamine neurons of the brain and the GABA neurons, the other feel-good inhibitory neurotransmitters that ameliorate anxiety. The reward circuit is activated by cigarettes, alcohol, cocaine, opioids, benzodiazepines, and sleep medications. The falling-in-love experience also involves the reward circuit. Constant use of this circuit leads to downregulation of dopamine receptors, which leads to the need for increased behavior or substance use to get the same effect.

The other matter here is that of personal regulation of the emotional and nervous system state. Addictions are commonly a function of auto regulation—the strategy of a one-person system of self-stimulation and self-soothing. Some compulsive behavior may be a strategy of external regulation—replacing an actual person or partner for outside stimulation and soothing. No matter, neither is truly prosocial or interactional unless both partners are using. If the latter is the case, partners generally do not complain of mismanagement of a third.

Also, while genetics certainly play a role in many of our behavioral choices, environment tends to be more of an influence, particularly with alcohol and some drugs. A child of an alcoholic family, for instance, may be genetically loaded for alcoholism, but more compelling is how the environment influenced what that child saw and experienced. Additionally, genetic predisposition often requires an environmental stressor or condition that promotes the expression of such genes.

The Central Culprit: The Interaction

Addicts, by dint of their one-person psychology, will often lie, bargain, apologize, argue, deny, and run around secretly hiding their behavior (and their goods). Addicts don't want to be found out. That last behavior is a surefire way to determine an addiction or compulsion.

In the above example, some may view Partner A's behavior as appeasing, enabling, or monitoring. That's a fair criticism. But keep in mind the ubiquity of addictive behavior in our society and in partnerships. Not everyone wants to pull out their hardline stance and admit a deal breaker is on the table. Extenuating circumstances may also exist that do not require such strong measures.

Addictions are relationship issues; their effect substitutes the emotional state changes often too difficult to obtain through relationship. I can relax, increase my excitement, loosen my inhibitions, stay awake, go to sleep, soothe emotional pain, feel hopeful, and focus myself—all without another person to help me shift how I feel. An addict can suffer several losses that will create a bottoming out of their denial system. One is the loss of relationship—partner, kids, family. Others include loss of employment, loss of freedom due to the legal system, and, of course, near-loss of life.

Let's focus on the first one—loss of relationship. Putting aside the deal-breaker full-stop limit of "It's either that or this relationship," other losses while in relationship can be quite compelling.

In the above example, Partner A is willing to withdraw from Partner B temporarily if Partner B fails to keep their agreement.

Partner A I'd like to make an agreement that, if you drink more than I can take, I'm going to put you on the couch for the night. I don't want you in the bed with me.

Of course, mileage will vary with this approach, depending on who will suffer more—Partner A or B. Clearly, this only works if Partner B suffers the abandonment.

Temporary withdrawal, as consequence, is one of the most powerful interventions partners and parents can use when disciplining a primary-attachment other. The relationship is leverage here, not objects. However, one must be careful and surgical enough to make the withdrawal timely, limited, and targeted to the behavior. Withdrawals should never continue for longer than a night or a few hours (with children, perhaps several minutes). Otherwise, the other will experience withdrawal as a punishment, which will simply arouse anger and resentment and, perhaps, payback. That is not the intent here.

Momentary targeted withdrawal is meant to be a consequence for hurting the relationship. Relationship goods are soon restored; otherwise leverage is greatly reduced in the future. We don't want to create an environment where there is nothing left to lose.

For this to work, Partner A would have to make good on their deal and put Partner B on the couch whenever they break their word and then reevaluate the strategy for effectiveness.

Corrections

Sometimes the matter of addiction becomes a straight-out deal breaker in which one partner must throw down and proclaim, "It's either that or the relationship." In secure-functioning relationships, using that as a correction is fair and just. However, the hardliner[6] must be ready to follow through or the results will be disastrous.

Attachment is the "I can't quit you" biology that reaches into our most primitive, existential survival fears going all the way back to infancy. It's a powerful force that all too often overrides principle and purpose. Holding to one's principles requires character, and that means one's ability to do the right thing even when it is the hardest thing to do. In this case, throwing down for the hardline partner is difficult because they are betting on the stickiness of the relationship as enough leverage to test the will of both partners. It's a worthy gamble and perhaps the only move that can work in the end.

If the hardline partner is not resolute in their determination to hold their line, the gambit falls apart and loses effectiveness in the future. As with any boundary, if a child or partner realizes the boundary is not real, they cease to take boundaries seriously and view the other as weak and unable to maintain their limit.

Variations of This Complaint

Compulsive eating, pornography, masturbation, gambling, and other behaviors must be evaluated by the couple as thirds that interfere with the primacy of one or both partners and those that simply do not pose a threat to the relationship.

In this book, we are only concerned about the mismanagement of thirds as experienced by at least one partner. I do not take a stance on these behaviors as good or bad, right or wrong.

---

6   This term is not meant to be pejorative.

"My Partner Is a Sex Addict"

The matter of sex addiction is a controversial subject. We can say that all addictive and compulsive behaviors are pro-self and not pro-relationship. They are pro-self because they necessarily override two-person systems as the person feels compelled to follow their own impulses, urges, and desires, despite consequences to their relationships.

Sex involves the neurobiological reward system mentioned above (dopamine + GABA) and as such can be classified as an addiction. However, and this is a big however, addiction is usually reserved for substances as there is dependency involved. Dependency is commonly a continuous need for more and more as the usual amount ceases to suffice. That means the neurobiological symptoms of tolerance and withdrawal exist. I'm not going to argue that behavioral compulsions and addictions are without tolerance and withdrawal. Anytime neurotransmitters are in oversupply, a downregulation of neuroreceptors follows. Thus the tolerance issue and the withdrawal symptoms.

With sex, the matter of addiction has become prevalent in the cultural nomenclature to the extent—as with all medical, psychological, and science terminology—these technical terms can be mismanaged by the public. For instance, the term *codependency* was coined as an Alcoholics Anonymous word to mean "co-alcoholic" or "enabler." The term was then furthered to mean "someone who lived through another person as an unhealthy form of dependency" (Beattie 1992, 2009; Black and Tripodi 2012; Bradshaw 2005; Mellody and Miller, 1989). Others, like me, differentiate the term from *interdependency*—"a basic need of all human primates to find common cause to mutually depend on each other" (Lee 2014; Lisansky Gomberg 1989; Weiss, 2018, 2019).

I see all variations of sexual behavior and misconduct in my couples clinic. Few rise to the level of true addiction. The addiction model does not integrate other predictors and etiologies of addictive or compulsive behavior. For instance, we can predict that certain attachment organizations will attract various behaviors and substances and for different reasons. We can predict that certain people with ingrained arousal regulation strategies—such as auto regulation and external regulation—will also lean toward certain behaviors and substances for stimulation and soothing. The existence of an underlying environmental influencer from childhood or a genetic loading does not fully explain or predict these predilections that become chronic over a lifetime. If addictions and compulsions also have a relationship component, we must see relationships as a powerful influencer in these pro-self behaviors.

The Complaint in Action

Partner A I want you to go into a program for sex addiction. You promised me you wouldn't use pornography, and you lied. And you're on Instagram all the time, looking at bodies of beautiful people. That's why we're not having sex anymore. You are having sex by yourself while looking at younger people.

Partner B I don't think I'm a sex addict. I told you I've used porn since I was a little kid. I'm sorry I lied. But you're so rigid about it. I . . . I mean, we don't have sex anymore because you reject me.

Partner A I reject you because you don't show any interest in me. Ever! We're roommates. I'm like a sibling to you.

Partner B It's difficult to get turned on when you're always angry with me.

Partner A I would be *less* angry if you showed some interest in me.

Partner B And now we're back in our loop. You don't because I don't because you don't. Nothing ever changes.

Partner A Treatment program. That's all I'm going to say. That worked for two of my friends—their partners are also sex addicts.

Partner B I really don't think I'm a sex addict. I don't sleep with other people. I don't go around peeping in windows or photographing sunbathers or flirting or sexting. I just use porn. Everyone uses porn!

I've caught you using porn—twice! I don't ask you to go into a sex addiction program.

Partner A I was curious.

Partner B Twice?

Partner A Yes. Very curious. (*Pause*) That's not the point. The point is that you don't look at me lustfully. You don't initiate sexy, romantic . . . stuff. You know what I'm talking about. You're just not that into me. Admit it.

Partner B I admit that I haven't been that into you, yes. But you play a role in this, too. You aren't sexy or romantic with me, are you? When was the last time you showed me love and affection? When was the last time you dressed up for me? I've invited you to be sensual with me in the tub and in the pool when we go away for a couple of days. You just say, "I'm good." And then just watch TV.

Partner A Well, maybe if you actually asked me in a good way. You just say, "Why don't we go down to the pool?" in freezing nighttime, or "How about joining me in the tub?" while you have sat there for an hour in a tiny tub with your dirty water. That's real enticing.

Partner B Why don't you watch some porn with me tonight, and we can do it while we watch?

Partner A That's disgusting. Why don't we just masturbate together and not even talk, touch, or look at each other?

Partner B Sounds like a plan.

Partner A Treatment program. Nothing else to talk about.

And scene.

This complaint, among others in the sex addiction camp, range from a serious addiction problem to what others might say is a compulsion, habit, or a way to self-soothe and manage anxiety.

The following is a list of eight paraphilias, or sexual behaviors, that are deemed mental disorders by the *Diagnostic and Statistical Manual of Mental Disorders* (DSM-5), with which you may agree or disagree:

1. Exhibitionistic disorder

2. Fetishistic disorder

3. Frotteuristic disorder (act of sexually rubbing/touching one's genitals against someone without consent)

4. Pedophilic disorder

5. Sexual masochism disorder

6. Sexual sadism disorder

7. Transvestic disorder

8. Voyeuristic disorder

Sexual addiction is *not* in the DSM. As mentioned above, the term *addiction* is tied to a neurobiological and sometimes genetic response to substances, particularly to legal and illegal psychoactive drugs. That isn't to say that so-called *behavioral addictions* escape neurobiological responses similar to substance abuse. For instance, the reward circuit, which involves dopamine and GABA neuropathways, lights up when falling in love, having sex, taking certain drugs, or taking part in any compulsion that rewards the person with excitation, relaxation, calm, or a pleasantly altered state.

The issue with sex addiction is that the term has entered the cultural zeitgeist, and like other psychology-like terms, is used as a complaint about another person's behavior. That isn't to say that someone who cannot stop masturbating or is driven to do so several times a day is doing okay or that the behavior isn't excessive and addiction-like. Or that a person isn't putting themselves and others at risk by compulsively seeking multiple sexual partners or compulsively looking at pornography. Any behavior that consumes a person's time and focused attention to the detriment of work, school, or relationships certainly is a problem.

But we also need to consider the various sensibilities of those who disapprove of behaviors such as pornography, masturbation, flirting, contacting and seeking attention online, or any other behaviors that personally offend some partners and not others. I *do not* take a position here on these sensibilities, as I believe people must judge for themselves what is or is not acceptable when in relationship with a primary attachment partner.

The most common issue here is that of thirds. One person feels displaced, left out, and in competition with a third that is taking space, time, attention, and energy away from the primacy of the relationship. There is no authority who can say that a complaint about a mismanaged third is unreasonable. There is no talking someone out of this perception or experience. That will only make matters worse. However, it may come down to a deal or no deal and that is always fair as long as both partners are remaining honest and aware of the consequences of declaring deal or no deal. Again, whatever we decide must be good for me *and* you, or it won't work.

In the above interaction, I see several issues, and hardly any of them are really about sex. **Remember, couples accrue threat due to the manner in which they interact under stress. It is not usually the subject matter.**

Why Does This Keep Happening?

All governance is predicated on previous agreements and permission to enforce them. The above couple does not appear to have made agreements that are strong enough (with both people fully on board) and so, enforcement is hindered. Also, this couple does not yet understand the ubiquitous and ongoing challenge of comanaging thirds, an issue that will continue to cause problems in other areas as well.

The Central Culprit: The Interaction

Now let's revisit the original dialogue and break it down. This is to help you learn to break down your own interactions and think to yourself, "If I alone could change the trajectory and outcome of this back-and-forth, what could I do differently if it were to happen again?" That is the way to handle these things in post review—figure out what *you*, not *your partner*, could've done differently.

Partner A   I want you to go into a program for sex addiction. You promised me you wouldn't use pornography, and you lied. And you're on Instagram all the time, looking at bodies of beautiful people. That's why we're not having sex anymore. You are having sex by yourself while looking at younger people.

Partner A missteps with the last two sentences by shifting topics. They would have done better to stick to one complaint and deal with that fully before adding another to the stack. That Partner B broke an agreement and how they did that is enough for one conversation. The danger of adding topics or subtopics is that it floods both partners with too many problems to solve at once and dilutes the first problem. It's vital to stay on message at all times and to pick your purpose when challenging each other. Our tendency to pile on is usually a function of frustration, repetition, and lack of repair. Also, the associative mind easily branches off into associated matters, which is great for chitchat about positive subject matter but terrible when partners are stressed or discussing distressing material.

Partner B   I don't think I'm a sex addict. I told you I've used porn since I was a little kid. I'm sorry I lied. But you're so rigid about it. I . . . I mean, we don't have sex anymore because you reject me.

Partner B makes a big error by countering a complaint with another complaint. This kind of response will simply elevate and amplify the already developing acrimony.

Partner A   I reject you because you don't show any interest in me. Ever! We're roommates. I'm like a sibling to you.

Now fully off topic, Partner A responds to their mate's deflection, and the original complaint—a broken agreement and dishonesty—is buried.

Partner B   It's difficult to get turned on when you're always angry with me.

Partner A   I would be *less* angry if you showed some interest in me.

Partner B   And now we're back in our loop. You don't because
I don't because you don't. Nothing ever changes.

Though Partner B is correct, they are in a loop, stating this fact isn't helpful at all. Instead, they should break the loop by refocusing their partner onto the original topic and quickly offer relief (e.g., amends, acknowledgment, repair). The apology should include having deflected away from the topic in the first place. "I'm sorry. I took us off course. You're right. I broke our agreement, and I wasn't honest. Full stop. I don't blame you for being angry with me."

Partner A   Treatment program. That's all I'm going to say.
That worked for two of my friends—their partners
are also sex addicts.

Unless this was part of the agreement—if you fail me, you agree to go to a treatment program—this, too, is a deflection as it really doesn't deal with the real problem: a broken agreement and dishonesty.

Partner B   I really don't think I'm a sex addict. I don't sleep
with other people. I don't go around peeping in
windows or photographing sunbathers or flirting
or sexting. I just use porn. Everyone uses porn!
I've caught you using porn—twice! I don't ask you
to go into a sex addiction program.

Yet a second deflective tactic by Partner B. Qualifying their behavior by making equivalencies with other behaviors they are *not* doing is a very weak argument. Furthermore, accusing their partner of using porn is not the central topic unless there was an agreement that went in both directions.

Partner A   I was curious.

Partner B   Twice?

Partner A   Yes. Very curious. (*Pause*) That's not the point. The
point is that you don't look at me lustfully. You
don't initiate sexy, romantic . . . stuff. You know
what I'm talking about. You're just not that into
me. Admit it.

Now they're back to the other subtopic, which again scrambles and confuses the field, meaning, they are all over the place. They also expect their partner to admit to something that is a guess on their part. We all create personal narratives to provide a container for our experience. The container, or the way a person organizes their experience, is always based on their own interpretation, which is influenced by history, memory, and usually a big fat empty space created by the other partner. That big fat space is a question mark that allows for filling in the blank, usually with the most negative meaning possible.

Partner B has created that space, that question mark, and is therefore responsible for the Partner A's misinterpretation. This is very important. We can say that Partner A made an assumption that their mate is "just not that into" them and then went further, demanding them to admit it. Bad form in doing both. Yet, Partner B is accountable for failing to provide evidence to the contrary and so bad on them.

Partner B   I admit that I haven't been that into you, yes. But you play a role in this, too. You aren't sexy or romantic with me, are you? When was the last time you showed me love and affection? When was the last time you dressed up for me? I've invited you to be sensual with me in the tub and in the pool when we go away for a couple of days. You just say, "I'm good." And then just watch TV.

This is the "I know you are, but what am I" game of turning defense into an offense. Forget about the validity of their counter, it is actually a deceptive tactic meant to deflect accountability and deal with the matter at hand. Partner B offers no relief save for the initial "I'm sorry I lied," which they buried immediately.

Partner A   Well, maybe if you actually asked me in a good way. You just say, "Why don't we go down to the pool?" in freezing nighttime, or "How about joining me in the tub?" while you have sat there for an hour in a tiny tub with your dirty water. That's real enticing.

Way off topic and becoming less friendly.

Partner B Why don't you watch some porn with me tonight, and we can do it while we watch?

Not a bad suggestion but the timing is way off and so is the topic.

Partner A That's disgusting. Why don't we just masturbate together and not even talk, touch, or look at each other?

Partner B Sounds like a plan.

Partner A Treatment program. Nothing else to talk about.

This argument may have been short, but its effects will be long-lasting. No mutual relief, nothing accomplished, mutual threat increased.

I should mention that the above couple is nongendered as are all couples in this book. Having said that, you may have already assumed gender or sexual preference while reading this section. I will bet your assumption is wrong.

Corrections

Let's play their dialogue differently, as if their agreements and understanding of thirds were intact.

Partner A You promised me you wouldn't use pornography, and you lied. And you're on Instagram all the time, looking at bodies of beautiful people. Your behavior is threatening me and our relationship.

Partner B You're right. I did promise and I let you down. I'm sorry. I wasn't honest. I'm not going to defend myself this time.

Partner A I don't want to beat you up about this but I'm hurt. I feel like we've become roommates or like I'm a sibling to you. I don't feel you want me anymore.

Partner B I understand. I feel the urge to blame you, but it's me. I have such a hard time staying engaged, I've always had that problem. I find it easier, more comfortable stimulating myself, you know? Pornography doesn't ask anything of me. I don't have to perform or show up. The Instagram posts allow me to be in fantasy, which isn't good for us but, I don't know. I feel ashamed.

Partner A Why do you find it so stressful to be with me? Do you feel I'm too demanding or critical? Do I feel unsafe to you?

Partner B No, I mean, I do feel like I'm disappointing you or letting you down because I'm not giving you what you want.

Partner A What do you think I want?

Partner B For me to initiate sex with you on a regular basis.

Partner A No, not true. I want you to initiate things, yes, but it's not just about sex. I want you to do things that make me feel wanted, attractive, important; that you want to be with me, intimately. That doesn't always mean sex. You misunderstand. If you would just talk to me instead of disappearing into your own head, that would make me happy. I think it would also be good for you because you keep practicing being alone. You think it's a good thing for you but it's not.

Partner B That's hard for me.

Partner A It's hard for me, too. You don't even know about my anxiety with sex. You don't know what I'm thinking or feeling because you don't ask. When I ask you it makes you angry, like I'm intruding on you or something.

Partner B Yes, it feels that way, but it's actually because I mostly feel ashamed of my thoughts and feelings. I get afraid you'll get angry or hurt, or you'll criticize me.

Partner A Well, try me. If I get angry or make it difficult for you in the future, just tell me and I'll back off. I want us to get closer. We're becoming strangers. I don't want to see that happen.

Partner B I don't either.

Partner A So tell me more about what you like about pornography, and why it's easier than engaging with me. Then I'll tell you about my problems with intimacy.

This is a much different interaction than the original one. Here, the dialogue is much more collaborative and focused on a mutual problem of avoidance, disengagement, and distancing. Both speak from their own struggles rather than simply pointing fingers at the other. They are working on the problem together and therefore able to quickly come up with a way forward that helps both of them.

Variations of This Complaint

Many people rely on devices to aid in achieving orgasm. That is *not* automatically a mismanagement of thirds. A partner may feel disappointed or insecure that their mate needs a device to reach orgasm, but then partners must discuss an alternative that is also possible. Alternatively, to get stimulated a partner might need to role play, hear "sexy" language, watch pornography, have a threesome, or do something else that their mate rejects, which leads to the following complaints:

"My partner prefers a device for sexual stimulation over me."

"My partner needs me to pretend I'm someone else to get turned on."

"My partner wants me to talk dirty to them."

All of these variations fall under, "Where are we going to be flexible and where is it a no deal?" Whatever the decision, it must be good for both partners or both will suffer.

"Our Kids Sleep in Our Bed"

Some people strongly believe in cosleeping with children either nightly or when extenuating circumstances, such as illness, nightmares, traumatic events (earthquakes, hurricanes, tornadoes), or other temporary situations call for it. I do not want to get into an argument with those who follow attachment parenting literature. That said, not all partners will agree with this system, and that's the point of this book. If one partner complains that a third is interfering with the primacy of the couple system, that is all we need to bring the matter up here.

The Complaint in Action

Partner A I am sleeping in the guest bedroom.

Partner B Why?

Partner A Because it's too crowded in our bed. I'm not able to be with you—intimately—at all anymore. I don't feel like a couple now. So, you can sleep with the kids, and I'll go sleep in the guest room.

Partner B Don't be such a baby. It won't be for much longer.

Partner A It's already been too long. We agreed the kids should sleep in their own beds a long time ago and yet, here they are sleeping with us each night.

Partner B They're not ready to be alone.

Partner A They're not or you're not?

Partner B COVID put a terrible strain on us. You know that. They've become used to being with us.

Partner A That's exactly my point. We're training them to sleep with us, and it's not ending any time soon. I don't actually believe you want to be with me anymore. We're not a couple. I think you prefer this over being alone with me.

Partner B That's not true. I'm with you all the time. We're working at home, we go shopping together, we eat together. What do you mean?

Partner A We're with the kids together, not alone. We're not alone together. There should be a boundary sometimes between us and the kids.

Partner B You're being silly. This time will go by so fast and then they'll be gone.

Partner A I'm moving into the guest room tonight.

And scene.

Why Does This Keep Happening?

Let's look at several possibilities here. The pandemic of 2019 changed lives and lifestyles. Couples, both with children and without, have all experienced varying degrees of stress and adaptation as a result of fear, isolation, school closures, and loss of employment. Many of these adaptions remain despite changing conditions. People tend to get used to their adaptations, for better or worse, and may resist further adjustments such as driving, returning to their office, traveling, or socializing.

In some cases, home scheduling and structure changed with environmental restrictions and demands. Couples with children had to make adjustments to include all-day care and homeschooling for their kids. Some partners, particularly those in the distancing group, moved out of the bedroom and began living separately in the same dwelling because the pandemic took away other reasonable distancing measures, such as traveling for work, going to the office, or just being able to regularly get out of the house. Other partners grew closer, spent more quality time together, and found new reasons for coupling. In general, some couples were distancing, some were clinging, and others were simply secure functioning.

Remember, the test of a good relationship is the amount of stress it can bear. People in my clinic often blame their circumstances for their troubled relationship. Though tough times and unexpected, unkind curve balls by nature cause grief, distress, and turmoil, a secure-functioning couple is expected to handle these troubling times with expertise, teamwork, and goodwill as they cope with problems, conundrums, puzzles, and challenges without focusing on each other as the problem.

And so, we have a couple who made adjustments during COVID that included allowing their children to sleep with them. One partner is dissatisfied by the mismanagement of thirds—in this case, the children—disrupting the primacy of the couple system. Partner A, whether or not you agree with their plight, has a valid complaint. Partner B may have a valid reason to stand their ground, but no matter, it won't go well because any mismanagement of thirds will lead to increased threat, resentment, and misbehavior (e.g., revenge). Therefore, Partner B better watch out.

In too many cases, partners who leave the bedroom can acclimate to the separation and maintain the separateness through avoidance and complacency. This leads to drift—again, a central problem in distancing relationships when partners inadvertently drift apart through a continuous practice of avoidance. They become siloed and eventually lose interest in the relationship. Additionally, because they are separated, they are left to their own minds, which will simply double down on personal narratives that justify the drift and eventual interest elsewhere.

The mind, folks, is not Disneyland. It's not the happiest place on earth. Our minds practice things, often negative things, that can keep us angry, resentful, and justified in our hostile or distancing behavior and can increase the threat level of the relationship.

The Central Culprit: The Interaction

An important part of correcting the interaction would be for these parents to curtail avoidance. What would have to change is Partner B's refusal to deal with the mismanagement of thirds as brought to the table by Partner A. They can agree to implement PePPeR (see chapter 1) by taking steps to predict and plan the children's move to their own beds and then prepare the children for it properly.

Let's redo the above interaction so that you might get an idea of how it could go in a secure-functioning relationship.

Partner A I am sleeping in the guest bedroom.

Partner B Oh dear. I know you're unhappy about the sleeping arrangement. I don't want you to leave our bed. Please. I want to be with you. Let's work something out right now, okay?

Partner B leads with relief by immediately recognizing the problem without asking questions. That goes a long way toward friendliness and collaboration.

Partner A Wow. Okay. I think it's high time we get them back in their beds so we can have our own space at night.

Partner B I agree. How about we move the older one tonight and get them acclimated to the new arrangement before we work with the younger one?

Partner A I think we could do both of them. They share a room, and it might make it easier for them—and us—if they have each other. Don't you think?

Partner B Hmm. Yes. Good point. I'm just afraid that our baby child will upset the other one, and they'll never get to sleep.

Partner A How about we try it tonight with both of them and see how it works out? We'll be up most of the night anyway because they won't like this at all. But it will be worth it. What do you think?

Notice how the conversation is very different from the earlier one. Notice also how they are interacting. Each checks with the other as if they are policy makers coming up with an approach that *might* work and remains open to discussion and adjustment.

Partner B Okay but be prepared to manage me as well. I'm not sure I'll do well with the little one crying. I feel so bad.

Partner A I'll take good care of you. I want to make sure you're okay. I worry that if we give in and don't follow through, it will send a bad message. If we back down, it just gets harder from there. You understand that, right?

Partner B Yeah, I do. It's just hard.

Partner A I know, baby. I know. We'll help each other, okay? Remember, this is our job. It's not always easy.

Partner B Okay. Does it have to be tonight?

Partner A No, it doesn't. But why not tonight?

Partner B Tonight's good.

Again, your back-and-forth may be different, but I hope this correction gives you the spirit of secure-functioning interaction.

Corrections

The only correction possible here is for Partner B to reassess their hold on sleeping in bed with the kids. Partner A may be correct in assuming that Partner B now prefers this arrangement and is leading the behavior with the children. In any case, Partner A is making their move in protest. While this withdrawal may make an impact, it also may backfire as only Partner A will be alone.

I said I wouldn't give my two cents on the matter of cosleeping with children. However, I will say that good reasons exist for partners maintaining the couple bed. One has to do with structure and hierarchy for the children. If parenting is partly theater, having a separate bedroom for the couple to have uninterrupted alone time provides children with the opportunity to view their own role as different from the parents, who as adults engage in a relationship different from their role as parents. They are a couple.

This separation prepares children for the outside world, where boundaries, role differentiation, and protocols exist. This then becomes a necessary adaptation for children to endure as to live is to continually lose privileges as we gain new ones. It is a parental responsibility to help children acclimate to loss and help them grieve and move forward.

Keeping children from necessary loss, disappointment, or grief delays their development and leaves them ill-equipped to deal with the vicissitudes of life. I'm not saying that parents should be harsh, punitive, or ill-timed with their decisions to implement necessary changes in governance and routine. I'm saying that when it comes to correction, parents should land on the side of strengthening their child's abilities and equip them with the confidence to move forward.

"My Partner Is Always Sick"

Sickness can be a third. It seems unkind to say that sickness, as a third, can be mismanaged, and yet you may face instances where it can be—at least in one person's mind. Nonetheless, this is a very touchy subject.

One partner may complain that their unwell partner is neglecting the relationship and using the illness as an excuse. Do we know people who might overfocus on symptoms or illness as a reason to avoid relationship or other responsibilities? The answer must be yes, but when can we be certain that is the case? Acute and chronic pain certainly takes up a great deal of bandwidth and resources. Chronic illness will likely involve depression, anxiety, loss of interest, low energy, lack of motivation, and some measure of obsessiveness. Pain and illness also commonly lead people to regress and feel helpless, hopeless, and in need of care.

Yet we know others who will use injuries or illness as a way to back away from moving forward in their lives, accomplishing goals, overcoming obstacles, or meeting obligations. Some tragically become permanently disabled and never again seek employment. We in the medical and psychological field worry about such people giving up on themselves. At the same time, no one but the person suffering knows what it is like to be in that body of theirs. So again, this becomes a very tough call.

Many people with disabling undiagnosed symptoms complain that when their medical professionals are stumped, they get blamed for feeling badly with the suggestion that it's all in their head. Others are frustrated because they know their symptoms are real, but no one is able to put a name to them or a cause or a treatment. I know many of these people. They are genuinely suffering and alone with no light at the end of the tunnel. Still others do have diagnoses, which may not offer any hope or positive outcome.

The Complaint in Action

These partners are frustrated that their home is cluttered and requires purging and redecorating. One partner suffers from ongoing autoimmune and inflammation problems, causing symptoms of fatigue, acute and chronic pain, and occasional mobility issues.

Partner A Honey, we're way behind on our deadlines with the house.

Partner B What do you mean? I've done the bedroom and the backroom like we talked about.

Partner A Yeah, but that took, what, three months to get done?

Partner B But I got it done. Give me credit for that, please.

Partner A Okay, thank you. That's great. But now there's the garage. It's filled with stuff you haven't gone through. We put my computer out there so I can work, and I'm worried that I'm going to trip and kill myself if we don't clean it out.

Partner B Okay, that's the next project then. I haven't been feeling well; you know that. My medications are also affecting me sometimes. I'm doing the best I can.

Partner A I know, I know. But we keep missing the deadlines we set. I can do things, but I'm stuck because you won't get rid of stuff.

Partner B I have to go through everything to see what we need and don't need.

Partner A Can we set a consequence this time if the deadline passes?

Partner B Huh?

Partner A If the deadline passes, can I just go in and throw away stuff?

Partner B No! You can't. That's not fair. No.

Partner A But then it's not fair to me either. You take forever getting to it. I've suggested someone to help you but you won't allow that.

Partner B You forget that my body is not working right now.

Partner A It's not just now. It's been this way for a long time.

Partner B What are you saying? You don't see me just sitting around, watching TV. I'm not lounging around, enjoying the times that I feel sick.

Partner A No, I know. I'm not saying that you're lazy.

Partner B Well then what *are* you saying? That I'm sick all the time? Because that's just not true.

Partner A I mean . . . you're often not feeling well, and we have things we have to get done. I can move things; I can do the physical stuff, but I can't do anything without you going through all your things. Either you get to sorting this stuff, or I have to get rid of it myself.

Partner B You *can't* throw anything of mine away! And I am sick. How many times do I have to tell you that? I'm not making this up. You know that. Are you suggesting that I am?

Partner A No. Not exactly. I mean, you're not always sick, but we keep passing the deadlines you set.

Partner B That's because I don't know how I'm going to feel day-to-day. Who are you? You do this all the time; you act like you care when it suits you but when it doesn't, suddenly I'm using my illness to get in *your* way. You don't give a damn about anyone but yourself.

Partner A That's not what I'm trying to say. You're twisting my words again. Now I'm the bad one. It's always about you and how you're feeling. It feels like an excuse sometimes.

Partner B So I was right! You think I make this up. I moan in pain, even throw up, can't concentrate, get depressed, and it's because I want to get out of doing things. That's what you're saying.

Partner A You're impossible to talk to.

Partner B *You're* impossible to be with.

And scene.

Why Does This Keep Happening?

You may notice the partners work on each other and fail to focus and work on the problem, which is how, and if, the two of them can speed up the process of sorting through the garage. Neither offers solutions. Instead, they both devolve into attacking each other.

Secure-functioning couples talk in a collaborative manner, focus forward, and work as a team. Because they are two-person oriented, partners know that what they say and do affects the other and therefore will affect themselves. They don't express thoughts or feelings in a manner that compels the other to defend themselves or their interests or attack back. That isn't to say the other cannot act defensively or improperly. Secure-functioning partners are obliged to cooperate with each other and not simply do what *feels* right or good at the cost of *doing* what's right and good. Doing what's right and good considers both partners, not just one.

Of course, there is no perfect anything. People will make mistakes, get defensive, speak in a manner that compels the other to defend themselves, yell, swear, and take other missteps detailed in this book. We're human. Secure functioning is not an ideal. It's a practice. Only practice will ensure a long-lasting relationship with anyone who matters. Any other practice is simply too unfair, too unjust, and too insensitive to last. Amends, repair, making things right, and getting back on a collaborative track is the only remedy for making mistakes. **We are all perfectly imperfect, which is why we plan on our imperfections and put behaviors and principles in place to fix what we break and learn from our mistakes.**

The Central Culprit: The Interaction

As might be expected, this couple's interaction quickly went off the rails. Let's take a look at when and how.

Partner A Honey, we're way behind on our deadlines with the house.

Partner B What do you mean? I've done the bedroom and the backroom like we talked about.

This response is a bit defensive, perhaps because Partner A didn't consider how Partner B would take the remark. As code, the intention may have been, "How come you're behind on our deadlines?"

Partner A Yeah, but that took, what, three months to get done?
Partner B But I got it done. Give me credit for that, please.

So, that assumption turns out to be true. The statement was a veiled complaint about the person. The response here, a defensive one, implies there's been a history of complaints about timeliness and completion and that Partner B doesn't feel that what they've done is being acknowledged.

Partner A Okay, thank you. That's great. But now there's the garage. It's filled with stuff you haven't gone through. We put my computer out there so I can work, and now I'm worried that I'm going to trip and kill myself if we don't clean it out.

Partner B Okay, that's the next project then. I haven't been feeling well; you know that. My medications are also affecting me sometimes. I'm doing the best I can.

Partner A I know, I know. But we keep missing the deadlines we set. I can do things, but I'm stuck because you won't get rid of stuff.

Partner A demonstrates their initial statement is off message and overly focused on Partner B's failure to sort. Also, they are beginning to misuse the word *we* when they mean *you*. Partner A's messaging is off enough to start an unnecessary fight. Had they begun with, "We're behind with the sorting," the problem-solving would have been more streamlined. If followed with something like, "Let's figure out something that might work better without overstressing you," Partner B would have less cause to be defensive. When either partner is under stress, or expected to be stressed by a particular subject, talk must be more direct, to the point, and highly focused on getting to mutual relief as quickly as possible. Languishing under stressful conditions will always cause problems—heart rates and blood pressures rise, resources dip, and bad things begin to brew just around the corner. No time to waste. Both partners need to scurry to mutual relief with a "for now" solution that works for both of them.

Partner B I have to go through everything to see what we need and don't need.

Partner B is unclear as to how this part is a "we need" and not an "I need."

Partner A Can we set a consequence this time if the deadline passes?

Partner B Huh?

Partner A again is unclear with messaging and appears to make a sharp turn to consequences meant for Partner B. It's not a bad idea, but the timing and circumstances seem inappropriate and noncollaborative. Their subtext here is troubling.

Partner A If the deadline passes, can I just go in and throw away stuff?

Partner B No! You can't. That's not fair. No.

Partner A But then it's not fair to me either. You take forever getting to it. I've suggested someone to help you, but you won't allow that.

Again, not collaborative. Partner A sets up a binary situation and a false solution. More than two solutions exist here, and two minds aren't working together to find them.

Partner B You forget that my body is not working right now.

Partner A It's not just now. It's been this way for a long time.

Uh-oh. Partner A takes another sharp turn and seems to imply that Partner B is slacking off or worse, malingering. This is going off topic big-time.

Partner B What are you saying? You don't see me just sitting around, watching TV. I'm not lounging around, enjoying the times that I feel sick.

Partner A No, I know. I'm not saying that you're lazy.

Partner B Well then what *are* you saying? That I'm sick all the time? Because that's just not true.

Partner A I mean . . . you're often not feeling well, and we have things we have to get done. I can move things; I can do the physical stuff, but I can't do anything without you going through all your things. Either you get to sorting this stuff, or I have to get rid of it myself.

Back to a binary solution.

Partner B You *can't* throw anything of mine away! And I am sick. How many times do I have to tell you that? I'm not making this up. You know that. Are you suggesting that I am?

Partner A No. Not exactly. I mean, you're not always sick, but we keep passing the deadlines you set.

Finally, Partner A clarifies, if true, that the other partner is the one who sets the deadlines. So confusing.

Partner B That's because I don't know how I'm going to feel day-to-day. Who are you? You do this all the time; you act like you care when it suits you but when it doesn't, suddenly I'm using my illness to get in *your* way. You don't give a damn about anyone but yourself.

Gloves are now off and, like most couples, both partners go full-bore into focusing on each other. Game over.

Partner A That's not what I'm trying to say. You're twisting my words again. Now I'm the bad one. It's always about you and how you're feeling. It feels like an excuse sometimes.

So not slacking off but malingering.

Partner B So I was right! You think I make this up. I moan in pain, even throw up, can't concentrate, get depressed, and it's because I want to get out of things. That's what you're saying.

Partner A You're impossible to talk to.

Partner B *You're* impossible to be with.

Corrections

If you ever face a similar situation, first determine the central problem. In this scenario, the problem wasn't either partner; it was the challenge of speeding up the sorting process. Instead of challenging each other—as Partner A did with Partner B's health—come to the table with possible solutions. When engaging in a back-and-forth problem-solving discussion, asking too many questions can be provoking. Better to make statements, suggestions, and offers. And remember, anyone who says no to an idea or solution *must* throw in with another suggestion or counteroffer.

Variations of This Complaint

Other medical or psychiatric thirds, such as chronic major depression, acute anxiety, panic disorder, phobias, OCD, sleep disorders, and sexual disorders (such as dyspareunia, vaginismus, erectile dysfunction, or premature ejaculation), might interfere with a partner's collaboration, cooperation, or mutuality.

For the most part, partners should seek proper medical or psychiatric treatment and even consider going together, at least to initial appointments. Keep in mind that thirds interfere only when one partner believes they are mismanaged. For example, a partner who suffers and does not seek medical advice or treatment and also fails to show up for the relationship may constitute mismanagement of a third (their health). The same goes for alcoholism, drug addiction, poor dietary practices, and other examples of inadequate self-care. As already stated, partners have a legitimate stake in each other's health and well-being.

Yet, there are genetic, environmental, stress-related, and sometimes unknown factors in illness. The fact is, we will all fall ill at some point in our lifetime, and partners must consider this—along with aging—in advance.

Too often, healthy partners will lose patience, become too unavailable, or just be too unempathetic to handle their mate's medical or psychiatric condition. The partners can mismanage vital moments when and where their ailing partner feels dropped. These moments where a partner fails to show up or shows up badly are very difficult to forget and therefore to repair.

Distancing individuals may fear indulging or coddling their suffering partner, as they wish they would keep a stiff upper lip and simply carry on. This stance is generally unhelpful and can lead to an amplification of partner symptoms. Along these lines, I have heard far too many stories of parents dismissing their children's mental or physical symptoms only to learn later their "pick yourself up by the bootstraps" turned out to be a serious mistake.

"My Partner Throws Me Under the Bus"

One of the principles of secure-functioning couples is protecting each other in public and private. Though this could easily go into the safety and security chapter, it's stronger here in mismanaging thirds. For instance, Parent A throws Parent B under the bus with a child, allowing the child to complain about Parent B, and Parent A to take the child's side. Other examples might include one partner embarrassing the other in public at a dinner party, one partner revealing private information about the other to friends or family, or one partner taking someone else's side against the other partner.

Most everyone knows what it's like to be thrown under the bus by someone else, particularly by someone who would otherwise be trusted. Unpleasant indeed.

The Complaint in Action

The following example involves one partner taking the side of others during a dinner conversation.

Partner A You once again humiliated me in front of everybody by repeatedly taking sides against me. Why do you have to disagree with everything I say? You don't do that when we're alone together. But you do that when we're in public. It feels so hostile to me.

Partner B I don't know what you're talking about. I'm a separate person, and I can have my own opinions. I don't have to agree with everything you say, and you don't have to agree with me.

Partner A You can say nothing. Right? You don't have to jump in with "Oh, I agree with so and so" and then challenge me. It's embarrassing! You don't even look around to see how other people feel about it. I can see other people are embarrassed for me.

Partner B I look around, and I don't see anybody looking any which way. I think you're too sensitive. You care too much about what others think.

Partner A I care that you care about me. It doesn't feel like you do. It feels like you join in with people against me.

You do that with the kids, too. I'll say something, and you'll either disagree with me in front of them, or you will take their side against me.

Partner B You've done that to me, too.

Partner A I have not. I've never taken the kids' side against you. I don't undermine your authority in front of them.

Partner B Sometimes I think you're wrong. Can't I have an opinion?

Partner A I'm not talking about having an opinion. I'm talking about undermining me in front of others and making me look stupid. There was no reason in the world that you had to weigh in all the time last night. And you disagreed with me in so many areas we've talked about and agreed on! What is that?

Partner B You were talking about things that, in my estimation, were making some people uncomfortable. I don't like conflict, you know that. It made me anxious.

Partner A So you're anxious about how other people feel, which is what you just criticized me for. You're the one who cares about how other people feel and think. I'm not that worried about it. And besides, I didn't really say anything controversial.

Partner B You were just making all these gender statements. It gets people upset.

Partner A What people? Nobody looked upset to me. I'm not an idiot that doesn't pay attention to other people. I'm not unaware of my surroundings.

Partner B I just think you're making a big deal out of nothing.

Partner A And I don't like socializing with you. It doesn't feel safe.

And scene.

Why Does This Keep Happening?

This couple doesn't have a policy to protect each other in public, whether with their children, parents, accountant, or friends at a dinner party. Because they do not have any agreements in this area, both are exposed and vulnerable to being hurt. Without a policy that clearly states what we're going to do and what we're not going to do in this or that situation, partners will fight again and again.

The Central Culprit: The Interaction

In the above case, Partner B, in a sense, is splitting hairs. It's not about having a difference of opinion. Context is everything and so is the manner in which someone says or does something. Partner A's complaint is they feel humiliated by Partner B. That alone should be enough to get Partner B's immediate and heartfelt apology, along with a remedy for the future. Instead, they argue, defend themselves, miss the point, and increase the level of threat in the relationship along with added memory and resentment going forward. Absolutely no upside and only bad downstream effects. Their interaction indicates a great many other problems. Let's take a look at some of them.

Partner A You once again humiliated me in front of everybody by repeatedly taking sides against me. Why do you have to disagree with everything I say? You don't do that when we're alone together. But you do that when we're in public. It feels so hostile to me.

Partner B I don't know what you're talking about. I'm a separate person, and I can have my own opinions. I don't have to agree with everything you say and you don't have to agree with me.

If Partner B was smart and understood secure functioning, they would have immediately said something like, "Oh no! I'm so sorry. What did I say to humiliate you?" Instead, they deny their partner's perspective and the fact that they felt injured. Partner B defends themselves by slightly changing the subject away from Partner A's point, which is "You humiliated me."

Partner A You can say nothing, right? You don't have to jump in with, "Oh, I agree with so and so" and then challenge me. It's embarrassing! You don't even look around to see how other people feel about it. I can see other people are embarrassed for me.

Partner B I look around, and I don't see anybody looking any which way. I think you're too sensitive. You care too much about what others think.

Both partners err here. Partner A should not bring in thirds here to bolster their point. In fact, doing so can be experienced as humiliating: "Hey, I'm not the only one who thinks you're an idiot. Everyone else thinks so, too."

Partner A I care that you care about me. It doesn't feel like you do. It feels like you join in with people against me. You do that with the kids, too. I'll say something, and you'll either disagree with me in front of them, or you will take their side against me.

Partner B You've done that to me, too.

Partner A I have not. I've never taken the kids' side against you. I don't undermine your authority in front of them.

Partner A again uses thirds to amplify their argument and also switches the topic to the kids. This is considered disorderly. As partners, when you get stressed, stick to one topic only. Partner B responds poorly by essentially throwing the accusation back and allowing the distraction.

Partner B Sometimes I think you're wrong. Can't I have an opinion?

Partner A I'm not talking about having an opinion. I'm talking about undermining me in front of others and making me look stupid. There was no reason in the world that you had to weigh in all the time

last night. And you disagreed with me in so many
areas we've talked about and we agreed on! What
is that?

Partner B You were talking about things that, in
my estimation, were making some people
uncomfortable. I don't like conflict, you know
that. It made me anxious.

Partner A So you're anxious about how other people feel
which is what you just criticized me for. You're the
one who cares about how other people feel and
think. I'm not that worried about it. And besides,
I didn't really say anything controversial.

Both partners seem concerned about performance and appearance—something that undoubtedly goes back to their families of origin. Despite their mutual sensitivity to what others think and feel, neither protects the other from that shared vulnerability. Instead they use it against each other.

Partner B You were just making all these gender statements.
It gets people upset.

Partner A What people? Nobody looked upset to me. I'm not
an idiot that doesn't pay attention to other people.
I'm not unaware of my surroundings.

Again, both misuse thirds as weapons. Partner A's initial complaint—they felt publicly humiliated when Partner B opposed them in the open—should have been sufficient. If one partner feels thrown under the bus by the other partner, that should be the only thing that matters. It shouldn't happen. Partners are allies. A team. It isn't a one-person system of personal rights, especially if those rights impinge on another's rights or sensibilities. Insensitivities and injustices should quickly be met with repair and relief and, perhaps, with a plan for preventing something similar from happening again going forward.

For example, let's agree that next time neither of us puts the other in a position to feel embarrassed, sacrificed, betrayed, or exposed. Would that be a good policy for us both? Is there a downside to that policy? Are there any bad downstream effects? Would it make us feel safer and more secure? If the answers are yes, then it's a shared principle of governance. It's a deal. Now, enforcement. If one of us slips up, the other cues or prompts that person and they must yield, cooperate, and change course, but in no case can that partner push back, explain, defend, or defy the agreement. To do so would be a great breach of trust.

Corrections

Let's review the three main components that can help you and your partner break the argumentative loop you may be in and start to get along.

Relationship structure. To get along, both of you need to view the relationship as a two-person system and therefore consider the other at the same time you consider yourself. Agree on that. Secure-functioning couples know that in order to survive, they must serve each other and not simply themselves.

Shared purpose. Partners need purpose-centered goals. Your daily relationship thrives with the real active shared idea that you are a team, an alliance, a union with purpose.

Guardrails. A couple needs those shared principles of governance (SPGs)—the guardrails—you read about earlier in this book to protect themselves from each other and everyone else. The manner in which you interact while under stress or in distress determines whether your relationship will cultivate more security or continue to yield the same loop of arguments.

In previous books I wrote about the *couple bubble.* The idea is that two people are in tight orbit with one another and agree to actively and continuously protect each other *from* each other and everyone and everything else. This is what we are talking about here.

I tell couples to be on the lookout for attempts to split them apart. The environment will at times attempt to do this, along with parents, children, friends, exes, and even therapists. It's their job to prevent this at all times. Attempts to split the couple are rarely maliciously motivated. Rather, it is often an attempt to exploit an opportunity. For instance, children will split to prevent getting into trouble or to get something they want. It's a good gig if they can get it. Good parenting prevents this from happening with consistent and thorough communication between all parents with an understanding that they should not be split.

Other Variations of the Thirds Complaint

 There are tons of variants when it comes to thirds. You and I could probably one up each other all day talking about these variants in one of my couple retreats. I'm sure you have a number of your own; however, the following are certainly common in my clinic.

"My Partner and I Don't See Eye to Eye about Our Children"

I cowrote a book called *Baby Bomb* with Kara Hoppe. In it, we describe how couples can prepare for their first and subsequent children. We introduce the concept of thirds and how important it is to preserve the integrity of the couple system. We caution partners about strong tendencies to recall their own early childhoods and battle over how to raise their children.

Whether parenting young or older children, the task is the same: to work as a team, as a parental alliance, always protecting the couple first. If the couple isn't consistently okay, the children cannot be okay. As previously mentioned, the parents, somewhat like actors in a theater, are exemplars for how relationships should operate, and their children play audience to their actions and reactions.

A high principle of secure functioning is full transparency and information sharing between parent-partners. Any other arrangement portends bad downstream effects between them and for the children. The parents are the roof of the relational home, and therefore everything they do as a couple affects the children.

The couple's union and alliance must be tight, or partners will be vulnerable to splitting. It's an old story: bad adult relationships often lead to partners co-opting children, and children following parental need for unholy alliances. Children want and need their parents to be happy. When they're not, children are compelled to step in. Their lives depend on parental happiness. It cannot be faked.

Partners ought not use their children as a battleground or as proxies for their own childhood memories of abuse or neglect, and they ought not invoke their children's names to bolster partner complaints against one another. Partners who disagree with each other's parenting style should not use their personal axes to grind as grist for their parent-partner complaint mill.

The next chapter delves more deeply into the subject of parenting and children. For now, be very aware of mismanaging thirds when it comes to your children. Throwing a parent-partner under the bus with children has dire consequences for all involved.

"My Partner and I Don't See Eye to Eye about Our Parents"

A very common mismanagement of thirds involves partners' parents or other family members. Some of these violations begin as early as the courtship phase, wedding planning, or the wedding ceremony. Throwing either partner under the bus with a parent or sibling as a third can have devastating consequences that may swiftly poison the well. These betrayals can turn into a nightmare that eventually destroys the couple's safety and security. Repair can be very difficult and, in some cases, impossible.

The primary attachment relationship is unique in that partners will rarely tolerate being relegated to third wheel. A secure-functioning couple represents an entirely different entity, country, and relationship ethics. They are supposed to be in charge of everyone and everything, including parents and other family members. They are no longer children, followers, or passengers in someone else's vehicle. They are the leaders and as such must lead. If the hierarchy is fuzzy, governance will be impossible, boundaries will remain unclear, and violations are certain.

Primary partners are the go-to people, the first to know things, and the ones to handle all thirds.

"My Partner and I Don't See Eye to Eye about Our Friends"

The next most common mismanagement of thirds concerns friends of either significant other. Friends can be a disruption if the couple allows splitting. Many partners maintain their separate friends and fail to unite their social networks. This can lead to mismanagement of thirds in that at least one partner will complain of misconduct. True or not, if one partner perceives impropriety in a partner relationship with a third, it becomes a problem for the couple. No one ever wins an argument over perception.

The best solution is for partners to share all information and quickly dispel fears of deception, secrecy, or splitting. Transparency is the best policy for mitigating suspicion and jealousy. The other strategy is to bring outliers into the couple fold and eliminate back-alley communications and dealings. If full transparency is not possible or is withheld, the third is definitely mismanaged and will continue to degrade the couple's safety and security system.

Chapter 10

Children

hildren are only as good as their parents are happy. By *happy*, I mean they have a good partnership in which they handle each other well, function as a team, and take very good care of one another. They are happy in their relationship with each other. Not all children get this need met, so this, of course, is an entirely subjective experience for all involved. And while it may sound unscientific to say that children need their parents to be in love, the spirit of the statement should be clear enough.

The couple system as it transitions into a parenting system becomes a hierarchy, meaning the couple system represents leadership and therefore must remain in good shape at all times. That system, when loving and healthy, likely creates a subsystem of children that will be loving and healthy. Therefore, the couple system must be in good order before adding more people. If the couple system is not in good order—and for a good stretch of time prior to children arriving—the couple is simply inviting more people into the mess.

Children can't fix your mess. In fact, children are one of life's major stressors, and an insecure-functioning couple will falter under stressful conditions. They will not be able to bear the load beyond a certain point before the wheels start coming off. The big stressors in life besides having children include changing careers, launching careers, building a new house, refurbishing an old house, moving to a new location, selling a house, buying a house, caring for sick or dying parents, coming into a lot of money, and losing a lot of money. All of these stressors lead to a tremendous load on the couple's capacity to manage stress as a two-person system.

Now, if the couple is coming apart at the seams without those major stressors, when the big stressors come—and they *will* come—the couple's ability and preparedness to expertly handle each other will be critical to their survival. The same is true for the children. If the couple goes down, the kids are not going to be good.

By "going down," I don't mean divorce. Divorce is not the driving factor in child unhappiness, traumatic memory, or sustained anger toward the parents. Rather it's the couple's ongoing unhappiness, rancor, contemptuousness, disdain, distancing, and unloving behavior that hurts kids.

Some couples start off the relationship with the explicit desire to have children, to raise a family. Some dream of starting a family but never of having just a romantic relationship or marriage alone. There is a difference. Those who dream of romance and love and marriage tend to focus more on the couple relationship, while those who want children, must have children, or dream of a family tend to put family or children first. Of course, this is not always the case. To be sure, people's feelings and attitudes change as they age.

Partners may dream of romantic love and then, once baby arrives, everything changes. They begin to feel the child is more important than their partnership. Alternately, if they become unhappy with their marriage or committed partnership, even if they never dreamed of having children, they begin to focus solely on the children. Other couples in distress, unsatisfied with their marriage or relationship, not only focus all their attention on their children, they commonly take one child each as their own favorite.

My personal belief on the matter is that a couple invites children into their relationship only when and not until they've achieved secure functioning and have become good parents to each other. They are good at handling and managing each other, and in the best way. It's as if the couple is saying, "We're so good at this couple thing. Let's add another person to this party we're having."

They have a shared purpose and vision for the future; they've installed SPGs. Finally, these partners begin to form a shared vision for parenting and how they wish their children to turn out. Shared parenting vision, when focused on the outcome for the children, is the best protection from future battling over differing parenting styles and preferences. Partners with a shared vision say, "We both want the same thing for our children. Our methods are different, but that's a feature, not a bug. We'll do what we always do when making decisions. We'll get each other on board, come up with solutions that could work for now, and then reassess."

It's sad—and, in my opinion, aggravating—when partners use children to avoid losing the relationship, to avoid losing their opportunity to have children biologically, or to avoid feeling lonely. They have motives beyond those that are within the protection of a well-functioning, two-person psychological system.

This is *not* to say that single parenting is irresponsible or the wrong thing to do! Dual (or more) parenting is no guarantee of a positive outcome. In fact, a poorly structured and operating couple system is awful for children, not to mention for the partners involved. Plenty of single parents do extremely well. I do worry, however, about single parents who are underresourced, undersupported, and isolated. Children need a well-resourced caregiver who is able to give their full presence and attention to the child. In addition, children require lots of stimulation in the form of responsible others, who remain available attachment figures and influencers in the child's life.

However, parents who are partners need to be a parenting team. The purpose to having two (or more) parents is not for the parents' convenience. It's because children benefit from having more than one caregiver—more than one mind, one approach, one personality, and one sensibility. Two (or more) parents and caregivers can add to a child's social-emotional enrichment and developing brain (Atzil et al. 2012; Azhari et al. 2020).

The fact that parents fight over parenting approaches is a couple matter of insecure functioning. **Partners must look to where they agree first before they fight over where they disagree. The best place to start is with shared vision.**

As parenting partners, begin with making a list of your vision for your children—health, well-being, honor, character, empathy, consideration for others, becoming good citizens and neighbors, and so on. Individually consider how you wish your children to turn out and then make separate lists. Compare your lists. It is unlikely that the lists will vary much. You will probably find that you agree more than you disagree. Now the question becomes, How do we achieve our goals?

The population of the world over the millennia has tended to be lazy and therefore vulnerable to authoritarianism. Why? Autocracies seem easier. Life is simpler if only one person is in charge. But is it better? In a more-than-one parent system (two, three, or more), is having only one parent in charge of the children better? It may be easier for some, but how is it for the kids? To be sure, co-parenting is difficult, and so is coupling. Remember, your kids are supposed to be coming to *your* party, which is awesome, right? Your kids are passing through. They'll soon be on their way, and you will still be a couple . . . or will you?

A co-parenting team (including biological, step, adopted, and foster parents, legal guardians, and multiple-parent partners) must be collaborative and cooperative. Neither parent is an expert when it comes to parenting because nobody really is an expert with your particular children. You are part of an improv, a constant trial-and-error process of failing and learning. And your children's brains are a fast-moving target. You have to be on your toes.

Finally, parenting is leadership. Parenting is theater. It is show, not tell. Your children constantly observe your relationship as their brains develop. They observe how relationship works. How to love, fight, make amends, make up, and forgive. They observe what is fake and what is authentic. What are truths and what are lies. They cross-reference continuously by observing the opposite parent's reactions, which show them how to feel about the other parent. This phenomenon is called *social referencing*, and it's something kids and adults do. My sense of my mother often comes from my father, and vice versa. My sense and regard for the same and opposite sex (as well as gender identity) comes from observing attitudes and behaviors from the opposing parent.

Your kids are watching, and what they observe they'll do both now and in the future. This is an ongoing, evolutionary process, so worry not about the past. You, their parents, are exemplars of what is possible, and that is true whenever you, the couple, get your act together, whether your children are very young or older.

Children need to see their parents in love, working together, and being in each other's care. Partners are masters of each other. If your relationship is in disarray, your children will be forced to step in and cease to be kids. Children are good when their parents are good and happy. Think back to your own childhood. Perhaps you can remember how you felt when your parents were happy, affectionate, and getting along.

"My Partner Disapproves of My Parenting"

The Complaint in Action

Partner A I don't like how you speak to our child. It's way harsh. You don't see how it affects them. I do. Whenever you talk in that manner, I see how they back away. You scare and hurt them. They're sensitive. Don't you see that?

Partner B And I don't like the way you coddle the kid. They're not going to learn anything if you constantly give them what they want and placate them. That's not the way I was raised. You may have had parents who always said yes to you. I didn't. A kid needs to learn that no is no.

Partner A This child comes to me crying after you yell at them. They say you scare them. That worries me, and it should worry you.

Partner B	Of course they come to you and cry. They know you'll take their side because you always do. Don't you worry that we'll have a child who won't take no for an answer? You're teaching them to disobey.
Partner A	And you're teaching them to be afraid of their parent. There are other ways to enforce limits with them. You don't have to yell.
Partner B	I don't yell. I use a strong tone of voice. I want them to know I'm serious. I'm not yelling.
Partner A	I don't think you hear yourself. You yell. You yell at me, too; when you're angry, you do.
Partner B	You think everything is yelling because no one ever fought in your family.
Partner A	We didn't have to fight. Your family is constantly fighting, even to this day. You all yell and fight.

And scene.

Why Does This Keep Happening?

Romantic partnerships are difficult, and parenting is no cakewalk. The most common problem between partners with children is witnessing one parent discipline or become upset with a child. It's as if we, the witnessing partner, are free to project, as if watching a home movie of our own early experiences with our parents. As a witness, we may identify with the child or the parent. Or, we may identify with the witness, ourselves as children, who observed these arousing interactions.

On an arousal level, heightened sounds, voices, movements, words, and phrases are threat cues that trigger a heightened state of alert and alarm. We want to fight or flee or, in some cases, collapse. Nonetheless, we're not neutral and relaxed. Generally speaking, we want to put a stop to the commotion right now. How we do it, however, will likely be automatic, reflexive, and memory-based.

We often forget how difficult parenting is as our children are rapidly developing, going through their own developmental crises and milestones. Their internal worlds are processed externally and put into our minds and bodies. We feel what they feel, and we often don't like it—the frustration, rage, desire, urges, impulses, fears, disappointment, neediness, distancing, rejection, contempt, selfishness, anxiety, worry, obsession, pickiness, opportunism, self-centeredness. Oh wait, that's the human condition. Quite often children express that which we were trained not to. We may feel that children should not be allowed to get away with emotions, thoughts, or actions that were verboten in our childhood. We sometimes see ourselves in our children and either don't like it or don't realize it.

How many times have we heard, "I don't want to parent like my parents did"? Since you now know that nature repeats itself, what do you think we're all going to do when stressed? Right, exactly what we've experienced in childhood. Sorry, but that's nature. That's where making amends comes in handy. I can lose it with my daughter as did my father with me, but I can go to my daughter and admit my wrongs (without qualification or excuses) and say I would like to do better next time.

In the above case, these partners either have forgotten their shared vision for their children or failed to cocreate one. Their shared vision would likely be aligned if they really fleshed it out. They would both likely want their children to be good people, good neighbors and citizens; to be ethical, cooperative, and collaborative with others; to be adventurous; to have good judgment and impulse control, fortitude, and compassion for others; and to be empathic and evenhanded. These are just a few possibilities. A solid shared vision keeps unions on track with what's important. Style, personality, approach, and other preferences are secondary to the vision, the expected outcome.

Perhaps both partners in the above example are right. They wouldn't see this because each is invested in being right and making the other wrong. Neither is checking their shared vision and then talking about approach. Both are remembering, acting, and reacting reflexively without real thoughtfulness. They are imposing their childhood cultures on one another and projecting disparaging narratives regarding each other's childhood culture. Neither is acting collaboratively or mindfully on the issue at hand, which is, "Should we set limits on our child and if so, when should we do that and how?"

This couple is not working on a problem involving the child. Rather, partners are working on each other. That is why they will accomplish nothing except to increase each other's felt sense of threat, and that will simply continue to accumulate more threat.

Again, the problem isn't really the subject matter, it's the manner in which partners interact when under stress.

The Central Culprit: The Interaction

Let's take a closer look at how they managed this exchange of ideas.

Partner A I don't like how you speak to our child. It's way harsh. You don't see how it affects them. I do. Whenever you talk in that manner, I see how they back away. You scare and hurt them. They're sensitive. Don't you see that?

This is a perfectly fine way to start this, as long as it's out of earshot of the child. Parents should not criticize each other in front of the children unless they are extremely skilled, secure-functioning partners who trust each other and intend to use it as a demonstration of partnership, collaboration, respect, and repair in the family community.

The way Partner A starts this dialogue *would not* be a good example of this, nor would this response from Partner B:

Partner B And I don't like the way you coddle the kid. They're not going to learn anything if you constantly give them what they want and placate them. That's not the way I was raised. You may have had parents who always said yes to you. I didn't. A kid needs to learn that no is no.

Big error. Partner B does not lead with relief, doesn't stay on topic, and attacks back. Remember, the first thing the responding partner must do when hearing a complaint is to relieve that person before going forward. It's not about politeness or formality but rather biology and wisdom.

If I'm facing my upset partner and doing anything other than first relieving them, that is going to be very bad for me. They are expecting some kind of relief now, not later. If I do not return my partner to a felt sense of safety and security right now, they (or anybody) will take that as threatening and unfriendly. This then will raise their heart rate and blood pressure, increasing threat perception and activating memory and the readiness to fight or flee.

Both partners are responsible for the trajectory of these interactions when stressed. Either could intervene and change the outcome if they held in mind that they are psychobiologically tied together—where one goes, so goes the other. The result of these spirals into self-protection is never positive. Failing to lead with relief, keep the other partner in mind, stay on message, keep to one topic only, or work on the problem only will always follow a predictable course.

So what should Partner B say instead? Something like the following:

Partner B   Yes, I do see how our child reacts to me, and I know I can be harsh. I don't wish to be scary. I only want to make sure they understand limits, and I worry that's not happening. I would really love your support somehow. I'm sorry for hurting you. This is really hard for me.

Now you might ask, But what if Partner B does not realize they are being harsh or scaring the child? I'd say, that would be highly unlikely. It's true that in moments of feeling threatened, attacked, and criticized, people will tend to overlook the truth of a complaint in order to protect themselves. And individuals with unresolved trauma can dissociate, particularly when enraged or in energy conservation withdrawal and collapse, and literally block out all self-awareness and even awareness of their surroundings (Chiu et al. 2018; Krusemark 2018; Spitoni et al. 2020). But most people can witness themselves, pick up surrounding information, and admit to knowing more when they become calm and feel safe. In some cases, individuals may continue to deny what they know because they never really ever return to safety and thus are in a continual threat state. Again, we're talking about those with a severe abuse history that remains unresolved. Let's continue with our analysis:

Partner A This child comes to me crying after you yell at
them. They say you scare them. That worries me,
and it should worry you.

Partner B Of course they come to you and cry. They know
you'll take their side because you always do. Don't
you worry that we'll have a child who won't take
no for an answer? You're teaching them to disobey.

Partner A is doing well again—staying the course and staying on
message. Partner B, on the other hand, is once again going off topic by
blaming their partner and remaining unresponsive to the original and
repeated point. What could they say instead?

Partner B They said that? Okay, that's not good. I don't want
them to be afraid of me. I'll go and talk with them
and fix that. Please let me take care of that. We
need to come up with something that will help
them accept disappointment so we can set limits
with them. I need your help with that.

This example demonstrates the partners are a team and each takes
responsibility for injuries that occur between them and their children.
This avoids triangulation between children and parents and allows the
offending parent to deal with the upset child or children directly.

**Repairing injuries or misunderstandings with children is separate
from letting them off the hook for bad behavior. The parent's willingness to show remorse and make amends for their bad behavior
only demonstrates secure functioning between the child and parent.
It does not excuse the child from responsibility.**

Partner B I shouldn't have yelled at you like that. I was
wrong to act that way, and I'm very sorry. I never
want you to be scared of me. I know what that's
like. My father was sometimes scary, and I don't
want that for you and me. Okay? I love you.

When that piece comes to a full stop, the parent might say, "Do
you know why I became angry with you?" as a cue for the child to
now admit their wrong. Be careful though and prepare yourself to be

disappointed if your child doesn't have an answer, as many younger children might not. This is still a teaching moment to be kept brief and to the point.

> **Partner B** It hurts me when I say no and you argue with me and disobey. I take it as you don't care. I care about you, very much, even though right now, at your age, I'm the boss. I need you to listen to me. I can't do this without you, you know. You and I, we cooperate with each other.

And exit the discussion. Too much talk by parents can make kids feel trapped. Make your point and exit. You will have a next time.

> **Partner A** And you're teaching them to be afraid of their parent. There are other ways to enforce limits with them. You don't have to yell.

Partner A continues to do a stellar job and has not gone off message once.

> **Partner B** I don't yell. I use a strong tone of voice. I want them to know I'm serious. I'm not yelling.
>
> **Partner A** I don't think you hear yourself. You yell. You yell at me, too; when you're angry, you do.

Partner A is still on point despite making the link to themselves. Why is this okay? Because it's more relevant than fighting over the child as a third. Issues involving children as thirds almost always point to the same issues that belong to the couple relationship, and the kids get used as proxies. So if Partner A's original complaint was yelling as a problem between the partners and they then brought the children into it (i.e., "It's not just me that feels this way, the kids complain of the same thing") that would be an improper use of thirds and now becomes a big mistake in the interaction. Make sense? Leave other people out of your arguments in general.

> **Partner B** You think everything is yelling because no one ever fought in your family.
>
> **Partner A** We didn't have to fight. Your family is constantly fighting, even to this day. You all yell and fight.

And this is where both go off the rails. Off topic and probably not coming back during this round. Game over.

It is easy for partners to go off topic by using a sidebar ("And another problem I have . . . You always interrupt me . . ."), the past (". . . like you did last week at dinner . . ."), or a defensive tactic (". . . because I'm the one who has to do it all . . ."). Each of these examples will delay, if not prevent, any mutual relief, solution, or agreement. This is not personal to any one individual as all people will act and react the same when oriented as a one-person system (I, me, mine or you, you, your). Collaborative, cooperative, and sensitive interaction must be maintained at all times, or threat perception and defense will ensue—wasting valuable time, energy, and good will.

If you and your partner find yourselves at an impasse like this, understand that when a conversation about a particular topic reaches the boiling point, stop. Take a breath. Count to ten. Pinch yourself. Then, with all the calm you can muster, look your partner in the eye. Remind yourself that they care and that they're probably out of options. Just because they default to frustration and attack, doesn't mean you do. Give yourselves time to cool off. When you both feel better, turn the talk around. Consider a different tactic and stay on target. For example, once the partners in the scenario above calmed down, one of them could end the interaction as follows:

Partner A or B Let's not drag our families into this. With the resources they had, they did their best. You and I are together in a different time and space. You want better for our kid as much as I do, and we can create a better plan of action to resource and empower them. I know we can. Let's gather ideas, brainstorm our best options, and decide on how we handle this issue as a united front when it comes up again.

Remember, all people wish to avoid loss of any kind. Keep this in mind the next time you attempt to get your way, want your complaints heard, or wish to influence your partner. Neither of you wants to lose, and if you believe for one second that your partner fails to have your interests in mind, you are going to fight! And of course, vice versa.

Corrections

If you and your partner find yourselves able to relate to this couple, understand that your first correction is to cocreate a vision for your children, not for yourselves as parents. What are the outcomes you desire? What outcomes do you want to avoid? At some level, most people will agree. When at one level you sense disagreement, move up a level to see if you can find agreement there:

Partner A I want our children to respect their elders.

Partner B I want our children to be unafraid of their parents and not hate them.

Partner A Wait, I want that too. But I want them to be respectful and to take limits seriously.

Variations of This Complaint

"I Don't Like How My Partner Parents"

By now you know that partners, when observing each other dealing with their kids, are free to remember and project their own childhood experiences with their parents or other attachment figures. It's a triadic phenomenon involving social referencing—for instance, when a child sees one parent upset, they look to the other parent for how they should feel about the situation. The information is visually and auditorily cross-checked unless no one else is in proximity. Partners are also doing that when listening or watching the other partner interact with their child.

Because partners naturally are different people, with different histories and upbringings, this is a ripe stage for reanimation of old experiences and attitudes. One parent, in most cases, disapproves of the other's discipline tactics, or lack thereof.

This marvel of memory will happen, particularly with the first child. Human beings are memory-based, automatic, and reflexive, and when under stress, they know only what they have experienced. If that experience is of an overly harsh parent that they or their siblings or their other parent disparaged, they might act out that harsh parenting style on their child, or they may be hypercritical of their partner doing so. If that experience is of an overly harsh parent whose behavior their siblings and their other parent condoned, they may parent as they were parented, believing they're doing the right thing.

However, if their partner either did not have harsh parenting or experienced a harsh parent who was considered by the family as having done the wrong thing, expect trouble. An overly lax partner who may have experienced overly lax or overly harsh or neglectful parenting as a child may be viewed as threatening by a partner who fears a permissive style is a wrong approach. Similarly, if a partner's experience is of early neglect and minimal parenting, that person may have a hands-off approach.

Studies of parent-child attachment behaviors demonstrate that parents who lacked attention or enrichment at various times in their early development tend to reenact the same parenting trends as their primary attachment figure during similar stages of their child's development (Beebe 2003; Mahler 1980).

Due to the many psychobiological factors affecting parenting decisions, particularly when under stress, the possibilities for mindlessly acting out or simply behaving according to our own parents' playbook are endless and also entirely predictable. Here we go back to the level of differentiation—one's ability to be autonomous and self-aware—in each partner to parent as they wish today, as an intentional team with a shared vision for their children.

When partners sit down and get to the nitty-gritty—explicating their vision for how they want their children to turn out—their differences dissolve. Next is the matter of how to get where they want to go. That is the challenge for a two-person system combining different personalities, styles, and ideas. From a developmental, psychobiological viewpoint, this is considered a feature for children, not a bug. If partners can work together collaboratively and cooperatively, accepting each other as *good enough* to get the job done, they can be awesome parents.

As I mentioned earlier, if you are parenting as a couple, parenting is a couples' project. It is no different from any other task or creative process the couple will face throughout their lifetime. Parenting is an improv within a frame of understanding and preparation. It involves lots of trial and error and using the constructive strategy I call PePPeR (see chapter 1)—predicting, planning, preparing, and revising if necessary—ahead of time and limiting possibilities of being caught off guard. Without PePPeR, parents will experience stress, which leads to automation and acting out.

For instance, we're going to go for a long outing with the children. What could possibly go wrong?

- Given our experience, what might Child A do when prepping for the outing?

- What might Child B do?

- How might these two specific children react while driving or flying to our destination?

- What fights might the two of us get into over the children?

Here we need to predict possible outcomes for all these if/then possibilities and build in guardrails that will guarantee the two of us have a good time. Let's think of it as a kind of war room, where we move all the pieces around: the situation, the environment, our moods and personal idiosyncrasies and peccadilloes. Let's even have a plan in case the unexpected happens.

A good parenting team predicts, plans, and prepares (PePP) for what could possibly go wrong. Now let's add the R to account for either of us having to either revise a plan or repair a mistake with each other. Being able to adapt to changing circumstances and being ready to repair immediately if one should misstep is a vital team operation. Messing up is part of predicting, right? Okay, we're all set to go.

"My Partner and I Are Blending Families, and It's Not Working"

People rarely seem to look ahead, predicting, planning, and preparing for things like marriage, having a child, and becoming a blended family. Think about it. Would you go into a new business without doing your research? Would you start a community center or a place of worship or a political campaign without first finding out everything you can about the venture? No, you wouldn't. But I'll bet you didn't do your research before you got married, had a child, or entered a blended family situation. I'll also bet you and your partner(s) didn't first come up with a mission statement, a purpose statement, and a vision statement. I'll wager that you did not plan for how you would govern each other and all others.

Aside from the fact that there is a multitude of literature and guidance out there on blended families and the common pitfalls most experience, I am fairly certain most people never read or seek out any of those materials before climbing aboard.

You can probably guess by now my position on blended configurations. I believe in a hierarchy whereby the couple is at the top level, and everyone else comes in second. Again, let me clarify that I do *not* mean the children are less important. If the partners do put themselves above the children (young and old), big problems can arise. This is about governance, leadership, and structure.

The new couple should represent an entirely new fiefdom with a cocreated culture and ethos that is uniquely built to spec by the partners. This relationship architecture should exist before blending families, not during the process. However, any time—even after the blending has been done—is better than not doing it at all. How partners will perform as parents should also be part of the design. Other considerations should include management of all thirds (see chapter 9)—exes, in-laws, friends, and children. Think *community*. Though nonbiological parents do not perform disciplinary functions in the foreground, partners are a parenting *team* and, as such, operate administratively, in the background.

So here you are, a stepfamily. Perhaps one of you is childless or both of you have children.[7] Any of these configurations can be problematic depending upon a bunch of variables.

---

7 Pets are not talked about here even though there are plenty of issues with
   partners with pets coming together, sleeping on beds, making a mess,
   making noises, causing allergy attacks, and otherwise generating mayhem.

Variations of This Complaint

"My Partner Is Childless"

This situation can be challenging in that one partner is without parenting experience. Add a hostile ex(es) and there's likely mismanagement of thirds taking place. Add to that the age, sex, and gender identification of the child(ren) and the family or origin history of the childless parent as well as their age and developmental stage of life and the challenge grows.

Then there is the parent-partner. What happened in the previous relationship? Who broke up with whom? Does the parent-partner feel particularly guilty about the child(ren)'s lot? Was the parent-partner a good parent? What is the custody arrangement if there is one? And perhaps more important, what does the parent-partner know about stepfamilies and how to set up the couple system?

Generally speaking, the nonbiological parent should not consider themselves a replacement for the biological parent. Nor should that stepparent be or become placed in a position of disciplinarian. That is the job of the biological parent.

The job of the nonbiological parent is to find the sweet spot that is both insider and outsider for the child; someone who can be an ally without triangulating the parenting team. The stepparent is in the unique position of being an adult model the child sees as making their biological parent happy. As sappy as that may sound, this awareness is commonly expressed by stepchildren.

The biological partner's job is to protect the nonbiological parent from all corners, particularly from angry children, angry exes, and all others that would seek to split the new partnership and target the new kid in town. The stepparent is an easy target for all those who resent the changes in the family structure. Once again, refer to chapter 9 on mismanagement of thirds—one of the most insidious causes leading to the demise of all adult primary attachment relationships. Biological families often buckle under the mismanagement of thirds. Stepfamilies very frequently fall to the same mishandling of third people, things, tasks, and interests, which threaten the relationship's safety and security system.

There are too many variables surrounding this singular configuration of biological parent-partner and childless partner to discuss here. I cannot stress enough the importance of predicting, planning, and preparing for this wonderful yet potentially perilous endeavor of blending families.

The couple must come first and the children second in terms of governance. If the couple is weak, children and others will seek to split partners into good and bad (with the "invader" as the likely target for bad). Elements of the environment will always attempt to split a dyadic system and that is not due to evil intent. All people resist change. All people can become opportunistic when motivated by self-interest and protecting against loss. Loved ones are no exception. If partners are thinking community—not mine or yours, but ours—and if the community is well-structured and well-governed, people eventually come around. This new fiefdom, this new architecture with its sound ethos and proper leadership at the top, should be designed to be as attractive and inclusive as possible for all those who will come to depend on it as home.

In other words, build it and they will come. Don't build it and there will be divides, splitting, resentment, and bedlam. PePPeR yourselves!

"I Don't Like My Partner's Children"

A nonbiological partner might have several reasons for not liking the biological partner's kids. One may be that the children are horrible monsters and nobody would tolerate their behavior. That aside, what are the children's ages? Very young children (one to seven) will likely be easier than adolescent kids (fourteen to twenty). Adult children (twenty-four to thirty) can be a handful in their own right. Let's find out why this might be the case.

Developmentally, children before the age of seven tend to view a new parent-partner with excitement. The family feels more intact. If the new partner is child friendly, they will likely find a welcoming friend in the child. At age eight, the child usually gets a brain upgrade; in other words various subcortical regions begin to build out as development soon moves frontward toward the prefrontal cortex. Development is always uneven, and the front is the last to be upgraded. With every so-called upgrade, human beings fall vulnerable to increased anxiety and depression. It is as if the mind's aperture opens wider to take in more information, making everything more complicated, including self and other. With this forward movement, the child (or, for that matter, anyone else going through an upgrade) can experience resistance and can regress, wishing to return to old times. The four-year-old wishes to be back in the womb, the seven-year-old wishes to be back in the stroller, the fourteen-year-old wishes to be seven, the fifty-year-old wishes to be thirty again. This constant movement toward complexity might help explain our penchant for nostalgia.

The eight-year-old is moving into something called *concrete operations*, whereby new cognitive abilities emerge, some of which put the kibosh on magical thinking. Every time we get a brain upgrade, we review our lives in 360 degrees, going over the past, present, and future. That means an eight-year-old might revisit their parent's divorce, which happened earlier, and begin to view it differently. Similarly, the child may reappraise the stepparent as well as their loyalty to the missing biological parent. Ages eight through thirteen can be daunting in that a child's brain is rapidly upgrading, and alliances begin to change. Preadolescence is a time parents might detect teen-like features in their child—a judginess perhaps, or increased awareness of fashion, music, teen interests, self-identification, and language.

Ages fourteen through twenty can be rocky as children are moving into adolescence proper with an increased need for privacy, increased self-consciousness, increased mood instability, increased acting out, and so on. Because the prefrontal cortex isn't fully myelinated until around age twenty-six (even thirty for some males), I consider persons under the age of twenty-six adolescents, as do insurance companies and psychopharmaceutical trials. It's still a different brain from the adult proper.

Age sixteen can be a very difficult time for all concerned. Not only is it junior year in high school for most children—arguably the toughest year—it is when most kids start driving and argue for more powers of separation from their parents. In fact, at every point in a child's life where there is an expectation to further individuate and separate from parents, many kids stumble with some regressing, if only temporarily.

These generalized points of development remain an important guide for parents of all stripes, but particularly for parents and stepparents who may be surprised that old losses come back to preoccupy their children with more questions.

Complaints about the children can arise from various structural causes such as the partners not regarding each other as equals in both power and authority. This does not pertain to delegation, dividing and conquering, or handing off duties to one another. Shared power and authority means the buck stops with the two of you. You each have final say unless you decide otherwise. Remember, secure functioning means that no matter how partners structure the system, they are both fully on board and in agreement. Childrearing should be a couple task, as partners are in charge. The couple must come first in terms of governance and well-being because children are depending on them. If the couple isn't good, the kids will not be either. If partners do not respect the principle of primacy and relegate either partner to secondary position (or less), children will pay the price. The couple system is the roof of the house; it shelters the children. **The partners are the generals. When generals fight and do not get along, soldiers die!**

Disliking a child or children may result from a stepparent's position on reprimanding or disciplining the kids. Take the following scenario for example:

> Partner A had a five-year-old child from a broken marriage. They desperately wanted a replacement parent for their child and picked a much younger, never-married, childless partner with the intention of having them fill in the gap left by the missing parent; by itself, a very poor reason to pair bond. The new parent-partner, Partner B, thought it was their job to discipline the child. Not only did Partner A disapprove of Partner B's discipline tactics, but the child also began to *hate* Partner B. The union quickly took a nosedive with Partner B being "fired" from the partnership.
>
> The poor child had nothing to do with this debacle. The blame lies squarely on the partners. No couple primacy, no protection or prior role setting for the stepparent by the bioparent, and an unprepared new partner.

When partners predict, prepare, and plan for a blended family, place themselves in a leadership position, and reorient themselves to a two-person stewardship governing a new community of others, there should be little reason for anyone to have a chronic dislike of a child. We do not always like our children, biological or not, but that should never remain a sustained condition.

Children are thirds. Dyadic systems can include thirds without a problem if the partners are managing thirds together and not separately. Thirds are generally, but not always, neutral. They can easily become negative or increasingly negative in the mind of the partner who feels marginalized. This is a tragedy when the third is a child.

So now you might ask the obvious parent-partner questions: Aren't I my children's primary attachment figure as well as you, non-parent-partner? And because they are children, aren't they more entitled to the primacy principle than my adult partner?

The answer to both questions is yes. Here we have competing primary attachment relationships, one between parent and child and one between partners. So who wins in a bid for primacy? This is where we have to loosen up a bit and look at the bigger picture.

When I talk to parents about these competing interests, I often clarify this is not a situation where two people are drowning and you need to decide who to save. If one of them is a child, sorry partner. But that is *not* what is at stake (and hopefully it never is). We are only speaking of the spirit of governance, which must be top-down.

Consider how you will prioritize this confusing thirds conundrum using this measure: Is the couple system failing to protect against triangulation and feelings of betrayal? Are partners allowing feelings of jealousy, envy, or resentment to take hold as a result of poor partner collaboration, consideration, and teamwork? If that is the case, the children will suffer.

The primary principle when involving other dyadic systems is complex and nuanced. You are managing several relationships simultaneously. It is *not* easy. Mistakes will happen. Mismanagement of thirds will occasionally take place. Just be prepared to make amends and fix the mistakes. To be sure, however, you have the capacity—and now the best tools—to protect your couple relationship *and* your parent-child relationship somewhat simultaneously, or at least close enough to avoid major players feeling thrown under the bus.

Again, your best prevention is always prediction, planning, and preparation for all that could—and probably will—go wrong. You can both be caught unawares—once. The second and subsequent recurrences are on both of you.

"My Partner Treats Their Own Child Better Than Mine"

The three things you can count on coming up in blended families are envy, guilt, and jealousy. Biological parent-partners are often besieged by guilt feelings for having messed up their kids' lives in some way or another. Whether the missing biological parent is absent due to death or divorce, guilt is usually involved. Guilt causes problems for everybody—the kids and the new partner. Guilt makes people do things that are meant to be loving but aren't. Envy may be experienced by one of the kids or the non-biological parent who feels a child is getting what they believe they should get. And both kids and parents can experience jealousy if they feel that something that is already theirs is being taken from them.

Most of these problems can be explained by mismanagement of thirds at the top tier of the administration—meaning, the couple. Otherwise, these feelings are normal and bound to come up in one corner or another in the blended community. Since you as parents are leaders and your job is to parent, talk about these feelings openly along with repair options (as needed) and possible solutions. Using PePPeR as a tool, consider opening that discussion with equity and justice in mind for you and every child, even the seemingly ornery one. Feelings of jealousy, envy, and guilt are not always fixable and may require patience and time and understanding. Actively observe how these feelings may be festering in you or another member of the family. Reflect on what the root cause might be.

Are these persistent negative feelings the result of a poorly thought-out family structure? Then get together as a couple and establish clearer rules. PePPeR yourselves for the next time it comes up.

Consider that the hurt party may be experiencing jealousy, envy, or guilt because of a mismanagement of thirds that has become overwhelming. It's never too late to talk about and implement a better management strategy as long as you pick your battles and stay the course as a united front.

Does the injured person(s) feel that you and your partner have been mishandling issues of unfairness, injustice, or insensitivity? Take a good hard look at the structure you created. Who is hurting? When and how does their hurt manifest and hemorrhage? As a couple, you must take them seriously.

You both have outside forces to consider, such as the unseated ex-partner. The biological parent must set and hold boundaries in order to protect the newer union. The absence of boundaries and protection of the new union is the single most common problem leading to relationship tumult. The consistent words and actions of the biological parent ensures that everyone respects the primacy of the new couple partnership as an almost universal reality. Primaries will *not* tolerate being secondary for very long. And even then, it is a big mess to clean up when it occurs.

There is a very good reason to start off on the right foot when launching into a blended configuration: the stage will be set *before* the actors take their places. However, if the stage is not set in advance, entitlements necessarily take hold and change becomes much more arduous. People do not like privileges taken away from them. **A big mistake a great many couples make is failing to set up shop before opening day. If the couple isn't organized and clear about their purpose and vision for themselves and the others, everyone is going to be confused and angry.**

The PePPeR war room idea comes into play here. What could possibly go wrong when we unionize each other and the kids? What are all the if/thens we must consider before going into the fray? Use your prefrontal cortices as nature intended—predict, plan, and prepare . . . and repair whenever necessary.

"I Hate My Partner's Ex"

I almost want to say, "Of course you do." Hating the ex is an old story—as is becoming the evil stepparent. People generally do not go peacefully when it comes to breakups. The angry ex-partner is legendary because few people like being left, even if they didn't like or love their ex-partner. Remember, the attachment system is a biological mandate and has *nothing* to do with love, but it sure *feels* like love, and there's nothing like losing a primary attachment figure. Attachment—the "I can't quit you" bond—is what makes us stay in bad relationships and make poor judgment calls. The attachment bond goes to our most primitive existential issue around survival. It's serious business.

Some blended families are blessed with exes who get along with everyone, are supportive of the new union, and are collaborative and cooperative with co-parenting. Some get there eventually; others make it clear that paybacks are hell.

If the latter is truer, even for the moment, the couple must seal itself off and create its own ethical standards, rules, principles, and structure. The principal partner must manage each ex, like all other outsiders, while remaining completely transparent to the current partner. The same is true for handling in-laws: the blood partner protects the non-blood partner at all times. The nonblood partner should *never* cross lines and attack or criticize the partner's original home team. You don't want to be on the wrong side of that political mess. Your partner's parents are *your partner's* problem, not yours. Protect your partner from your family in the same way, and everyone will be better off. I know this is easier said than done. That doesn't mean it still isn't the best way to do business with families.

Chapter 11

Money

Money is one of the "big five" issues (along with time, sex, mess, and kids) that couples fight about. One person spends too much, the other spends too little; one person controls all the money while the other gets an allowance; neither partner agrees to a common joint fund, or just one of them does; one person has lots of money from a family trust, and the other doesn't. Like all the other complaints, this one comes in a variety of combinations and configurations.

So where does secure functioning come into play in these situations? Secure functioning focuses on partner agreements based on the couple's notions of fairness and justice. Unfairness, injustice, and insensitivity arise when one partner raises a money issue with a complaint. And if one partner complains about unfairness around money (or anything) the couple has a problem to solve.

"My Partner Is Always Anxious about Money"

The Complaint in Action

Partner A You are spending way too much money. We don't need to go to the most expensive grocery store. We don't need to send the kids to the most expensive school.

Partner B Hold on just a minute! I spend just enough money to keep this household running and for everyone to be fed, you included. It's a regular food market, not fancy. What are you even talking about? You and I both agreed on the school. You had plenty of time to do your own research, and you didn't. You left it all up to me, like you always do. And then you said yes.

Partner A I told you I didn't approve of the school.

Partner B Then why did you say yes? Are you saying you didn't look me straight the eye and say yes?

Partner A Yes, I said yes, but only after you did this to me!

Partner B Did what to you? Talk common sense? Is that what you mean?

Partner A I mean what you're doing right now—beating me up about it. You know that neither of us went to a private school. And you know that I don't have time to investigate schools when I'm this busy at work.

Partner B Our child is at this school because our child is special needs. You're talking like this is some upscale private school.

Partner A Okay, okay, I know. I'm just constantly up at night worrying about how we're going to pay bills. We don't have any savings. What if there's an emergency? If I don't make enough sales this year, we could lose our insurance benefits. We don't have anything tucked away for our retirement or our child's future.

Partner B Will you *please* stop with all your worrying. It goes nowhere. I don't hear you complaining when you decide to buy yourself a new pair of shoes. And you don't hear me complaining, either. We've always had enough to get by, and you're always worrying.

And scene.

Why Does This Keep Happening?

This couple gets caught in a loop. It's pretty much the same loop every time with minor differences. Still, no one walks away happy or at least relieved.

For many, money represents love. Perhaps money and things were the currency of love during their childhood. For others, money equals value and respect. It's society's currency of value, which translates into self-worth, appreciation, importance, and even prestige. **For all, money is inherently connected to safety and security. Without money, life becomes about survival if you're an independent adult.**

Partner A's felt sense of safety and security is threatened in the matter of money—saving, predicting, planning, and preparing. Does Partner A have historical issues around money? Very likely. Does Partner B have any historical issues around money? Again, likely. As it usually is with couples, where there's one there's the other. Each partner has the bite that fits the other's wound. Might Partner A have an untreated anxiety disorder? Possibly. Regardless of all these factors, these partners are in each other's care. How well do you think they are communicating and caring at this point?

Partners are coexecutives of their mutual safety and security system. Therefore, both are responsible for thinking ahead for what could possibly go wrong. Here too, predicting, planning, preparing, and revising (PePPeR) are the four essentials for managing all things—finances, living together, childrearing, vacations, holidays, meetings, social gatherings, healthcare . . . everything!

This couple doesn't manage things together.

The Central Culprit: The Interaction

Doubling down on counterattacks and getting off topic cause chaos to ensue between the partners. Both play a mighty role in a highly charged standoff around a perfectly reasonable topic every couple should be able to discuss together. I will focus on where and why the micro-exchanges within this dialogue go faulty.

Partner A You are spending way too much money. We don't need to go to the most expensive grocery store. We don't need to send the kids to the most expensive school.

Partner B Hold on just a minute! I spend just enough money to keep this household running and for everyone to be fed, you included. It's a regular food market but not fancy. What are you even talking about? You and I both agreed on the school. You had plenty of time to do your own research and you didn't. You left it all up to me like you always do. And then you said yes.

Partner A starts off okay but would do better with something less likely to pose a threat. Perhaps, "I'm so anxious about the money you and I are spending." That buries the real intent, which is to say, "You are spending way too much money." The "we" statement levels the field and is less accusatory, and the anxiety part focuses attention on the partner's perception and feeling rather than making a statement of fact.

If they had an agreed-upon budget amount for both of them, and the other partner exceeded that limit, then Partner A's original statement would be accurate with supplied proof. But Partner A makes the mistake of instigating a fact-based argument without facts, points their finger squarely at Partner B, and launches into a list of unnecessary expenses.

This leads to Partner B's response, which is a counterattack. Punch your partner, you get punched back. The counter response is hearty because it includes an indictment of Partner A's lack of collaboration.

However, Partner B is equally responsible for the trajectory of this interaction segment and is in danger of being disorderly by bringing up a different subject: Partner A's lack of collaboration and joint decision-making.

Partner A I told you I didn't approve of the school.

Partner B Then why did you say yes? Are you saying you didn't look me straight the eye and say yes?

Partner A Yes, I said yes, but only after you did this to me!

Partner B Did what to you? Talk common sense? Is that what you mean?

Partner A doubles down by making more errors, such as admitting they disapproved of a decision that they actually agreed upon. This is another easy setup for Partner B's response, which is to continue the alternate topic of noncollaboration with an added issue of dishonesty to which Partner A finally admits. And now Partner A adds to the disorder by bringing up a new topic, which is Partner B's demeanor. This not only takes the couple further off track, it also weakens Partner A's position by blaming Partner B for a personal lack of agency and honesty. Partner A is just making things worse.

Now, Partner A could easily put the couple back on course at any time by resetting the discussion to the original topic—spending too much money. And admitting sooner that they become highly anxious around finances would probably shorten this back-and-forth. Then Partner B could say, "I know you're anxious about the spending. Let's talk about what you and I are actually spending." And Partner A could at any time do the same in an effort to get relief with the original complaint.

Partner A Okay, okay, I know. I'm just constantly up at night worrying about how we're going to pay bills. We don't have any savings. What if there's an emergency? If I don't make enough sales this year, we could lose our insurance benefits. We don't have anything tucked away for our retirement or our child's future.

Partner B Will you *please* stop with all your worrying. It goes nowhere. I don't hear you complaining when you decide to buy yourself a new pair of shoes. And you don't hear me complaining, either. We've always had enough to get by, and you're always worrying.

Finally, Partner A admits the real motivation for the complaint: they worry about saving, planning, and preparing for the future. These are legitimate concerns. But Partner B makes a terrible mistake next by dismissing their partner's distress and adds insult to injury by getting back at and blaming the other for spending money, which is off topic.

Do you see how disorderly these interactions are? Do you see how this starts unnecessarily as an attack without repair? As such, the couple walks away without relief, without a plan or temporary solution. They walk away with an increased lack of safety and security, increased resentment, and more memories of threat. We can assume these interactions repeat regardless of the subject matter. That's because anything stressful will lead to the same manner of doing business with each other.

Whenever interactions become disorderly, go off topic, bring in thirds, focus on self-interests only, or center on the partner as the problem and no relief is offered, disaster will follow. Guaranteed. All people will encounter the same results regardless of who they are, where they came from, or any other factor involving humans. This isn't you or me, one person or another, you or them, it's all of us. Stop overthinking what's obvious. Just about every day I hear, "But . . . but, you don't understand. There's something deeper here." And there isn't. True, there is personal history, culture, trauma, personality, attachment, genetics, neurobiology, and a host of other very important factors to consider when attempting to understand a specific human being. However, in this area of two-person comanagement of stressful interactions, all humans will act and react badly when experiencing threat. **One only needs to understand human nature to know that when any of us feels under attack, misunderstood, helpless, treated unfairly, or abandoned, we will sooner or later become two-year-olds on steroids.**

Inflammation caused by repeated interactions builds threat and leads to a natural mental sorting into big bucket issues, past and present, and then becomes part of our narrative. "I'm in pain, and I don't know why. Oh yeah, it's because of you."

Corrections

One person's anxiety will become the other's anxiety as well. Rather than overfocus on each other, focus on the issue causing anxiety and find solutions to rein in whatever is causing repeated chaos. That doesn't mean you yell at the anxious person to pipe down. It doesn't mean that you suggest they go on medication. It doesn't mean that you attack that person with statements like, "You're too anxious," or "You worry too much," or "You're too sensitive," or "You have nothing to worry about." These are all dismissive reactions to a real problem that just does not go away because you wish it to.

Instead, reassure your partner or commiserate with them. Let's change the dialogue from above:

Partner A You are spending way too much money. We don't need to go to the most expensive grocery store. We don't need to send the kids to the most expensive school.

Partner B Okay. Let's talk about it but take one thing at a time, starting with the grocery store. What would make you more comfortable?

Partner A Why can't you go to a cheaper store like everyone else?

Partner B Fair. The food you like so much and the food that offers the healthiest options is the one I go to. We would have to give those things up. Or, I could go just to the one for the foods we like, along with the healthy choices, and go to a cheaper store for the other stuff. What do you think?

Partner A Okay. That's a good idea . . . the last one, I mean. Because we're not rich. That grocery store is a luxury we can't really afford.

Partner B I know, I get it. But this idea works for you, yes?

Partner A Yes.

Partner B Now the school. You may not remember, but let's talk about it anyway. We decided, or so I thought, that this would be the best alternative for our child. Would you like us to revisit what's best?

Partner A It's just that I'm worried sick about our finances. I'm up at night thinking about emergencies, our retirement, insurance, I mean, I'm a mess.

Partner B (*Moving next to their mate and taking their hand*) I know, I know. I'm so sorry. We're in this together. Let's figure something out so you're not so burdened. I can go back to work. I'd like that. I can work from home. We can cut down on some of our expenses, including groceries. Let's brainstorm where we can cut.

Partner A I'm sorry for being such a pain. I know I'm anxious all the time.

Partner B You're not a pain. I understand your anxiety, and I know you're looking out for our financial well-being. Let me help. Okay?

Partner A Okay. Thank you . . . really.

Partner B We're a team.

Your job as secure-functioning partners is to manage stress and distress together. Find ways to calm and soothe each other so you can address the cause of the anxiety. Be careful not to negatively interpret your partner's motivations or their underlying psychological problems. That would not be calming or soothing. So what can you say to manage a stressful topic like money and avoid an argumentative loop like this one?

First, carefully prepare your first words, as if your partner is innocent. Be curious, not furious. Avoid the attack. Accusatory words and phrases are charged, and their impact pushes people into a defensive position from which they might not retreat. Instead of charging forward, like Partner A, with "You are spending too much money. We don't need . . ."

and facing a counterattack, like "Hold on just a minute!" think of what you really want from your partner.

Think of the words and emotional tone you wish your partner would use with you. Then open a dialogue in a nonthreatening way. Set your intention so you both can see the appeal and stay focused. Start with a request or goal you have ideas on how to approach. Make sure you're in the same room and have each other's attention. "Hon, when can we sit down together for twenty minutes? Remember when I agreed to track our spending this quarter? Well, I actually see where we can make some cuts without much pain, but I want your input. How does Saturday after breakfast look?" Whether you feel resistance or acceptance, offer to help them with something they feel stressed about. Remember, you're in each other's care.

Variations of This Complaint

"My Partner Is Cheap"

One person's definition of *cheap* can be another person's characterization of *prudent*. My father was a big tipper. He believed in rewarding people and that often endeared him to others. He lavished people he didn't really know with gifts or financial help if he heard someone's child was in need or if an acquaintance needed money for a vital surgery. I looked up to my dad and thought of him as big-hearted and altruistic. As I grew older, I began to view his altruism as having more complexity, and a lot of it served a personal need to feel important.

Yet, as an adult, I often feel like a cheapskate in comparison to him. My wife, Tracey, would never regard me as such. Yet she is as much of a liberal tipper as my father, and I sometimes feel smallish when my impulse falls short of hers.

We all have our personal relationship to money. Much of that relationship is connected to love, worth, and selflessness. For many, money is deeply rooted in survival. This is especially true for those who grew up in poverty or in families that lost their money.

Some partners argue they are frugal and concerned with overspending or spending unnecessarily. But their partners may argue that translates into caring more about money than pleasing others, including the partner. Other partners actually do spend more on themselves than their mates. This often coexists with separate bank accounts and/or financial inequity where one partner has more money and feels entitled to do with it what they wish. Still other partners have expensive tastes and expectations. The following three Partner A/Partner B scenarios further illustrate these points.

"My Partner Says I Overspend"

In this scenario, Partner A came from a family of modest income and opportunities. A hard worker, Partner A expected to work in the service industry—like their parents—which would afford them only a modest but respectable income. Partner B came from a family of greater wealth and entitlement, and the matter of their overspending repeatedly came up. It wasn't that Partner B was a spendthrift. They were simply accustomed to having more money.

"My Partner Is Miserly with Money"

In this case, Partner A was unaccustomed to lavishing partners with gifts or material goods and was unfamiliar with other niceties, such as romance and affection. Such was Partner B's lot in the relationship. One might say that Partner A's notion of a love relationship was quite different from that of Partner B, who considered Partner A cold and ungenerous.

"I Make More Money Than My Partner"

Here, Partner A's arrangement with Partner B is based on who makes the most money. Partner A believes that whoever makes more should get more. Partner B finds this unfair but has gone along with the arrangement.

The three Partner A/Partner B scenarios above have one thing in common: a structure where partners are not in full agreement. All of them went into the relationship failing to consider what they were getting into. So now, what to do?

In the first scenario, partners have to decide what's most important for each of them and the union. The fact that Partner A chooses a career path that probably won't make them rich is a value and quality-of-life matter. This couple will start moving forward toward repair by, again, listing their individual values and discussing the shared values that will become part of their rules of governance as a couple. Some people work only for money while others feel that making a difference is a greater reward for their work than simply money.

The second scenario is a different matter. Some people are unfamiliar with romance, affection, and other loving behaviors that many consider as generally accepted. These individuals might be interpreted by some as cold, clueless, boorish, or simply detached and utility-minded. Other possibilities aside, in couples, where there is one, there is always the other. It is difficult to imagine an affectionate, romantic, and gift-giving partner unionizing with such a character as described. Stranger things happen, yet partners are usually much closer together in these orientations than what we see on the surface. More likely, one partner is more special-event-minded than the other—they cherish birthdays, holidays, and anniversaries as gestures of celebration. To some, these particular days have little meaning. This is where one's childhood experiences can make all the difference. Individuals who experienced some measure of attachment neglect may literally believe they are missing celebrations in their lives. No expectation, no disappointment. Their partners, however, may have a very different reaction to forgetting, neglecting, or devaluing a beloved special celebration.

Secure-functioning partners may not care about their own celebrations, but they *must* care about the other's sensibilities, expectations, and wishes. And thus, in the second scenario, Partner B perhaps forgoes celebrating certain events if Partner A does not regard them as special, and Partner A respects and responds to Partner B's desire for rejoicing in their special moments. Everybody gets what they want.

One last point: some folks insist on doing special things for partners who protest against such things. I consider that effort to be as one-person oriented as the partner who consistently fails to honor a wish to celebrate or receive a gift. Neither is commensurate with secure functioning—you are in *each other's* care, not simply your own. You serve each other's desires, wishes, needs, and wants as the other would like to be served. In that way, you both win.

The third scenario is perhaps more common. One partner is wealthier than the other, or one partner is the sole wage earner. The person who *has* money and property wants to keep it and believes the other has not earned the right to make claim to it. What's mine is mine, and what's yours is yours. But what if the arrangement is that one partner is expected to quit their job or career to be available to the other partner or their children, thus giving up their wage-earning ability? For some, the wage earner continues to have the entitlements they believe comes with earning a living. Consider the logic and wisdom, however, of the idea that the person making the most money is entitled to spend the money as they wish. Perhaps it feels good to be the sole monarch, but it sure is foolish and shortsighted in a couple relationship.

I believe that in a union of equals, unfairness is an invitation to be robbed. It is a wide-open opportunity for betrayal and revenge. Inequity is just not a smart way to set up an organization that depends on trust and mutuality. I don't know about you, but I'd rather have a partner who has the same things to gain and lose as I do. That is a basis for trust right there.

Let's get back to structural arrangements made between partners *before* they unionize. In free unions between autonomous adults, an unleveled playing field can portend trouble ahead. **If partners are to be mutual stakeholders in their fate as a couple, they need to avoid inequity anywhere, as it will eventually lead to resentment and bad behavior.**

Most human beings balk at inequity and unfairness, although it's true that some folks expect and endure it—remember what I said about the human proclivity toward authoritarianism? It is attractive to those who wish to remain passengers only.

In secure-functioning relationships, however, you have no passengers. Both of you drive and steer the union. Both celebrate your gains and mourn your losses as equal and active participants and shareholders. Head there in your daily words and actions. You'll both feel safer and enjoy the security of being aligned.

Chapter 12

Transparency

Secure-functioning partners fully and completely share all information with each other. They maintain their transparency at all times. But while principles are perfect, people are not. Thus, people will screw this up. Partners also determine what *must* be shared. Since partners are at the top of the food chain, they are the governors, the executives, the bosses, the leaders, the big kahunas; shared information becomes an essential commodity for doing business and for governing. The right and left hands must know the same things.

If you are somebody who likes to keep information to yourself, make that clear with your partner and find out if they feel the same. If you both decide on nontransparency, I hope you will predict, plan, and prepare for what might go wrong with that deal (see chapter 4). You both might end up rethinking your strategy for survival. If you are someone who likes to keep their cards close to their chest, talk to your partner and come up with how that will play out for the team. If you are someone who is afraid of transparency because of the anticipated consequences if you don't fess up, at least talk to your partner and plan for what could possibly go wrong with that tactic.

People commonly fear saying what is true. They're afraid their partner will disapprove, disagree, criticize, judge, object, or obstruct. Perhaps they're afraid of losing respect, the partner's love, or the relationship. They might feel small, guilty, ashamed, admonished, or punished.

Saying what is true goes back to early childhood. We likely faced consequences for withholding information or lying. In childhood, let's face it, we were small and therefore vulnerable to the reactions of our caregivers, friends, teachers, and other authority figures. Yet, in an adult partnership of equals, transparency isn't about staying out of trouble, obstructing your freedom, or reporting to your parents. It's about freedom of information so that partners can function as a full, operational team of allies. Sharing all information willingly with one's partner is an adult act of interdependence whereby partners choose to be each other's confidants, most trusted persons, and equal stakeholders in what and who they manage. I mean, come on—what's the point of partnership if you are going to be a solo player?

Full trust is an awesome responsibility to give another human being: "I trust you with my life because I can and choose to. My life is in your hands now." To trust another with one's life is an extremely vital human need and, my friends, the very definition of secure attachment.

If you are not putting your full faith and trust in your person— someone you chose as your life partner—what the hell are you thinking? If I put only some of my trust in you, I put myself in real jeopardy because that is precisely how and why I can get screwed. If I invest only some money in you, I'll get what I paid for—limited investment, limited return. Think about it. It's not smart, it's not safe, and it's no way to enter a union based on terms and conditions.

I deal with betrayals daily in my couple clinic. By far the most damaging betrayal of all is the withholding of vital information that, if known, would change everything. If and when revealed, this particular type of betrayal commonly causes PTSD in the discovery partner. At best, this condition lasts at least a year but can linger much longer if the secret keeper continues to mishandle the truth by withholding, denying, defending, lying, and gaslighting.

The withholding of vital information is a betrayal that is very difficult to repair. That is because the discovery partner is in a very real position of now never knowing what is true. The secret keeper has provided evidence of serious deception and a willingness to keep their partner from having agency that comes with knowledge. **Withholding vital information is especially pernicious in that it is an entirely unilateral act of a one-person system that deprives an equal partner of choice.**

Shared information is a big deal because in free and fair unions among equals, information is vital currency for surviving and thriving. It is essential for governance. It is essential for ongoing, daily trust. Transparency and the free flow of information are foundational to a couple's safety and security system. If those crack, what else is there? I cringe if you are magically thinking, *love*. Please . . . don't even.

If you are afraid of full transparency, get ready to put your adult pants on before reading the complaints that follow. If you want to avoid rather than repair real damage, embrace the principle of full and complete transparency because that should be right up there with your relationship coming first.

"My Partner Lies"

Lies come in various forms—fibs, fabrications, deceptions, exaggerations, denials, broken promises, tiny inconsequential lies, bold-faced lies, compulsive lies, and lies of omission and commission. Aggregates of many studies claim the average person lies one to two times per day (Arico and Fallis 2013; Serota and Levine 2015; Serota, Levine, and Docan-Morgan 2021). The top 1 percent of liars lie more than fifteen times per day. Men tend to lie more than women. Married partners tend to lie more than single partners.

Children learn to lie at a very early age. Some of the most popular kids in high school are also the biggest liars. It would appear that lying well is a sign of intelligence. Of course, not all lying is evil or meant to harm others. It's a form of self-protection. When it is a fib as in "Hon, I have no idea who ate the last cookie," we may not like it if we find out about it, but most of us can usually survive it without serious consequence. When it's a big bad smooth-talking boldfaced lie—something used to gain a personal benefit at someone else's cost—that is roundly frowned upon by the majority of people.

My wife, Tracey, and I made a pact to tell each other the truth and be fully transparent with each other. Refer to the "Agreements and Guardrails" section in the introduction so you'll understand what I'm about to say.

I agree to say the truth and be fully transparent because that's who I want to be. I'm not a child, and I no longer like to hide. So, truth and transparency make life easier for me, allow me to be myself, and are the right principles to go with when the right thing is the hardest thing to do.

For example, I come home late from the office. I go to the pharmacy to pick up medications, and I get a pint of ice cream. I love ice cream. I sit in front of the pharmacy, in my car, eating ice cream, watching a television show on my phone.

Tracey calls me and says, "Where are you?"

I say, "I'm sitting in front of the pharmacy, eating a pint of ice cream, and watching a TV show."

"Take another bite and get your butt home," she replies.

"Okay." And that's it.

Is this embarrassing? Yes. Would I like to lie? Not anymore. This is much easier.

Today, if I take too long coming home from the pharmacy, she guesses I bought and ate some ice cream. If true, I never deny it. "Bad boy," she'll say. "Stop doing that!"

The Complaint in Action

This example I'm about to illustrate is of one partner who frequently lies about spending money and the other partner who lies about social media contacts and text messages.

Partner A We agreed that we would tell each other ahead of time before spending over $500 on something. I looked at our credit card bill and saw three charges over $500. You're supposed to ask me first.

Partner B I knew you'd give me a hard time. I was going to return those things, so it wouldn't have mattered.

Partner A Wait. First, that's not the point. You are supposed to ask me first. We agreed. Second, you hardly ever return anything, and you haven't returned those items. Third, that's not an excuse anyway for not asking me first.

Partner B Well, okay. My bad. You don't always tell me things either.

Partner A What don't I tell you?

Partner B (*Puts a hand out*) Give me your phone.

Partner A Why?

Partner B Just give it to me.

Partner A (*Hands over the phone*) What?

Partner B (*Searches a bit and holds the phone up*) What is this? Who is this? Why is this?

Partner A Nobody. That's . . . that's . . . oh, that's an old friend from high school.

Partner B An old friend?

Partner A Yeah. What's wrong with that?

Partner B This old friend, as I recall, was an old flame. No?

Partner A (*Studies the screen and thinks*) Yeah. That was a long time ago.

Partner B What did we say about contacting people from the past and text messaging without telling each other?

Partner A I know; that we would check, I mean, let each other know. Okay.

Partner B And then, let's see . . . you say here, "We should meet for coffee some time." Hmm. Would that be you and me meeting them or just you?

Partner A Well, yes. You and me, together. We'd all meet for coffee.

Partner B You're lying.

Partner A No I'm not. That's what I was thinking.

Partner B You can't complain about my overspending when you keep breaking our agreement. We're even.

And scene.

Why Does This Keep Happening?

Both partners in this example are pro-self, not pro-relationship. **Partners who break agreements court disaster because they've proven that they are ungovernable and therefore cannot be trusted collaborators.** What's the point of making agreements if they're broken? Creating rules if they are disregarded? Crafting principles of governance if they are ignored? The result is the Wild West, where anything goes. The safety and security system breaks down into anarchy. It's simply self-destructive.

In this example, both are guilty of either making faulty agreements or showing their disregard for law and order. They are both operating as one-person systems of me, my, and mine. There is no we or us. No real collaboration. Their decisions are feeling-centered, not purpose-centered. Partner B is mistaken. They are *not* even. Now they both lose. They lie to cover up their one-person choices and get further away from each other by making moral equivalencies—"If you can do this, I can do that."

The Central Culprit: The Interaction

Beyond these one-person system flaws, many other problems exist in their back-and-forth as well.

Partner A We agreed that we would tell each other ahead of time before spending over $500 on something. I looked at our credit card bill and saw three charges over $500. You're supposed to ask me first.

Partner B I knew you'd give me a hard time. I was going to return those things so it wouldn't have mattered.

Oops. Excusing oneself from an agreement by blaming the other for being difficult is not a great excuse. It's dangerously close to gaslighting.

Partner A Wait. First, that's not the point. You are supposed to ask me first. We agreed. Second, you hardly ever return anything, and you haven't returned those items. Third, that's not an excuse anyway for not asking me first.

Partner B   Well, okay. My bad. You don't always tell me
things either.

Deflection is a common deceptive technique. This is deflection.
Now listen as both avoid honoring their agreements.

Partner A   What don't I tell you?
Partner B   (*Searches a bit and holds the phone up*) What is this?
Who is this? Why is this?
Partner A   Nobody. That's . . . that's . . . oh, that's an old
friend from high school.

Clearly deceptive. Hesitation followed by too little information.

Partner B   An old friend?
Partner A   Yeah. What's wrong with that?

Deflection again.

Partner B   This old friend, as I recall, was an old flame. No?
Partner A   (*Studies the screen and thinks*) Yeah. That was a
long time ago.

Dismissal and denial.

Partner B   What did we say about contacting people from the
past and text messaging without telling each other?

Never a good idea to put your partner on the witness stand or talk
down to them as if they were a child.

Partner A   I know; that we would check, I mean, let each
other know. Okay.

Against the ropes with nowhere to go. Partner A continues to offer
the least amount of information, which appears deceptive. Partner B
gets away with their deceptive tactic of diversion.

Partner B   And then, let's see . . . you say here, "We should
meet for coffee some time." Hmm. Would that be
you and me meeting them or just you?
Partner A   Well, yes. You and me, together. We'd all meet
for coffee.

No longer credible. When information is withheld, ad hoc admissions fall flat.

Partner B You're lying.

Partner A No I'm not. That's what I was thinking.

Doubling down. Bad idea.

Partner B You can't complain about my overspending when you keep breaking our agreement. We're even.

Wow. And for the final twist, Partner B gets away with minimizing the spending Partner A wanted to talk about in the first place. What a low-level ploy. It sort of works from a thieving standpoint: You screw me, I screw you. Now we're even.

Corrections

First, be sure you have reviewed the "Agreements and Guardrails" section of the introduction to shore up your agreement process. This couple probably did a shoddy job of it. When you do, make sure you and your partner answer and agree on these important questions:

- What principle do we want in place regarding transparency and truthfulness?

- What consequences do we agree to establish for breaking agreements?

Fulfilling this task thoroughly and thoughtfully may be difficult and time-consuming, but it is well worth the effort. Cocreating principles of governance—how you will govern each other—is the best way to create ease and peace in your union. You are holding each other to principles you set that protect both of you and ensure good things will happen, bad things will not.

Variations of This Complaint

Lying causes lots of damage, particularly when it is chronic and involves information vital to the other partner. Withholding information (lying by omission) causes damage because, when discovered, it adds another layer to the betrayal as the uninformed partner must discover that information for themselves. Omissions lead to future suspiciousness and for very good reason: the withholder provided evidence that they could cause future harm.

Lying to a partner's face causes a specific harm in that the liar proves their ability to cover up by strongly asserting their lie, eliminating any possibility of confusion. Repeated offenses dig a grave that becomes almost impossible for the offender to dig out of. Plenty of people with lying partners have come face-to-face with at least one of the following variations. You're not alone if one or more of these statements resonate with you:

"My partner withholds information from me."

"My partner turns things around on me."

"My partner gaslights me."

While none of these are good behaviors, gaslighting is far and away the most pernicious. As you may recall from chapter 7, gaslighting is an attempt to shift blame, shift focus, or make crazy the one who catches the liar in the act of lying. Gaslighting deflects the lie and refocuses the problem onto the suspicious partner or onto someone or something else. More effort and thought must go into gaslighting than lying as it requires more complexity.

People are more likely to lie when cognitively depleted. Lying is less energy expending in these instances. But some liars lie when fully resourced because they have always done so. The practice exists from childhood as their caregivers likely lied as well. In some cases, caregivers didn't lie but were either unable to detect their child's lies or were too avoidant to pay attention.

There are some cultures where lying—at least in some instances—is socially sanctioned. There are some families where everyone lies. And there are some children who had the misfortune of never being caught.

Lying is normal and part of being human. Everyone lies. But lying is a social liability, particularly in primary attachment relationships where interdependency is central to unionizing. Lying creates a ripple effect by disrupting and inhibiting trust. Liars can't be trusted, and liars never trust anyone. It's a self-enclosed world of aloneness and self-preservation at the cost of pro-relationship engagement. **People lie because they believe they can. And the biggest liars are likely some of the most avoidant, isolated, and cynical people on the planet.**

"My Partner Is Conflict-Avoidant"

By far, the most conflict-avoidant individuals are also avoidantly attached; they are anxiously insecure folks who distance themselves from others. The reason for this is largely due to the chronic interpersonal stress experienced by these individuals. Engagement with caregivers was complicated by expectations leveled by caregivers who themselves were overly pro-self rather than pro-relationship, operating as one-person psychological systems. Relationship-centered interactions were undervalued as were conditions of mutuality, fairness, and sensitivity. Therefore, these children expect to be *needed*, not *wanted*, for performance and appearance purposes. In other words, engagement can be misinterpreted as demand for a one-way purpose, and therefore, the choice is to comply or avoid but not to oppose.

Children always adapt to their social environment. Examples of such adaptations in avoidant families include complying, flying under the radar, withdrawing, and absorbing the old familiar clichés that work until they don't: "Be careful what you say," "Keep to yourself," "Don't rock the boat," and ultimately, "Do what you want anyway but don't get caught." Now any one of these behaviors or stereotypical beliefs alone could describe anybody but taken together, along with other patterns of avoidance, they pretty much describe a group of defenses that point to what we, as research clinicians and scientists, see when studying babies and their developing attachment organization. We know how these organizations develop because we also study their caregiver interactions in stressful situations (Van Rosmalen, Van Der Veer, and Van Der Horst 2015).

While conflict avoidance is perfectly understandable, particularly given the etiology of the defense, the habit is almost always experienced by others as frustrating, threatening, and noncollaborative. It's bad practice in adult relationships. If you are conflict avoidant, use the PePPeR technique you learned in chapter 1 to break this loop. Because conflict avoidance, as with any chronic defense, protects the self from perceived harm, the only way out is to actually turn against the defense by realizing it does the opposite of protecting the self. It's like when the alcoholic, who finally gets that alcohol will ruin their life, starts to turn against it and actively takes steps to stop drinking.

If, and only if, you are able to get yourself there can you reliably give your partner permission to prompt you when you're avoiding engagement. Additionally, you can catch yourself just after choosing avoidance and then immediately reverse yourself. You will train yourself and allow yourself to be trained. If you are convinced that avoidance and conflict avoidance are your friends, your nonengagement will continue to blow back on you as conflict.

Bottom line? There is no way to avoid conflict in the human world. To accept relationship with people is to accept conflict. Only engaging can effectively manage conflict. Embrace conflict; don't seek or avoid it.

The Complaint in Action

The below interaction is sexless and genderless, yet I'll bet you will automatically assign gender or sex to the partners. Check yourself on this. If you think this, or any other example in this book refers to an assigned sex or gender, consider it your bias, not mine.

Partner A   I need to talk to you about what happened this morning.

Partner B   Not now, I have to get ready to go out.

Partner A   It'll only take a minute.

Partner B   No it won't. It never takes a minute.

Partner A   Well, you're just making it longer, aren't you now.

Partner B   What?

Partner A It really hurt my feelings this morning when you just got up without saying good morning or kissing me or at least touching me. You just got up . . . got dressed . . . and left the apartment. Even after we've talked about this a million times.

Partner B I believe I kissed you.

Partner A Well, I believe you didn't.

Partner B Huh. I'll try to do better. Okay?

Partner A Not okay. You've been saying you'll do better, and you don't. I'm tired of being a broken record. Why can't you be in a relationship with me? Instead, you're mostly in your head and not with me. You're somewhere else most of the time.

Partner B I'm with you all the time.

Partner A Oh my God . . . Where do you have to go right now? It can't be work.

Partner B I'll be back soon.

Partner A Wait, we're not done.

Partner B Like I said, never just a minute.

Partner A (*Grunts in frustration*) You're maddening!

Partner B (*Shrugs*) What? What's the big deal? I said I'll try to do better. What do you want from me? Just let it go. You hold on to everything. I'll forgive you for detaining me right now. You can forgive me for not saying goodbye this morning.

Partner A Where are you going?

Partner B I said I'm going out, and I'll be back soon. (*Looks at phone*) Gotta go. 'Bye. See? I said goodbye.

And scene.

Why Does This Keep Happening?

The above is a good example of mutual amplification of threatening behavior. The more one partner distances, the more the other pursues. The system is reacting to itself, creating a balance from an imbalance. Partners are forcing each other to be more threatening. The primary imbalance is created by chronic conflict avoidance in one partner. The refusal to engage properly creates the conflict and provokes abandonment threat in the other. Only equally conflict-avoidant partners could escape this problem. Still, we could expect a problem at some point down the road.

Secure functioning requires both partners' leadership and active engagement. No passengers. No free lunches. No backing down or giving up. This is a two-person team. It can't afford a partner taking a break, avoiding, running away, or giving up. Any other arrangement unfairly puts the burden on one person, and it becomes dangerous to the union. Looking at it this way, it really can't happen.

Conflict avoidance, general avoidance, distancing, and dismissiveness often go together. People in the distancing group come from pro-self family cultures in which attachment behaviors are undervalued. The intention is rarely to hurt the partner. Rather, their partner's requests are misinterpreted as demands to perform a function that benefits only the other person.

Of course, secure attachment behavior benefits both partners; however, it is not perceived that way by distancing folks. Their early experience is centered on performance, appearance, and parental self-esteem. Parental self-interests too often came first. Independence was expected often with a disdain for neediness, clinging, or dependency.

Insecure people on the clinging side are equally pro-self despite their ability to act and sound pro-relationship. They may be more related, but their fears of abandonment, withdrawal, and rejection make them as self-centered as those in the insecure distancing group.

Everyone is, in fact, self-centered and selfish. This is part of the human condition. Secure functioning means being simultaneously self- and other-focused—taking care of self and other at the same time. And that is a two-person psychological system.

The Central Culprit: The Interaction

Let's revisit the original dialogue and see exactly where avoidance comes into play.

Partner A I need to talk to you about what happened this morning.

Partner B Not now, I have to get ready to go out.

Could be true, but probably not so much.

Partner A It'll only take a minute.

Partner B No it won't. It never takes a minute.

That could also be true.

Partner A Well, you're just making it longer, aren't you now.

Clever retort.

Partner B What?

Partner A It really hurt my feelings this morning when you just got up without saying good morning or kissing me or at least touching me. You just got up . . . got dressed . . . and left the apartment. Even after we've talked about this a million times.

Partner B I believe I kissed you.

Typical conflict avoidant defense. Much better to run, not walk, to relief, so Partner B could say something like, "I'm sorry. I know we've talked about it so many times," then kiss Partner A several times lovingly and sincerely and ask if they would be willing to say something immediately if Partner B should forget: "I'm not making you responsible, I'm just going to need some help initially because it isn't automatic for me yet."

Partner A Well, I believe you didn't.

Again, a pretty funny rejoinder.

Partner B Huh. I'll try to do better. Okay?

Please avoid phrases like "I'll try" or "I'll work on it" or "I want to . . ." They never work, they don't relieve, they mean nothing in the world of deeds. They're just words. Words are cheap, and those are among the cheapest. Just . . . don't.

Partner A Not okay. You've been saying you'll do better and you don't. I'm tired of being a broken record. Why can't you be in a relationship with me? Instead, you're mostly in your head and not with me. You're somewhere else most of the time.

Partner B I'm with you all the time.

Typical avoidant response. When I studied infant-caregiver attachment and then adult attachment, so many avoidant individuals claimed at least one caregiver was always around. What they meant was physically around but not engaged, a common misinterpretation of attachment neglect.

Partner A Oh my God . . . Where do you have to go right now? It can't be work.

Partner B I'll be back soon.

Too little information.

Partner A Wait, we're not done.

Partner B Like I said, never just a minute.

Clever, perhaps, but snarky.

Partner A (*Grunts in frustration*) You're maddening!

Partner B (*Shrugs*) What? What's the big deal? I said I'll try to do better. What do you want from me? Just let it go. You hold on to everything. I'll forgive you for detaining me right now. You can forgive me for not saying goodbye this morning.

Here's an avoidant's idea of gift giving: "How about I don't give you anything, and you don't give me anything, and we'll be even."

Partner A Where are you going?

Partner B I said I'm going out, and I'll be back soon. (*Looks at phone*) Gotta go. 'Bye. See? I said goodbye.

Clever callback, perhaps, but dismissive, cold, and aggressively distancing. As I say: with couples, where there's one, there's the other. People do what they do because they believe they can. Partner A must choose their ground and take a stand. But first, they must be absolutely clear as to what stand to take. Is the stand for principles that serve only the self, or is it for the union? A secure-functioning union means you do what's good for both. Your ground is always stronger when your argument, or stand, serves you both.

Perhaps Partner A decides to take their stand by not being there when Partner B returns. There's no coming back together until an accord is met. That's a bite, not a bark. Message to Partner B? "What you are doing is unacceptable—literally. No deal."

That stance, if it's honest and true to a principle that serves mutuality, is the only way to say, "You can't do that."

Corrections

The real burden here is on the conflict-avoidant partner. Secure-functioning relationships are pay to play. Don't pay, you shouldn't expect to play or reap any rewards. Conflict management through engagement costs energy, patience, consideration, collaboration, and yes, cooperation. It's not easy, but it doesn't have to be so hard. Disengagement, regardless of whether it's easier, is not an option if a team is to survive and thrive.

Partners must remember that we're automatic creatures. We're mostly not present. Consider the notion that you are training each other, by agreement and permission, into new behaviors and out of old ones. Doing either by oneself will take forever or just won't happen.

In section 1, I talk about when it is time to take a stand. The above example demonstrates such a time. Perhaps it is time for Partner B to discover that Partner A is not at home when they return. Actions speak louder than words. If a partner keeps repeating behavior that damages the safety and security of the union, that should be a deal breaker. Children and adults can acclimate to negative emotions expressed by a resentful other. One's anger doesn't demonstrate, "You can't do that" for everyone. For many, it's sadly insufficient. Threats can be equally ineffective and even problematic to the safety and security system. At some point, folks must show, not tell, that something is unacceptable. The most nonviolent method is to remove oneself, either out of the bedroom or out of the home. Withdrawal as a consequence is a measured act in terms of the length of withdrawal.

This act should not be done out of anger. Rather, the decision should be made out of resolve. One takes a stand, not only for oneself, but for the union. Be clear on your reasons for physically removing yourself from the premises. Your stand should not only make sense for yourself, but for your partner and the relationship. That is your strongest position—always.

If your choice is to remove yourself—or your partner (if safe)—it should remain decisive and based on principle, not feelings. You're taking a stand for the relationship to exist. Yes, it's a risk, but remaining physically available and escalating the rancor between the two of you runs a higher risk of verbally violent interactions and also degradation of the relationship going forward. This takes courage and conviction and should not be acted upon without firmly acknowledging that your stance is for the good of the relationship.

Partners are the only two pillars holding up the alliance that is the relationship. Sometimes, one must take a stand for secure functioning when the other will not.

Another Variation of the Transparency Complaint

"My Partner Won't Say What They're Thinking or Feeling"

Though some may argue, this variation clearly lands as a transparency issue. People have a great many reasons for not saying what they're thinking or feeling. Let's begin with the most obvious: they don't know what they're thinking or feeling.

For starters, many people do not develop a witness mind—a network of brain areas that witnesses or observes oneself in any given moment. Without the witness mind, we may lack insight and awareness of the mind chattering or detailed body sensations and emotions. We can be fully present and still not be aware of our own thoughts and feelings. In psychology, we call this alexithymia, the inability to put words to feelings. However, it may not be just lack of words but a lack of self-awareness.

Certain brain areas specialize in body awareness. Emotions are a collection of body sensations and thoughts. If we had caregivers who did not recognize emotions in us as young children or give words to the physical expression of emotion, then our child selves may not have learned to recognize this aspect of our internal world. Similarly, if our caregivers themselves didn't express or talk about feelings and thoughts, the result may be the same.

In some rare instances, the brain areas responsible for experiencing, understanding, noticing, and giving words to thoughts and feelings malfunction. Still, the great majority of alexithymics are the way they are not due to nature but to a neglect of nurture.

Another common mistake is to diagnose your alexithymic partner as being on the autistic spectrum or a narcissist. Whatever the cause, expecting an alexithymic to give words to feelings and emotions, or getting angry when they have nothing insightful to add, will simply lead to anger and shame. Not everyone is good at expressing them-selves, expressing their thoughts and feelings. Partners are expected to read their partners through explicit and implicit channels, not just through words, but through knowing their partner's baselines and reading changes in the face, voice, movements, and gestures—both what they do and what they *don't* do and when. You don't expect a nonverbal being, like a baby or pet, to tell you what they think or feel. You have to look for the nonverbal communication and intuit their correct meaning.

We learn about ourselves through others. Read your partner prop-erly, give words to what you see or hear, and help your partner learn from the outside in. That's how we *all* initially learn anything.

Another reason people don't share thoughts and feelings is conflict avoidance: "Why should I share my thoughts and feelings now when nobody was ever interested in my thoughts and feelings as a child?" "I learned early on how unsafe it was to share thoughts and feelings." These beliefs are most often learned in very early childhood. They are now very much reflexes rather than thoughts. So if a partner pushes too much, becomes overly frustrated or angry, that simply drives the low- or nonresponsive partner into further mutism.

When partners maintain a safe and secure environment, they naturally influence each other. They become more like each other. However, there still need to be cocreated mutual agreements around a shared purpose to bring partners to at least a midline. Remember the rule: where's there's one, there's the other. For instance, usually where there is a partner who talks too little, there's a partner who talks too much. Where there's one who is minimally expressive, there's one who is highly expressive. Where one is more introverted, the other is more extroverted. One is faster, the other slower. One never gets angry, the other always gets angry. One expands, the other contracts. One worries, the other maintains calm. One is negative, the other positive.

And it's not just due to baseline predisposition. Insecure-functioning partners will amplify each other's worst inclinations, creating an illusion of extremes. Rather than help each other, they make each other worse.

So learn. Learn your partner's most extreme inclinations and help them come to a more middle ground. Things are rarely what they seem. Our narratives seem to serve us only because they are based on mostly false assumptions, and they are never ever pro-relationship.

Chapter 13

Intimacy

The title of this chapter is a word that the couple clinician probably hears most often embedded in complaints. *Intimacy* is often synonymous with sex, though other times it means "affection" or "vulnerability" or "transparency." It's mostly a catch-all term, like *communication* which, by itself, doesn't mean anything because it could mean everything. I believe people just do not have words to describe what they find missing or wrong sometimes with regard to feeling understood, heard, seen, connected, wanted, loved, special, chosen, and merely not alone.

"I've Given Up Being Affectionate, Loving, and Romantic Because My Partner Isn't"

Giving up is by no means a good strategy unless you are both ready for full dissolution of the relationship. If you're currently remaining in an adult romantic partnership, don't give in to this toxic option unless unhappiness is your goal. Giving up is self-harming. Like avoidance, it never ends well.

The Importance of Leverage

Partners must have leverage when enforcing secure-functioning principles. Quitting, giving up, systemic withdrawal or withholding of goods will deprive you of your leverage. Better to provide everything you expect your partner to provide. When your partner fails to come through, confront them by using your fairness-justice-sensitivity sledgehammer and say, "You can't do this, and I can't do this, so don't do it" or "I've agreed to do this, and you've agreed to do this, so do it." If your partner does anything other than yield and comply, then withdraw with the explicit understanding that "this failure to meet our agreements, heed our principles" will not stand.

Since attachment is a biological mandate to maintain our bonds, it should be used wisely as leverage to hold each other to account. First, however, SPGs and a shared value system must be in place for this to work. Otherwise, withdrawal will simply be perceived as a threat to abandon your partner.

For instance, by dedicating myself to serving you and your interests, protecting you from everyone (including myself), and ensuring your happiness and well-being, I have leverage. I'm not your servant, your slave, or your child; I'm a fully functioning autonomous adult who expects you to be the same. That's the deal. If I simply withdraw my goods, my dedication to serve you, I lose my leverage. If I empty the pool of water, it ceases to be a pool. It's now just a hole in the ground. It's worthless. Like the couple as a Venn diagram (see page 132), the circles part, interdependence is no longer a reality, and leverage is lost.

Secure-functioning partners do the right thing when the right thing is the hardest to do. The right thing is what partners decide in advance. By operating autonomously and sticking to the principles decided upon, regardless of feelings or attitudes, the right thing happens, and now there's leverage.

"We're Always in Our Own Silos"

Distancing partners commonly set up shop by admiring their own independence as if it's a signal to the other: "I'm easy, I don't expect much, and I really don't need anything." The message also means,

"Don't be difficult, don't expect much, and don't need anything from me." We get what we pay for, remember? Independence here is code for "Don't bug me. Keep to your side of the street. If I need you, I'll holler. Otherwise, be seeing you."

Partners give up spending time together to be alone without distraction. That is technically called *primary intersubjectivity* in the attachment field. They also stop enjoying things and activities as a couple, such as games, sports, movies, plays, travel, or other adventures. The technical term for this is *joint attention* to a third thing for mutual enjoyment. With joint attention, interaction is part of the mix. Siloed partners, however, overly rely on separate alone time or being together but in separate worlds. This is called *parallel play*.

Nothing is wrong or bad about parallel play unless it becomes the couple's main diet. At least one partner is bound to feel lonely in a manner different from being alone. Being alone can make one lonely. But being alone *with* someone for extended and repeated periods is a particular kind of loneliness. It's a kind of lonely that harkens back to many childhoods in which parents or caregivers were physically present yet unavailable for engagement.

Siloed partners are already set up for drift (see chapters 6, 8, and 9), a trajectory that aims at eventual dissolution. Drift is initiated and then spurred on by chronic distancing and avoidance. This, like so many problems described in this book, can only occur with two people signing on in some way.

The Complaint in Action

Partner A I feel like we're two ships passing in the night. Like we're just roommates. It's getting kinda lonely, don't you think?

Partner B I don't think that's true.

Partner A We don't really look at each other anymore. We don't talk about anything really, except the kids and work.

Partner B We don't have any time.

Partner A Is that really true though? I mean, like right now, you're over there doing your thing, and I'm over here doing my thing.

Partner B Yeah?

Partner A I don't know. Is this how you imagined it would be?

Partner B I like how it is.

Partner A Close your eyes.

Partner B What?

Partner A Just do it. Close your eyes. I want to play a game.

Partner B (*Closes their eyes*)

Partner A Now, without looking, tell me what I'm wearing right now—from head to toe.

Partner B T-shirt and sweatpants—what you always wear.

Partner A Eh, not tonight.

Partner B Come on.

Partner A What's my favorite color?

Partner B (*Eyes still closed*) I don't know. Blue?

Partner A No. On which side of my chest is my mole?

Partner B (*Opens their eyes*) You have a mole?

Partner A (*With a slight laugh but playful in tone*) You don't know anything about me, do you?

Partner B (*More clipped but still playful*) I know you. What are you talking about? Stop it.

Partner A (*Playfully*) Put that down and come over here. Let's be together.

Partner B (*Becoming irritated*) I want to finish this.

Partner A (*Still playful*) You can finish later. Just come over and be with me. Come on.

Partner B (*Irritated*) Enough. Stop. This was fun. Let me finish.

Partner A (*Without anger*) Okay.

And scene.

I actually smiled as a witness to this interaction, not because it was successful but because it was sweet, and at least one partner did it well. No threatening words or phrases, no threatening tone or attitude. They had, however, a distinct lack of collaboration and mutual play. One might hope that Partner A does not give up this bid for connection going forward. Sadly, partners too often give up when their bids for connection get ignored, dismissed, devalued, or rejected.

Why Does This Keep Happening?

I often say that if two people come back from a vacation and only one of them claims to have had fun, one of them was on a different vacation. Such is the case in the above vignette. If only one partner is feeling lonely or disconnected, something is wrong with the couple, not with the lonely partner.

Secure-functioning partners take responsibility for the other's sense of happiness, well-being, safety, and security. The other's distress is a call to action. Partner B doesn't see it that way. They believe their own evaluation or sense of these things is all the reality check they need. This is a huge mistake in judgment. In couples, relationship evaluation, temperature readings, and claims about the relational state are true or not true only if both partners agree; otherwise it is a one-person system.

The Central Culprit: The Interaction

Let's review:

Partner A I feel like we're two ships passing in the night. Like we're just roommates. It's getting kinda lonely, don't you think?
Partner B I don't think that's true.

Wrong response. It's about as meaningful and helpful as one person complaining it's cold and the other saying it isn't. Okay, we've established we're different people, and . . . ?

Partner B's response is distancing and dismissive, which actually reinforces Partner A's sense of disconnection.

Partner A We don't really look at each other anymore. We don't talk about anything really, except the kids and work.

Partner B We don't have any time.

True or not, the reply remains dismissive.

Partner A Is that really true though? I mean, like right now, you're over there doing your thing, and I'm over here doing my thing.

Partner B Yeah?

People so often do not understand that a nonresponse is perceived as negative to others. Partner B remains largely disengaged. Instead of relieving their partner, they are at least passively amplifying their distress, which leads to more disruption, not less.

Partner A I don't know. Is this how you imagined it would be?

Partner B I like how it is.

Despite Partner B's indifference, Partner A remains cool, interested, and friendly. Outwardly, there's nothing wrong with Partner B's statement, "I like how it is." But taken in context, it sounds too indifferent and oppositional.

Partner A Close your eyes.

Partner B What?

Partner A Just do it. Close your eyes. I want to play a game.

Partner B (*Closes their eyes*)

Partner A Now, without looking, tell me what I'm wearing right now—from head to toe.

Love this game.

Partner B T-shirt and sweatpants—what you always wear.

Partner A Eh, not tonight.

Partner B Come on.

Partner A What's my favorite color?

Partner B (*Eyes still closed*) I don't know. Blue?

Partner A No. On which side of my chest is my mole?

Partner B (*Opens their eyes*) You have a mole?

Despite this being a likely attempt at humor, it doesn't lead to self-awareness. Partner B should at least follow with, "I get your point." But they clearly don't want to.

Partner A (*With a slight laugh but playful in tone*) You don't know anything about me, do you?

Partner B (*More clipped but still playful*) I know you. What are you talking about? Stop it.

Partner A (*Playfully*) Put that down and come over here. Let's be together.

Partner B (*Becoming irritated*) I want to finish this.

Partner A (*Still playful*) You can finish later. Just come over and be with me. Come on.

Partner B (*Irritated*) Enough. Stop. This was fun. Let me finish.

Partner A (*Without anger*) Okay.

As I share in the "Corrections" section below, Partner A plays this well and will need to keep at it going forward.

Corrections

In the above case, Partner A remains appropriately playful, inviting, and friendly and, when shown a limit, backs off without retribution. However, I would change my assessment if Partner A drops this matter going forward. The complaint presents a specific problem of loneliness, but the interaction reveals a definite flaw in the relationship—denial, distancing, dismissiveness, and avoidance. This will kill the relationship if not addressed as a serious matter. It's akin to one person saying the house is on fire while the other says it isn't without first checking. It's . . . not . . . smart.

I would also change my opinion of this interaction if Partner A were to show signs of misattunement with Partner B. People on the clinging side of the attachment spectrum will misattune, meaning their heightened sensitivity to withdrawal, abandonment, and rejection leads them to act out their vulnerability by becoming aggressive, punitive, snarky, sarcastic, and mean.

That said, Partner A must make Partner B understand that as secure-functioning partners, the relationship must come first before all other people and matters. Partners are in each other's care and therefore one-person attitudes will always result in trouble soon or down the pike.

I will often tell distancing folks who resent intrusion by their loved ones that it's possible to arrange things so that nobody cares to intrude because nobody longer cares about you. Interdependency, connection, and relatedness are necessary human "inconveniences."

Variations of This Complaint

Each of these variations involves some distancing or clinging.

"We never talk intimately."

"We never talk about important things."

"My partner never really sees me."

"My partner doesn't understand me."

"My partner makes me feel lonely."

"We're never alone."

Where there is one (distancing), there will be the other (clinging). Though people come to the table with inclinations in either direction, they can also amplify or attenuate their predilections, depending on the partner they choose and their dynamics in union.

"My Partner Tells Me to Get More Friends"

A partner who tells the other to get some hobbies, find their own interests, or get some friends is likely either concerned about their partner's mental health—they believe their partner to be depressed or inert for some reason—or they feel guilty or bothered about their own need for distancing. Then again, both may be true.

Usually, when a partner who is satisfied with their life repeatedly receives this advice, they take it as criticism. Some distancing partners, intolerant of their own and other's perceived lack of drive, extroversion, or active lifestyle, push their mates to "get out there, be more social, and be more motivated or active." This is rarely well-received. If a partner is recommending personal changes for which the other has little or no interest, the pushing will be perceived as judgy, critical, and unfriendly.

When I see this in clinic, the pushing partner is commonly projecting their own bias or the biases of their early caregivers onto the other.

Individuals in the distancing group of attachment formation tend to be more performance- and appearance-driven. Their family culture was likely similar. Some people lack differentiation (becoming one's own person) from their early adaptations to caregiver expectations. Those expectations, drives, shoulds, and should nots remain deeply embedded in memory without having ever been investigated or reviewed with the adult mind. For many, these childhood adaptations remain unquestioned, unexamined, and unchallenged. Individuals then carry parental expectations forward into adulthood. The degree to which those individuals lack self-awareness is the degree to which they maintain a lack of differentiation with their partners and children.

The Complaint in Action

Partner A I'm going out with my friends tonight. I should be back by about 11:00 or 12:00.

Partner B (*Reading a newspaper, feet up, with the TV on*) I'll be here when you get back.

Partner A Why don't you go down the street and spend time with . . .

Partner B Nope, I'm fine.

Partner A You don't have any friends. You don't go anywhere.

Partner B I like being with you. I'm not interested in finding new friends.

Partner A That's so weird. It's not healthy to just hang around one person.

Partner B (*Matter-of-factly*) I don't. I have my siblings and my dad. And I have our cat. And I have you.

Partner A It just doesn't seem normal.

Partner B Thanks.

Partner A I don't want to feel bad about going out.

Partner B Then don't . . .

Partner A Go out?

Partner B . . . feel bad. It *would* be nice if you stayed with me.

Partner A That's what I mean.

Partner B What? I didn't say you couldn't go out. I'm allowed to say I'd like you to stay, aren't I? That's your guilt talking. You feeling guilty?

Partner A I wouldn't be if I knew you weren't just sitting around waiting for me.

Partner B I'm not waiting for you. Do you *want* me to wait for you?

Partner A No, I want you to do something for yourself.

Partner B (*Becoming frustrated*) Look, you're starting to piss me off. Go have fun, don't feel guilty, and stop telling me I'm weird.

And scene.

Why Does This Keep Happening?

These partners have different preferences. Nothing new to see here. One appears more social than the other. One likes to go out, the other is happy to be home. If, in another scene, we witnessed an unwillingness to meet in the middle—one won't go out, or the other won't stay in—and either or both complained, that would be different. But here, neither partner is complaining about doing something separately. The complaint appears one way only from Partner A, who feels guilty about going out alone to be with their friends.

Rather than deal with feeling guilty, they criticize their mate for being friendless and a homebody. They make a personal problem a mutual problem unnecessarily. If Partner B did or said something to provoke guilt, that would be another matter. But their narrative here is devoid of guilt-inducing messaging.

Sometimes, when feeling ambivalent about something, people will blame their partner as a way to escape insecurity. For instance, Partner A could be battling with their own indecision to stay or leave and confuse it for guilt. They could project their ambivalence onto the other in an attempt to solve their indecisiveness. If Partner B had somewhere to go, it would perhaps tip the scales toward leaving. Or if Partner B did indeed create resistance by complaining of being left, Partner A could blame them for making it too difficult to step out, even if they secretly wished to stay. In any case, Partner A seems to be acting out an internal conflict of some kind and making it about the other.

This is a common phenomenon in couples that usually centers on attachment insecurity. Secure-functioning partners are not joined at the hip. They are autonomous individuals who orient themselves according to a two-person psychological system of mutuality, not dependency or fusion. They are not organized around fears of separation and reunion, abandonment or engulfment. When those issues become center stage, those fears will foster insecure functioning. In some cases, partners can become quite disorganized and disoriented when faced with separations and reunions. Ambivalence, which can easily become fear of any loss whatsoever, can then lead to emotional dysregulation for some individuals.

Emotional dysregulation in one partner often turns into mutual dysregulation in the couple. The result is head spinning because the source of the problem is usually in one person's head only, but because the internal conflict—a deep insecure panic of sorts—is nebulous for that person, its external, explicit form never resembles the actual disturbance: "I'm upset, and I don't know why, but I believe it's because of *you*." Now, we all do that to some extent—some more than others. Still, this confusion between inside and outside, what's going on inside my head and what's actually going on outside my head, can easily cause mayhem in the relational field. Problem, problem, who's got the problem?

The solution is curiosity: gathering knowledge and studying your partner but never for the purpose of defending yourself or blaming them. Knowing each other's core vulnerabilities will allow you to help each other sort words and behavior into meaningful communication.

The Central Culprit: The Interaction

In the interaction above, Partner B seems to almost help Partner A at one point, but they don't go far enough. That's because they are likely unaware of Partner A's internal struggles with their own independence. Had they known about it, their narrative would have been quite different. Let's take a look at an upgraded version of the same interaction.

Partner A I'm going out with my friends tonight. I should be back by about 11:00 or 12:00.

Partner B (*Reading a newspaper, feet up, with the TV on*) Okay. Have a good time.

Partner A Why don't you go down the street and spend time with. . . .

Partner B You're worried again about leaving, aren't you?

Partner A (*Clears throat*) Yeah.

Partner B Honey, I'm fine being here, and I'm happy you're going out with your friends. Are you feeling ambivalent about going out?

Partner A (*Moves toward partner and sits down*) I am. I don't know why. Part of me wants to see them and get out of the house, but another part wants to stay with you.

Partner B That's tough. I hate when that happens to me.

Partner A If I stayed, would you want to watch a movie together?

Partner B Depends on which one, but sure. I'm probably going to want to be sleeping by about nine tonight. Would that be too early for you?

Partner A That helps. I'm going to go meet them. Can we watch a movie tomorrow night?

Partner B Sure. I'll be able to stay up a little later, too.

Partner A Great. I adore you.

Partner B And I, you.

In this version, Partner B already knows about one of Partner A's core vulnerabilities and uses that knowledge to help focus the problem, rather than allow it to be misdirected.

Corrections

Most partners are predictable, like most people. But some people just refuse to learn about and predict each other so they can plan for future interactions, particularly when previous ones go south. It would seem that partners tacitly believe they shouldn't have to know each other in detail and in-depth, as if that isn't part of the job description. For example, I may want to be known and understood, but why should I want to know you beyond what I think is necessary? I know you, right? I know what's wrong with you, I know what bugs me about you, I know how you could be better . . . I know all I need to know.

Human beings are insufferably lazy. We do only what we believe necessary and reserve our energy for those things. If we don't believe examination of the self and other is necessary, no way will we do it. We may be interested in the very beginning of a relationship, when we're possessed by our own curiosity and desire to experience this brand-new person. Once we get the gig, we—all of us—withdraw that effort and turn our attention elsewhere.

Romantic unions rely on information that other unions may not require. The romantic attachment relationship recapitulates our earliest dependency relationships. Like it or not, this union *is* the caregiver-infant attachment relationship redux with one exception: this time, the power balance is symmetrical. But it is *still* a dependency relationship. In contrast, a business relationship isn't, nor is a friendship or an adult family relationship. I've said the couple union is like a team, a troupe, an alliance, and yet it is actually more than that. Romantic attachment is very, very personal, grounded in primitive personal needs and expectations. There is, in fact, *no other* adult relationship like it.

Therefore, the implicit rules of this type of relationship are quite different from those of all other types. The adult primary attachment relationship is a mental representation of home; therefore, make the home the way it should be today, the way you want it to be, and not simply the home you had as a child. Make yourself the way you want to be today, not the way you were in your family of origin. You and your partner make up the rules together based on what you both want today for your new household; in other words the mental representation of what you want, not what you had. We're talking about two people cocreating an architecture from the ground up based on what is both good and best for both of you, not just one of you.

Most people do not examine themselves or their early experiences or develop a witnessing mind that allows for self-awareness. For some, that function just never developed. For others, the process feels foreboding and too painful. Most are too busy to make the effort. Only those who are forced into self-examination do so. That force is usually suffering: "I've lost something, and I'm forced to examine how and why that occurred." Or, "Unless I deepen my self-knowledge, I will soon lose something." Please, do not wait until you are absolutely forced to take a good look at yourself, not just as you are now, but how you got here. Do not delay being actively curious and knowledgeable about your mate. Be an expert. Be competent. Learn about yourself and about all humanity by studying your partner carefully and in detail. You won't regret it.

Other Variations of the Intimacy Complaint

 The following variations could go into the chapter on safety and security, particularly if the concern is health and longevity. I place them in this chapter because they can affect intimacy.

"My partner is out of shape."

"My partner doesn't dress nicely anymore."

"I can't get my partner to exercise."

"My partner eats too much junk food."

I began writing this book as the 2019 coronavirus pandemic began, and at the time I am writing here, early 2022, COVID-19 and its variants continue relatively unabated. As such, new personal habits have taken over the general public. Worldwide we have become accustomed to interacting over the internet. People are more inclined to bathe less often and stay in comfy clothing and have given up the time and effort to look better than natural. Less formal, more natural can also mean less attractive to one's mate.

Existential threats can alter how one cares for oneself. For instance, alcohol use is at an all-time high. Weight gain is a common complaint. Because many people stay home and work, they are more sedentary. During the height of the pandemic in 2019–2020, people had less sex. Some of this is trending differently now that vaccines and boosters have been introduced, calming people's fears that death is looming over them.

Many of my couples are currently fighting trends to be overly indulgent and leisurely by working out, dressing up as often as they can, and going out to socialize. Pandemic aside, the above variations have been around for a much longer time. I don't think COVID has made a significant difference complaint-wise.

If the complaints regarding being out of shape, exercising, or junk food refer to *real* concerns about a partner's health, then the legitimacy of the complaint is clearly in the land of mutual stakeholding. Partners should have the right to have a say in each other's health and health habits as they are interdependent survivors. Each has an invested interest in the other's health and longevity for obvious reasons. As annoying as it might be to have someone pick on you, remind you, and nag you into proper self-care, telling them it's none of their affair won't work under these circumstances—your investor-partner has every right to see their investment cared for properly.

Things change somewhat if the complaints focus less on health and more on performance and appearance. For instance, if the couple defines and claims mutual interest in each other's fitness as some couples do, partners can legitimately call foul if one or the other gets out of shape. I wouldn't make that particular agreement, but that's not my relationship.

Similarly, if beauty and presentation are principles we agreed upon to uphold, no problem. However, we're edging toward dicey territory because of changing perception, age, and other possibly unforeseen factors in the future. What then?

The real problem for every complaint variation not centered on health and longevity is either a poorly made agreement or no agreement—with only one partner pushing performance or appearance values. That, in my experience, has never gone well.

The non- or lesser-driven performance- or appearance-valuing person is likely to feel devalued, dismissed, judged, criticized, and very, very angry. Unfortunately, we're in a territory shared by those partners with high-performance expectations applied to sex—quality, quantity, and variety. In other words, we start to approach deal-breaking terrain. Relationships tend to break when high expectations meet disappointing performance, especially when that high expectation isn't shared by the other partner.

I never argue with people's expectations, nor do I take issue with desires, wishes, or preferences. I *do* think that some people's expectations lack two-person thinking and sound judgment because the expectations are too often one-sided with feigned or strained attempts at sounding mutual and collaborative. Still, it isn't my place to judge what's fair or right. My role is to clarify and help partners make agreements that serve both partners' interests.

I've discussed the cultural adaptations found in the distancing and clinging groups of insecure attachment both in this chapter and chapter 12 on transparency. Attachment insecurity influences some, most, or maybe all of these complaints to a greater or lesser degree. I would assume that the greater the influence, the more unfair the expectation. The more pro-self, the less pro-relationship the complaint.

Chapter 14

Sex

S ex is perhaps the single most common complaint among couples. Couples break up over issues of libido, sexual preference, experimentation or the lack thereof, frequency of sex, sexual performance, the use of porn, and the list goes on. While sex is about pleasure and connection (and it can also mean a long list of other things to people), a lot of shame festers in this area. Tons of misinformation fuels an already fiery area of love relationships.

Yet when it comes to struggles, some of the real culprits that arise with our partners in the area of sex are based in psycho-neurobiology. As in many other areas, most sexual problems are not what people think. When we have an understanding of our psycho-neurobiology—and we exercise many of the skills I've offered in this book—we can work through sex issues so we can both enjoy it, rather than view it as a constant that threatens to break us up.

Let's look at some of the primary psycho-neurobiological issues that can explain why sex becomes a big problem for couples beyond the challenges of bedtime routines, management of thirds, and other areas we've discussed that may be in need of repair.

Attachment and Sex

Attachment theory concerns itself with a subjective experience of safety and security with regard to one's primary attachment figures, such as a caregiver or an adult partner. A secure-attachment relationship is one that is relatively free of anxiety—around either abandonment or engulfment. An insecure relationship is anxiety-prone with concerns of abandonment and withdrawal (clinging type) or engulfment and freedom impingement (distancing type). Though attachment theory is not directly concerned with sex, one can clearly imagine its impact on it.

In attachment, two measurable behaviors are commonly applied to determining classification. One of them is *proximity seeking*, which is my behavioral interest in seeking you out. I can say, "Hey, I want to talk to you," or I can just look at you repeatedly or offer a different nonverbal signal to beckon you, perhaps something coquettish, seductive, or flirtatious. Texting you, calling you, sharing social media memes with you—all are behaviors that can be proximity seeking.

The other behavior is *contact maintenance*; that is, how long I can stay in physical contact with you before needing to get up and do something else. An example of this is how long I can maintain eye contact with you before saying, "Okay, that's enough. Time to look elsewhere and do something else." Or I hug you and then tap, tap on your back, which is a signal, "Okay, that's enough." Contact maintenance is the length of time that I can stay in physical contact with you. It is also the length of time I can maintain emotional presence with you.

Many people have little problem moving around their partner when the contact is too much, often by just using their hands to move them, sometimes like a doll, in a manner that is friendly and loving without triggering any kind of abandonment, withdrawal, or rejection. They are able to do this without fear, awkwardness, or discomfort. They don't feel trapped or worried about what the other person will think.

Some partners do a lot of proximity seeking. They often want to be with their partner if their partner is busy on their phone or doing something else. One might picture a young child with their caregiver who becomes preoccupied or inattentive. The child may express a plaintive whiny cry, "Be with me," tugging on the caregiver's clothing. "Be with me. Put that down. Be with me. Be with me." This behavior is not the fault of the child. Either the caregiver is not available, is preoccupied, or there's something wrong with the caregiver, and the child is worried.

Partner differences in proximity seeking and contact maintenance can make for a big deal. Variances in these areas are neither good nor bad, right nor wrong. They're just differences that partners must understand and tolerate, while finding a way to meet in the middle.

These differences are huge when it comes to how we approach sex.

Arousal and Sex

As a couple, we also carry differences in terms of how we respond to arousal—and this affects how we relate to sex. We've looked at what it means to be in a window of tolerance vs. becoming hyperaroused (the fight, flight, or freeze danger system) or hypoaroused (the be still or collapse life threat system). Some hypoaroused cases are worrisome as they become more of a physical problem—when someone cannot fight, cannot flee, or cannot function. Extreme energy conservation, withdrawal, or collapse is hazardous to our mental and physical health.

During sex, we begin by being both relaxed *and* alert. Our nervous system has opposing but complimentary arousal pathways. The *sympathetic* pathway is responsible for energy, excitement, motivation, and attraction. Without sufficient sympathetic tone online, we can't reach orgasm. The *parasympathetic* track is responsible for relaxation, proper blood flow, and readiness. Without sufficient parasympathetic tone online, we can't become erect or lubricated. However, if you believe that sex is defined by erection, lubrication, or orgasm, physical problems can, and likely will, result.

Perhaps you are saying to yourself, "But our arousal, eroticism, and sex lives were perfect and alive when we first met." Here's the deal: **When we are courting, we are literally on love potion drugs that can override our sexual baselines.** Our sexual drive and passions can become supercharged in the early frame of romance and courtship.

That override will become apparent when those drugs wear off, and we begin to automate our partner. They become part of memory and lose their novelty. We think we *know* them because we become familiar with them. We default to our baselines in our attachment reflexes and arousal strategies. We carry on as if we are *family* and not *strangers* who must continue to learn about each other. So many partners become disappointed that their love life, their shared eroticism, isn't as it was in the beginning. But this is a trick of the comparing/contrasting mind that is too aware of what is missing! Partners are moving through time. They are changing. But if they get stuck in the automatic brain, the energy-conserving nature of being human, the strong pull toward searching constantly for novelty outside the realm of the familiar and ordinary, disappointment is certain.

The mind's proclivity for going back is simply nostalgia—a search for the easier, better, more satisfying time in life. The reason we want to go back is because we're afraid of where we are and where we are going. If people can accept that their relationship is constantly changing and maturing—and that's a good thing—they have no need to look back and imagine it as, "Ah, the good old days." As mentioned earlier, part of the reason we always go back—and this starts in childhood—is that whenever we get a brain upgrade, whenever our brain develops and we move into more complexity, we see more, experience more, and we tend to want to go backward to when life was simpler.

- *I've seen everything, and I don't like it.*
- *I'd like to go back to the womb.*
- *I'd like to go back to when I was seven.*
- *I'd like to go back to when I had hair.*
- *I'd like to go back because I've seen the future.*

Every time we develop more complexity, we review our lives in 360 degrees: that's the way it goes. That happens throughout the lifespan.

That's going to happen when we start to compare and contrast our sexual experiences as well. That is part of what the brain does: it compares one thing to the other. If we buy into that comparing brain, we're going to be mighty disappointed. **Many of the fights and struggles arise with our** partners in regard to sex because one or both partners carry the expectation that it should be as it was in the beginning. No one is going to win those arguments because your relationship can never go back to how it was. It's a forward-moving ship that requires presence of mind, attention to what is, and detailed appreciation of the present moment.

You've matured as a couple. You've automated each other, and you are no longer novel to one another. Going back is unrealistic. We develop and sex matures into something else. The sex life you build together, now that you know each other, is a whole other thing that can be fulfilling and interesting and beautiful.

The Brain and Sex

I have already made numerous statements about the human condition and the brain, but I will restate them here in a list because they are important to hold in mind:

Human beings are by nature:

- Moody

- Fickle

- Aggressive

- Lazy

- Self-centered and selfish

- Impulsive

- Opportunistic

- Easily influenced by groups

- Xenophobic

The human brain:

- Conserves energy—we do the least necessary

- Is based on memory

- Compares and contrasts

- Is aware of what is missing

- Is survival-oriented—sensitive to threat cues

- Has primitive (or fast-acting) areas that run on automatic and are highly error prone, acting/solving by recognition

- Has ambassador (or slow-acting) areas that are energy consuming, body/motor interfering, lazy, error-correcting,[8] and easily exhausted

- Is highly error prone, inaccurate, slow, and exhausting, as language and speech consume considerable energy

- Is highly unreliable—memory is affected by the present state of mind and easily altered over time

- Creates perception, which constructs one's reality and is affected by the present state of mind and memory and is therefore unreliable

- Creates personal narratives that serve and protect the individual's interests only

- Acts like a radio stuck on with both signal and noise (nonsense)

- Is constantly tricking us into believing what it produces, especially when threatened

- Is repetitive—most people never become aware they are repeating what was seen, heard, and experienced early in life

The brain and sex are intertwined. We could say that sex is largely in the brain, which directs the body and can inhibit the body from performing properly. A great many brain structures are involved in sexual attraction, desire, and performance, including the high cortical areas, or ambassadors, and the subcortical areas, or primitives. Both of these areas can interfere with sexual function, but it's going to be the ambassadors that cause a lot of trouble with desire, pleasure, and performance (Tatkin 2012).

---

8 The brain's ambassadors do not always error-correct the primitives. When the ambassadors are under-resourced (inadequate blood, oxygen, and glucose), they malfunction.

The ambassadors, or what Daniel Kahneman calls System 2 (Kahneman and Egan 2011), are part of an energy-expending, error-correcting system of thinking that is slow and deliberate. In particular, the ambassadors include areas of the prefrontal cortex. To make it simple, these areas are goal-oriented and inhibitory. Some structures will predict your next mistake or error, and, in terms of performance, that can be disastrous. If a dancer thinks too much, they can mess up, as can a musician, a comedian, a painter, an athlete, or a lover.

A similar problem arises from the neuroendocrine system that responds to stress. There is an inverse relationship between the brain's hypothalamic-pituitary-adrenal axis and the experience of *flow*, a subjective feeling of relaxed focused attention—a losing of oneself in an activity (Peifer et al. 2015).

Flow and Sex

The performative nature of most sexual encounters (post courtship) and flow are in natural opposition to each other. When the subjective experience of demand, expectation, inhibition, fear, threat, shame, or guilt intrude, flow is no longer available to partners. Flow can be had by one partner alone, through autoregulation (self-stimulation). However, it is best had through co-regulation, or rather, by both partners simultaneously. As when partners dance well together, lovemaking is a felt experience of flow. But please, this does not mean that partners must focus on physical operations or simultaneous orgasms. No, no. Flow is a relaxed and attentional state of mind and body. This occurs during friendship, engaged discussion, and curious exploration and discovery of the other person. Flow is free of self-consciousness. We might view it as other-consciousness or outward focus and meditation on our partner. The musician focuses on the music, not themselves playing the music.

Yet, few couples understand this business of flow, of outward curiosity and delight in continuous discovery of their partners. Instead, they are in their heads, in a fantasy ("I must use something to stimulate myself"), in the past ("This never ends well"), or in the future ("This will be over soon").

I have no gripe against orgasms for orgasms' sake. They are good for what ails you—pain reduction, lowered anxiety and depression, temporary relief of restless leg syndrome, ability to sleep or stay awake, increased bonding through endogenous chemicals (neuropeptides oxytocin and vasopressin). Great, and not at all a problem. However, if partners mistake that goal-directed activity for lovemaking, that could definitely be a problem.

Lovemaking is being present and attentive to each other, not to yourselves. It's losing yourselves in the present moment, which is improvisational and process directed, with the two of you accepting the inherent strangerness that exists at all times and a continuous, never-ending desire to know each other more fully and deeply.

The Near Senses and Sex

One last tidbit on another common hazard partners can experience, and it is something people mostly do not talk about: persnickety sensitivities in the near-senses field—taste, touch, smell, sound, and near vision (seeing your partner up close). Partners rarely pair bond if something is terribly wrong in the near senses and a partner experiences aversions. However, a lot of evidence shows that these sensitivities can arise after courtship when partners are in a committed relationship.

This matter of near-senses aversion can be a very sensitive topic—one that is often shame inducing. However, I assure you that things are rarely what they seem. If behavior can wag the tail of feelings, feelings can wag the tail of sensory perception. Act in a friendly, loving way, and you'll begin to feel friendlier and more loving. Start to feel threatened by your partner, and your sense perceptions may begin to alter. Perhaps you suddenly don't like their touch. Or you're now turned off by their smell. Or you begin to suddenly find fault with the sound of their voice or some detail of their face or body. What's going on?

This strange experience can occur with a small number of people in the insecurely attached distancing group. Fears of engulfment, being trapped, or a felt loss of agency and boundaries can result in this sudden dislike of the other person on a sensory level. For these people, only an honest self-analysis of one's relationship history will reveal if sensory issues commonly arise after fully committing to another person.

One's sensory perception could begin to find aversiveness where it previously wasn't because of something called "amygdala disliking" (Gallo et al. 2014; Lundstrom et al. 2008; Zald 2003). Sensory aversion, which is related to amygdala disliking, is a phenomenon that can also occur when a partner overrides their dislike for a particular sex act and performs it anyway so as not to disappoint. These overrides can have long-term consequences that lead to general aversive reactions to the partner and can include all touch due to an increase in disgust. The same can happen if a partner is unhappy or threatened—such as when they feel trapped, expected to perform, or forced into being physically intimate. This latter cause and effect of sensory aversion should serve as a cautionary hypothetical for those who force themselves to perform sexual acts they find repulsive.

My recommendation for dealing with near-sense aversions is to first talk about them. Talking about sensitivities does require a high degree of relationship safety and security. You know your partner best, so be sensitive about choosing a private place and time the two of you can have a face-to-face chat. Your partner is in your care, so find the grace to be kind, quick, and direct: "Hon, I'm struggling to say this because I know you brush and floss, but could you rinse with mouthwash before we make love?" or "I know you work hard, and I love that about you. The sweat? Not so much. Can you please take a quick shower before you come to bed at night? I'll be waiting for you."

Be prepared, too, that when you are honest with them, they may surprise you by being honest with you. Fair play may be a way for your partner to release their shame and save face. They are still in your care, so stay calm. They may need time to process the incoming information, and you may, too. In the long run, agreeing to remove small barriers and make small adjustments isn't about changing or shaming a partner, it's about helping your relationship grow closer. No secrets.

To be clear, the above has little if nothing to do with preference regarding pleasant touch, smell, taste, sound, or visual perception. One may prefer their partner's vocal tone when relaxed, or a particular fragrance, or a particular way they touch a body part. This section of the book does not deal with likes or dislikes so much as near-sense aversive reactions or sudden changes in near-sense perception.

Many people may not like their partner noticing or commenting on their breath, body odor, body parts, skin, or genital area, but free speech regarding near senses is an important health feature. You and your partner can smell or taste a bacterial or viral infection on each other's skin and breath. A discovery like that may require one of you to take a trip to the dentist, ENT doctor, gastroenterologist, gynecologist, urologist, or endocrinologist. You are privy to see unusual or concerning skin eruptions on each other that might necessitate dermatological attention. You and your partner can detect changes in skin temperature suggesting a fever or changes in blood flow in the other's extremities or can discover other signs and symptoms in a partner's voice that again might warrant further investigation.

In these examples, I am not talking about a chronic narcissistic preoccupation with imperfection. That particular feature is unfriendly and distancing. Certainly anyone might object to and feel hurt and angered by a partner who looks and comments with critical or judgmental eyes, ears, nose, and taste buds. Are you such a person—highly judgy and shaming? If you are the chronic critic, be aware that the people around you will rule you out as fit for comment. You ruin your credibility through your lack of acceptance, kindness, and sensitivity. Your partner, most importantly, will eventually lose trust in your opinions because they will see that your near-sense issues are yours alone.

Intimacy involves curiosity, truth telling, interest in the other, good will, and trust. Partners who can speak frankly about near-sense matters can speak openly about other areas of intimacy such as sex, shame, or private thoughts and feelings. Secure-functioning partners talk freely about all matters, body fluids, sexual desires and fantasies, dreams and nightmares, and shameful past behaviors and experiences. Why not, when you are secure in each other's care?

DIY Sexual Intake for Couples

Before you go any further, I suggest taking a moment for a playful investigation game. Try this while sitting across from each other, perhaps while sipping some wine or your favorite relaxing mind-altering substance. It is something I might introduce in my clinic with couples (without the mind-altering substance). I'd have partners sit across from each other, maintaining eye contact, while I ask one partner a question that would have them guess what their partner would say to a sexual inquiry. For instance, what would your partner say truthfully as to what they love best when having sex? I would then corroborate the answer with the target partner and then ask the same question to the other partner. The questions (see below) become increasingly more personal, private, and perhaps embarrassing. The purpose is to provoke a flow of information that likely never happens between partners.

Cross Questions for Sexual Exploration

Sit across from each other. When asking and answering each question, imagine what your partner would truthfully say to a neutral, third party. Let the games begin.

- What would your partner say privately as to what they love most when having sex?

- What would your partner say they would never talk about regarding sex?

- What would your partner say embarrasses them most about sex?

- What would your partner say embarrasses you most about sex?

- How often would your partner say they masturbate?

- How often would your partner say you masturbate?

- How often would your partner say they use pornography?

- How often would your partner say you use pornography?

- What device(s) would your partner say they use when masturbating?

- What device(s) would your partner say you use when masturbating?

- What would your partner say privately is one of their sexual fantasies?

- What would your partner say privately is one of your sexual fantasies?

- What would your partner say about how you smell?

- What would your partner say about how you taste?

- What would your partner say about how you touch them?

- What would your partner say about your sensuality?

- What would your partner say about your willingness to experiment?

- What would your partner say about your willingness to be guided during sex?

Sex à la Mode

Here is another exercise you might try. You could do this for discovery, affection, or any number of agreements the two of you are trying to make, but let's start with sex.

I want you to answer these questions separately. You are being asked what kind of sex you want, the way you want it, how much, and how often. Answer honestly and distinctly. Be sure to be specific.

- What would you like for your order? Be specific. What kind of sex would you like? Do you want à la cart? Do you want an entrée and, if so, with what side orders? Do you want the family meal (actually that sounds creepy)? Do you want the chef's choice, the Hungry Person Feast, the buffet? What would you like as an appetizer? Consider appetizers as foreplay. How many appetizers would you like?

- What portion size would you like your meal to be? Skinny, dieting, normal (whatever that is), or hungry person? How long would you like your meal to last? What would you like for dessert?

- How often would you like this meal delivered? Once a day? More? Two or three times a week? Two or three times a month? Perhaps you don't want a regular order. Would you prefer to make the call once you're hungry? You decide.

Now share this with your partner. Compare your orders. How far away are you from your preferences?

Lovemaking is more than sex. Intimacy is more than bodies pressing together. Curiosity, truthfulness, and unabashed leveling evoke intimacy and closeness. Intimacy and knowledge go together. **Sex without curiosity, exploration, discovery, and up-to-date knowledge of the other and the self leads to mechanical sexual behavior, boredom, and eventual loneliness.**

Now let's take a look at a few of the complaints partners have concerning sex with their partners.

"Having and Talking about Sex Is Really Uncomfortable"

As is common with a great many couples, partners become injured—sometimes due to unartful talk or behavior. Because most people view sexual experience differently, have different expectations, and mostly do not talk about sex during sex, error rates in communication, perception, and attribution go sky high during periods of extended physical intimacy. Remember, folks sometimes have very different preferences and tolerances for proximity-seeking behaviors and extended contact maintenance.

The Complaint in Action

These partners have avoided sex for a very long time. Both say they would like more sex, but neither does anything about it. They complain that it has become too awkward and painful.

Partner A I don't even like talking about it.

Partner B I don't either. But do we want a sexless partnership?

Partner A   No. I don't want that. You never make any moves on me. I was always the one who got things going. I'm not doing that anymore.

Partner B   Yeah, but you started to reject me. I just gave up.

Partner A   That's because you always approached me when I was already in the middle of doing something or when I was about to sleep. Isn't that suspicious?

Partner B   Okay, but admit that you're always too busy to have sex or you are just too tired.

Partner A   That's not true! You'd come up behind me while I'm on the phone and expect me to get horny immediately. Or you'd wait until I was ready to sleep after I'd tell you to come to bed way before. You'd wait until the last minute.

Partner B   Forget it.

Partner A   No. Let's be honest. You'd also make mean comments to me about my weight or how I should get back into shape. That really hurt.

Partner B   You want to honestly talk about hurt? Well, I never felt you were that into me or my body. It felt like a chore for you; something you just had to get over with so you could go to sleep. So like I say . . . forget it. Just forget it.

And scene.

Why Does This Keep Happening?

Avoidance is quite often the death knell of a relationship. What we avoid eventually gets us sooner or later. Avoidance increases anxiety, though it is used as a stopgap attempt to lower anxiety. What we avoid looms larger with time until it becomes too big to handle. This couple avoids talking about their sex life. What likely began as a series of misunderstandings, errors, and unrepaired wounding became a systemic avoidance of the entire matter.

To repeat, the issue isn't really sex. It's that sex is one of those areas where insecure-functioning partners make more errors and missteps.

These very same errors and missteps appear elsewhere in the partner interactions but perhaps more intensely so in the bedroom. Only one solution exists and that is to deal with the elephant in the room.

It only takes one of you to broach the subject and the other to cooperate. This need not be a long discussion at all. In fact, bring up the matter in brief and keep doing that over time. Most people avoid it because they imagine getting stuck, trapped, overwhelmed, and exhausted by a long, drawn-out, difficult talk. Consider nibbling instead of gulping, binging, and stuffing. Take a stroll. Don't sprint or marathon through any topic. Big topics, areas of importance, require small bites, lots of chewing, and plenty of digesting time between the two of you. Learn to pick up and drop topics, particularly hot ones—holding on and letting go.

Learn to bring up difficult subjects when both of you are in a good mood and seem well-resourced. Focus on one aspect only and be ready to switch topics or activities if and when either of you feels or appears underresourced, fatigued, stressed, or overwhelmed. Keep your eyes open and on each other for cues that it's time to shift gears, and if possible, shift together instead of distancing from each other.

All people replenish better together than alone if the conditions are correct (i.e., when they face no demand, expectation, pressure, rejection, or punishment). Partners are coregulating each other's mental-emotional states as they interact. Like facing one another while balancing on a tightrope, if one goes down, you both do. Paying close attention to your partner when discussing difficult subject matter is vital to good teamwork and is always wise if you want to accomplish anything.

And remember, work the problem, not each other.

The Central Culprit: The Interaction

This couple makes a familiar error by focusing on each other rather than the problem they wish to solve. It starts off well with Partner B asking, ". . . do we want a sexless partnership?" and Partner A replying, "No. I don't want that." But then it devolves into pointing fingers, which point right back, and now the two are in the weeds and probably won't get out for a long time.

Partners in a two-person system must think of themselves as having shared interests and must always find where they agree and focus there. What do they want to achieve? What do they want to prevent? They must protect the system and consider themselves and each other simultaneously.

Most people err by speaking in a manner that communicates care for the self only or focuses on the other only. This leads partners to remain wary, prepared for hurt and blame, or to feel overly responsible as "the problem." Many individuals think it's a sign of health and strength to express their feelings about the relationship or their partner without considering the partner at the same time. In doing so, however, they revert to a one-person psychology in which no shared interest, no obligation exists to protect the system itself.

I believe this false notion of self-activation is rooted in our modern self-help culture of independence as counter to codependence, both of which are a denial of interdependence. "I have to take care of myself" has come to mean, "In order for me to have a self, I must not consider you." That stance is always going to be perceived as threatening. Interdependence is the awareness of holding self and other in mind simultaneously. In order for us to get along, to remain allies, to work together and govern, create, and rule, we must think as individuals responsible to and for each other. Any alternative is adversarial.

Ask yourselves the next time you review an interaction that goes off the rails: would we have behaved this way if we were just getting to know each other? Would we be as informal, presumptive, inconsiderate, insensitive, or reckless as we have been recently? If the answer is no, guess what? You've been operating in a one-person psychology as you did in your family of origin. You're operating in another time zone with someone you've mistaken as familial.

Secure-functioning partners remain strangers who are constantly learning about each other. They exist in real time, in the present moment.

Corrections

In the following dialogue, which models a better approach to the original complaint, notice how each partner talks about themselves in a manner that doesn't indict the other. Both are thoughtful, considerate. Neither gives the other cause to be defensive. No one is pointing fingers at the other. They're just friends, talking casually about themselves and their mistakes. Neither expresses feelings about the other that would lead to threat or further avoidance.

Partner A   Hey, about our sex life.

Partner B   Okay, that was sudden.

Partner A   I've been thinking how much I've wanted to avoid the subject. I worry I could avoid it forever if I let it. But I don't because I want to understand why it's so difficult for me to talk about. I think it's become something I've just adapted to and, you know, I don't want to just move through life avoiding things that I think matter to me. I think I miss having sex with you.

Partner B   Hmm.

Partner A   (*Pauses and maintains eye contact, waiting several beats*) You and I, we both avoid difficult subjects sometimes. I can't imagine you haven't thought about this either.

Partner B   Well, no, I've imagined it. I just thought, maybe it's best to let it be.

Partner A   (*Calmly*) Do you think it is? I mean, best for us to just let it be? Should we both just pretend we don't think about sex or not have sex or whatever? Is that best for us?

Partner B   No. I don't think that's best. I don't know any more why we don't, you know, have intimacy with each other like we once did. I get sad about it every now and then.

Partner A I do, too. And I never tell you. I get lonely, and I don't tell you that either. Do you ever get lonely?

Partner B (*Eyes begin to water*) I do. I don't tell you either.

Partner A (*Takes partner's hand*) I'm sorry I don't talk to you like this. I feel so sad we've avoided this and so many other things, but I don't want to do it anymore, okay?

Partner B Okay.

Partner A I want to solve this thing—our lack of intimacy— with you. Okay?

Partner B Okay. I'd like that.

That evening at dinner . . .

Partner B I think I hurt you a while back.

Partner A What do you mean?

Partner B I think I hurt you some years ago when I mentioned my ex being wild in bed. I don't know if you remember, but it was ill-timed, and I think you took it to mean I was unhappy with you.

Partner A Yes, I remember. I did take it to mean you wished I was looser. I was a lot less experienced than you. I thought, I don't know . . . I thought I wasn't at all sexy.

Partner B You were . . . you *are*. I was stupid. I think I meant something different by it, but I knew it hurt you and said nothing. I thought you were none too happy with me. I kept groping you, thinking it was going to turn you on. I've been thinking about it, and I was . . . I . . . my dad always groped my mother in front of me. She would laugh, but I don't think she appreciated it.

Partner A I miss you touching me . . . not grabbing me like you're talking about, but the gentle times . . . when you took it seriously.

Partner B (*Looks longingly into their partner's eyes*) I'm sorry. I am still very attracted to you. Do you believe me?

Partner A I'm not sure yet. Keep saying it, though.

Partner B Let's continue talking in bed later. I have some
other thoughts about us.

Partner A I'd like that.

The couple in the interaction above understands both their separateness and their agreed-upon dependency on one another to
remain friendly, safe, and secure at all times, and when not feeling
those things, to fix any breach in that covenant. A two-person system
requires mindfulness, attention, consideration, and ongoing mutuality.

Sometimes life requires us to jump in with all the courage and
grace we can muster, particularly when we care deeply about our
relationship and know that we may be losing our connection.
Partner A took that chance. As awkward as their entry was, they
immediately admitted how they have often wanted to avoid the
subject, a vulnerability that allowed Partner B an equal amount of
courage and grace and felt safety to enter what is going to be a sensitive conversation. The difference here is they get through step one
with a positive finish.

Variations of This Complaint

"Sex Feels Awkward between Us"

Awkwardness between partners comes in different forms
and from various directions and reasons. Perhaps one
partner is less experienced than the other. Perhaps both
partners lack experience. Partners who wait for marriage
or for some other standard to be reached before having sex will define
sex differently. For some, sex is intercourse. For others sex includes
nudity and genital contact; no nudity but genital contact; nudity but
no genital contact; or no deep kissing. I once worked with a religious
couple who insisted on waiting until marriage before having intercourse,
although manual and oral stimulation was permissible. Surprisingly,
for another couple anal sex was okay but not vaginal intercourse.

We get most of our ideas about sex early in life, including shame
and guilt regarding sex, masturbation, and our bodies. Someone who
raised us or was influential in our youth may have warned us about
opposite or same-sex partners. They may have told us that sex is not to

be enjoyed or that it is to be compulsory to please a partner. Or maybe they said that sex is special, magical, and precious.

Nothing's wrong with feeling awkward. Being together in awkwardness is simply being together in this state or that. We are rigid characters when our sex is precious in our own minds. We have ideas, expectations, memories, and comparisons—most of which are not even ours but are what we have heard from others or in music lyrics, read in books, talked and gossiped about, or seen in movies, on television, or on the internet. It's insane. It's not friendship, kindness, curiosity, or freshness. It's the mind doing what the mind does, which is to take us from the present moment and into our heads. Understand and accept the awkwardness *as is*. Notice it, simply allow it to be, and it will pass. What is awkward now will change with a friendly joint effort. Avoid awkwardness and it will increase.

If one or both of you feel awkward, be together in awkwardness. No one will die. Nothing bad will happen. Deal with shame together with kindness and compassion. Be patient. Be friends and allies. Feelings come and go, as do thoughts. Say them out loud to disconnect from their importance, not to amplify them. Share them as momentary puffs of smoke or clouds, not as steady-state facts of being. **Your thoughts and feelings are not who you are and do not determine what you can or cannot do. Your purpose is to be fully present with and fully attentive to your partner.** Stay out of your head by making your partner the object of your meditation. Be in life: it's short and will be over sooner than you might think. Be in real time. That is all. Just watch, notice, and allow thoughts and feelings to arise and fade like wind or waves. Sex is for making babies and orgasms. The rest is about being here, with one another, in loving-kindness. The rest is the best.

"My Partner Is More Concerned about Performance Than Intimacy"

The preciousness around sex can lead to high expectations, performance anxiety, and stilted sex. Many awkward situations revolve around precious attitudes around sex as something that is separate from and beyond all other human interactions rather than an interaction of playfulness, exploration, curiosity, discovery, improvisation, and friendliness. Sex without presence and attention is something other than intimacy, although intimacy is not essential at every moment in a couple interaction. Flow can be had without interactive regulation between individuals. Flow can be autoregulatory in that play is really by oneself (no real person necessary).

For many, awkwardness is offset by alcohol or other drugs. When alcoholics or drug users become sober, awkwardness often comes to the fore. Some drugs (and medications) increase awkwardness and anxiety. Psychostimulants, such as amphetamines and cocaine, can enhance libido but can also diminish sexual performance as well as interfere with body function. Alcohol can disinhibit individuals but can also cause loss of body function and a diminished sensorium.

Once upon a time, a muscle relaxant drug called Quaalude increased libido and for many, was a sure-fire sex drug. For others, it led to sleep. Drug users once lauded MDMA, or Ecstasy, as a sex drug among other things. That, too, caused people to go in the other direction with heightened anxiety and perseverance, which led to more talk than sex.

Partners will use pornography and say good things about it. Like drugs, porn is another method of using a third thing to help with libido, novelty, and excitement. But it can also cause trouble if one partner starts comparing themselves or the other to an actor on-screen. Pornography use alone, without a partner, can help a partner gear up for sex or can be overused as a replacement for the partner. That leads to other problems.

For men, chronic pornography use can lead to erectile dysfunction or delayed orgasm when with a partner. The latter may be helpful if premature ejaculation is a concern. Yet, for men in the distancing camp of insecure attachment, chronic porn use will often lead to increased avoidance of a partner. Awkwardness and anxiety worsen for these folks because they are practicing (autoregulating) with something that has no interpersonal stress component and has an endless stream of novel, moving objects—both of which the brain loves.

"The Passion Is Gone from Our Sex Life"

And then there is plain old sober sex where we are at baseline with ourselves as we presently reside. Our superpowered sex drive settles into our baseline level without the extra testosterone, dopamine, noradrenaline, phenylethylamine, vasopressin, and oxytocin. In fact, this is when our attachment issues—if we have any—come to the fore. Sex, for some, may actually become *more* threatening with increased distancing or clinging. We begin to automate each other, which means we cease to view one another as novel. The anxiety that was once there in the beginning—the fear we won't get the gig—drops away, and life gradually returns to base expectations and activities. We mistakenly begin to see ourselves as family and quit seeing each other as strangers, and largely unknown to the other. Now we either forgo sex altogether, or we have to reassess the whole sex thing.

"My Partner Fantasizes about Other People"

This particular complaint may have several variations. One partner is concerned that the other is fantasizing about someone else during lovemaking. Or partners have admitted their fantasies to each other, and that discovery burdens one of them. Or a partner imagines that the other is often fantasizing about other people or things.

The problem with complaints about fantasies? We have no way to legislate against them. Feelings, thoughts, images, fantasies, and memories . . . happen. They arise without permission. We can redirect our attention through our eyes and ears and other sensory gates such as touch, smell, and taste. But we cannot, and never will, be in full control of our thoughts and feelings.

Thus, worrying about what someone is thinking, feeling, or fantasizing may be a waste of energy. The same goes for your own anxiety about your thoughts, fantasies, and emotions. Worry and attempts to control them simply amplify their effects.

The Complaint in Action

Partners are lying in bed together in the morning following sex.

Partner A Now that you told me that you sometimes fantasize about other people while we're having sex, it really, really bothers me.

Partner B I'm sorry. I thought you invited me when you asked. I still have a hard time with the idea that you never do and never have.

Partner A Were you fantasizing about someone else this morning?

Partner B No, I don't think so.

Partner A (*Gets up and out of bed rapidly*) I can't do this. (*They begin to dress*)

Partner B (*Mouth agape*) Why are you so upset?

Partner A Because you fantasize about someone else when you have sex with me. I don't like that. It's creepy and makes me sad. It's offensive to me.

Partner B I'm turned on by you. It's not personal, and I'm not doing it that much. I'm sorry. I'll try not to do that.

Partner A I won't know if you're doing it or not. I don't want to be with someone who doesn't want to be with me.

Partner B I never said that. I want to be with you. You're incredibly sexy and attractive. I don't understand why you're this upset.

Partner A It's like you're cheating on me.

Partner B Okay. I get it. I shouldn't have said anything. But you asked. I thought I was being truthful and honest. I didn't mean to offend you.

Partner A (*Finished dressing*) Well, you did. And there's no taking it back. I want someone who thinks of *me*; wants *me*.

Partner B Is there anything I can say to make this right?

Partner A What can you say? That you won't fantasize about anyone else? I won't know, but now I know that you do. (*Leaves the room*)

And scene.

Why Does This Keep Happening?

When a partner confuses thoughts and feelings with deeds, expect conflict. While it's entirely reasonable to expect someone to control their actions and behavior, it's a bit fascistic to expect a person to control their thoughts and emotions because it's nearly impossible and therefore unfair as a measure of right and wrong, good and bad.

A similar conflict is when a partner wants a certain behavior from their mate *and* wants a particular feeling or emotion to accompany that behavior. For instance, I want you to do this thing for me, but I need to believe you want to do it or it won't count. The partner behavior is being measured by a quality or quantity of a particular expressed emotion.

This is, of course, conditional, such as when you apologize but sound as if you really don't mean it. There's some legitimacy to that complaint. Or when you ask, "Do you love me?" and the response is delayed, dismissive, flat, dull, not believable, or contradictory. I am specifically talking about asking your partner to *say* or *do* something with the expectation that they express a level of delight, joy, excitement, or other sign of emotional attunement. As far as you're concerned, the act will not count as a good deed if they do not show they *want* in the same way or degree as you: "I will only accept that if I believe you want it as I want you to want it." Again, the idea here is emotion is either equal to or more important than action or deed. That attitude not only eliminates much of what secure-functioning partners actually do for each other, it discourages acting in service to the partner.

"I want you to come to the party with me and not complain while you're there" is quite different from "I only want you to come because you want to be there with me." What if that partner is going for some ulterior reason? What if they're going because next time they want you do something you'd rather not do?

If everyone is to do only what they want and feel, aren't we back to what is wrong with most romantic unions in the first place? Feelings and emotions cannot be a part of governance. Governance is created and maintained to prevent bad feelings and allow others to bloom. Without it, bad feelings blossom, good feelings wither.

The Central Culprit: The Interaction

In the above example, Partner A confuses what is controllable for what is not, leaving both caught in a bind. If Partner A wants to make sure Partner B is fully present during sex, that might be doable and even something good for both partners. The mind is a radio stuck on "On," a good reason most of us have limited attention spans. It's constantly churning, running, making noise, distracting us, pulling us in multiple directions, and demanding we watch its movies and listen to its lectures and its calculations.

Let's see how the initial interaction could be improved. Observe the changes and see if you can similarly correct your approach. Always work toward quick and effective repair.

Partner A Now that you told me that you sometimes fantasize about other people while we're having sex, it really, really bothers me.

Partner B I'm sorry. I get that. But hey, look at me.

Partner A Why?

Partner B Just look at me, into my eyes.

Partner A (*Turns and looks into their partner's eyes*)

Partner B I love you and only you. I don't want to be somewhere else when we're making love. I only want to be with you. How about this? If either of us notices the other's mind wandering, we remind each other to stay present.

Partner A Okay. What if I don't like so much eye contact? I mean, I don't think I can get aroused this way.

Partner B Let's just try it, and see what it's like. It may be hard for me, too. But we can check with each other, right? If you think I might be off somewhere else, you can just ask me to come back.

Partner A I like that.

Partner B Just don't . . . you know, keep asking me what I'm thinking though, okay? That might be, you know, disruptive.

Partner A (*Laughs*) But I like to know what you're thinking.

Partner B I know. That's fine. Just not during sex. Just remind me to be present. Okay?

Partner A Okay.

Partner B And I'll do the same with you because now I worry you will be off worrying about what I'm thinking. Get it? You won't be with me.

Partner A I think I get it, because I kept thinking this morning that you were fantasizing about someone else.

Partner B Exactly! That's you leaving me. I felt that.

They kiss and start making love . . . again.

Corrections

If you pay close attention in quiet and stillness, you'll notice your mind rapidly shifting between feeling (sensations, emotions, mysterious body states, reactions to smell and taste), hearing (outside sounds, inside sounds, self-talk, thoughts, judgments, urges), and seeing (outer vision, inner vision, pictures, memories, images). To remain present is both relative and intermittent. However, one can train one's eyes to look, notice, and observe. One can direct one's ear to listen to sounds from their partner. Partners can *see* if the other is present by their gaze and remind each other to come back when drifting away. This can only work with prior agreement and permission to do so.

Had either Partner A or Partner B realized what *could* be done instead of what *could not*, the interaction would have gone differently.

Variations of This Complaint

"My Partner Looks at Other Attractive People"

Wandering eyes can annoy anyone who wishes to remain engaged and feel important. Sitting and talking one-to-one with anybody whose eyes keep rolling around feels incredibly rude and insulting unless we're playing the who's who game. It's difficult not to feel that that person would rather be elsewhere or is looking for something more interesting than your company.

Yet, rather than focus on the inattentive behavior, many partners focus on the third; that is, the attractive person or persons catching the other's eye. That is because the wanderer is actually mismanaging thirds with their inattentiveness toward their partner. That points the partner to the third and arouses jealousy and threat.

The real problem isn't the attractors in the wanderer's visual field (a fancy way to say good-looking people), it's the avoidance of the primary who is in their immediate orbit. Hence, many a wanderer is also in the distancing, avoidance group of insecurely attached persons.

The dismissed partner wrongly (but understandably) mistakes attraction with avoidance—a common mistake made by many. Your wandering partner is actually avoiding sustained contact and engagement with you. Because they don't like you? No. Because they can't sustain contact and engagement with anyone, particularly a primary partner. And you thought it was personal.

Stupid things partners do most often *feel* personal, but mostly they're not. These are automatic reflexive behaviors that repeat because of habit and safety or security impulses to self-protect from something threatening. Most people, most of the time, do not *know* what or why they are doing what they are doing. If pressed, they will likely make something up because they actually don't know. All they know is they're in trouble.

Please review the sections on human error potentials here in this chapter and in chapter 1. Remember that real time is faster than consciousness and that we are primarily, on any given day, fully automatic, mindless, reflexive, and operating with lightning-fast recognition memory systems that are close to robotic. We look like we're listening and understanding, but that is mostly not the case. We believe we are clearly speaking and communicating, but that is most untrue as well. We think we remember correctly, but we actually don't—at least we cannot prove it. We believe our own narratives without realizing they're made up with scant fact wrapped in a whole lot of fiction.

Our narratives help organize *our* experience only. We're threat animals who, by nature, collect and sometimes hoard painful experiences that drive us to be ever more cautious and aware of future harm. It's the constant, unyielding fact that we are in our own worlds always attempting to hold hands with other worlds while remembering we're always strangers striving to get to know each other. The reality of that separateness is disturbing and sometimes frightening, but it's also another thing we all have in common. We are not each other; we're only very much like each other.

Secure functioning, which in couples represents a two-person psychological system of fairness, justice, and sensitivity while maintaining continuous attitudes of collaboration and cooperation, is a simple idea. It's an idea I did not make up. The idea is represented in all unions among free people who unionize for a purpose, perhaps a mission, and certainly for a unified vision that serves all equally.

In systems that require interdependency, participants must sometimes surrender the personal for the interpersonal and for the purpose we share. I believe most everyone can operate this way even though the path and practice are quite difficult.

I struggle even today with my own personality flaws, my temper, my impulsivity, my selfishness, my arrogance and narcissism, my stubbornness, my tendency to think I'm right, my island nature, my wave nature, my anxiety, my depression, my insecurity. Secure functioning isn't a panacea, nor is it particularly natural.

I *can* say that the path to secure functioning has made and continues to make me a better person, a better partner, a better parent, and a better friend. Despite failing so many times at doing the right thing when it's the hardest to do, the rewards have been awesome and continue to be so when I override my base impulses to be the lazy, self-centered, impatient person I can be.

I can say with all honesty that secure functioning is very hard to do and still the rewards are awesome and make the effort worthwhile. Secure functioning benefits you, your partner, your offspring, your friends—everything and everyone. Secure functioning is what the world needs, especially in our time.

Always Stay in Each Other's Care

My sincere hope is that you and your partner embrace the primary takeaway from this book: secure functioning is the only way to ensure a long-lasting relationship that is interdependent and fully mutual. Interdependency means that as the participants of a union you are full and equal shareholders with the same things to gain and the same things to lose. Any other arrangement is either dependency or codependency, slavery or autocracy. This form of unionizing is available to everyone, no matter your sex, gender, religion, ethnicity, race, personal history, or any other distinguishing factor.

Secure functioning is an agreement between two (or more) people to play fair and square at all times and, when an agreement fails, to make proper amends and then make things right. Secure functioning is a two-person psychological system of teamwork, full collaboration and cooperation, and is based on fairness, justice, and mutual sensitivity. As participants you must communally create your purpose, values, ethos, and vision as a couple; the shared principles upon which you both will govern each other. These principles should be considered higher than basic human emotions, urges, impulses, opinions, or biases afford. In fact, in order for a union to hold, you both must place your agreement and shared principles higher than yourselves to maintain your secure-functioning relationship, or you will fall prey to every other human story of resentment, rancor, revenge, betrayal, and dissolution.

Secure functioning is for adults who understand that discipline, character, and adherence to principles must override our human nature to protect our interests when it suits us. This has been the long story of human beings throughout human history. Basic human nature leads us to otherize, deny, devalue, blame, justify, avoid, punish, lie, cheat, steal, aggress, stay little, be right or righteous, dominate, and appease. In contrast, secure-functioning principles require us to rise above our basic human tendencies. We may not be able to achieve this higher path in all corners of our lives, but we should at least be able to manage it in our most valued relationships.

Secure functioning is a simple concept. Creating a secure-functioning relationship is ongoing and sometimes even, for reasons unique to each one of us, supremely difficult. Is it worth the effort? For me—the self-centered, lazy, impatient, ill-tempered person that I am—a continuous payoff is unquestionably wonderful as I get to be a better person each day.

Epilogue

Even by the time this book is published, the world will likely continue to struggle with the deadly pandemic that struck in March 2020. Hopefully, one day we will finally be out of the woods. But that is not to say that there won't be other occasions where public health is a concern, and we are forced to come up with safety measures and agreements with our partners. Health is a relationship issue.

Some partnerships split apart when COVID hit hard while others became stronger and more resilient. Sexual activity declined worldwide, as did birthrate. Particularly hard hit were families with young children and teenagers still at home, unable to attend school. Many of these young people became depressed and anxious due to lack of social engagement. Parents also struggled because day care was no longer available due to fears of viral exposure. Many parents had to perform home schooling, an activity for which nobody had planned.

Those who were single and had no family or friends living with them felt overly isolated and depressed. Alcoholism and drug use were on the rise as were psychotropic medications to help with mood and sleep. Many people gained weight, learned to bake, and binge watched movies and TV shows. Video communication programs, such as Zoom, became the mainstay of communication with family, friends, and clients. Physicians, psychiatrists, and psychotherapists performed via telehealth only. Live television, including late night comedy shows, news, and awards ceremonies, were also performed through video communication programs, allowing us to become closer—in some weird way—to people whom we had very little personal knowledge of or connection with, such as celebrities.

Still, many of us learned a lot during this harrowing time of social isolation, constant existential fear, and socio-political upheaval, and one key lesson was the importance of close relationships. The couples who became closer adapted to home life together without the common comings and goings so many of us had become accustomed to. Many of those who had relied on travel rediscovered a slower pace, increased comfort and relaxation, while others complained of feeling trapped, housebound, and plagued with cabin fever. Though discomforting, some found it enlightening to discover that one's relationship happiness had been so dependent upon regular distancing habits, such as traveling, working at an office, or driving for work.

Perhaps the awareness of outside danger, such as a lethal pandemic, reframed mindsets and attitudes that recentered their focus on partnership, camaraderie, and finding the novel in the ordinary. Modern life has become far more complex, distracting, and busying than human beings have ever faced. Once upon a time, before the dawn of personal electronics, we were actually more mindful and present. Most likely today, the average person is rarely living in the moment, fully present and attentive, particularly to another person.

Even when there were signs of COVID letting up and life returning to some kind of normal, a great many people resisted going back to their offices, preferring to work at home. At the time of this writing, no one knows what the future will bring with regard to this pandemic, nor does anyone know what is to come with other global anxieties. Much of the world is gripped by fear and dread. And still, hope and happiness for many continues to be found in relationships.

The fact of the matter is that existential threats have always existed since the beginning of human history. Currently it is the pandemic, along with extreme socio-political divisiveness, global warming, and other as-yet unknowns. All the more reason to find one's safe and secure place. That can be something someone finds by themselves or with another person (or two or three).

And that, really, is the point of this book—to find happiness, well-being, and ease at home. Remember, home *is* your partnership. In a world that is ever changing, unpredictable, indifferent, and filled with dangers, the two of you are the constant, the stable, the dependable, the predictable, the fully invested, and the guardians. You are the warm blanket for the things that go bump in the cold of night. While all about you there are those who are losing their heads—the two of you still stand in solidarity, ready to handle anything and everyone.

Acknowledgments

First and foremost, I'd like to thank my editor, Karen Aroian, who has been my friend and gentle guide throughout this project. I would also like to thank my staff at the PACT Institute for all their support and tolerance of my missing so many meetings. Thank you, Beverly Baker, Lauren Kozak, Shea Depmore, Marla Katz, Michelle Syverson, and Evelia Hunter.

I am forever grateful to my mentors and friends who encouraged me throughout my career: Allan Schore, Marion Solomon, John Bradshaw, Kip Flock, Ellyn Bader, Peter Pearson, Harville Hendrix, Terry Real, Esther Perel, Helen LaKelly Hunt, Stephen Porges, Helen Fisher, Lou Cozolino, Dan Wile, Jeffrey Zeig, Dan Siegel, Pat Ogden, John and Julie Gottman, Rick Hanson, and Edward Kassman.

And to my stepdaughter, Joanna May Beinfeld, who continues to teach me in the ways of generational change and sensitivity.

References

American Psychiatric Association, ed. *Diagnostic and Statistical Manual of Mental Disorders*, 5th edition (DSM-5). Washington, DC: American Psychiatric Publishing, 2013.

Arico, A. J., and D. Fallis. "Lies, Damned Lies, and Statistics: An Empirical Investigation of the Concept of Lying." *Philosophical Psychology* 26, no. 6 (2013): 790–816. doi:10.1080/09515089.2012.725977.

Atzil, S., T. Hendler, O. Zagoory-Sharon, Y. Winetraub, and R. Feldman. "Synchrony and Specificity in the Maternal and the Paternal Brain: Relations to Oxytocin and Vasopressin." *Journal of the American Academy of Child & Adolescent Psychiatry* 51, no. 8 (2012): 798–811. doi:10.1016/j.jaac.2012.06.008.

Azhari, A., M. Lim, A. Bizzego, G. Gabrieli, M. H. Bornstein, and G. Esposito. "Physical Presence of Spouse Enhances Brain-to-Brain Synchrony in Co-Parenting Couples." *Scientific Reports* 10, no. 1 (2020): 7569. doi:10.1038/s41598-020-63596-2.

Beattie, M. *Beyond Codependency: And Getting Better All the Time.* New York: Simon and Schuster, 1989.

———. *Codependent No More: How to Stop Controlling Others and Start Caring for Yourself.* Center City, MN: Hazelden Publishing, 1992.

Beebe, B. "Brief Mother-Infant Treatment: Psychoanalytically Informed Video Feedback." *Infant Mental Health Journal* 24, no. 1 (2003): 24–52. doi:10.1002/imhj.10042.

Belanoff, J. K., K. Gross, A. Yager, and A. F. Schatzberg. "Corticosteroids and Cognition." *Journal of Psychiatric Research* 35, no. 3 (2001): 127–45. doi:10.1016/S0022-3956(01)00018-8.

Black, C., and C. Tripodi. *Intimate Treason: Healing the Trauma for Partners Confronting Sex Addiction.* Las Vegas: Central Recovery Press, 2012.

Bradshaw, J. *Healing the Shame That Binds You*. Deerfield Beach, FL: Health Communications, Inc., 2005.

Brooks, K. P. "Social Experience and Physiology: Effects of Social Relationship Qualities on Allostatic Load." PhD diss., UCLA, 2012.

Chiu, C.-D., M. S. Tollenaar, C.-T. Yang, B. M. Elzinga, T.-Y. Zhang, and H. L. Ho. "The Loss of the Self in Memory: Self-Referential Memory, Childhood Relational Trauma, and Dissociation." *Clinical Psychological Science* 7, no. 2 (2019): 265–82. doi:10.1177/2167702618804794.

de Jesús Rovirosa-Hernández, M., M. H. González, M. Á. Guevara-Pérez, F. García-Orduña, A. de los Ángeles Aguilar-Tirado, A. Puga-Olguín, and B. P. Vásquez-Domínguez. "Menopause in Nonhuman Primates: A Comparative Study with Humans." In *A Multidisciplinary Look at Menopause*, edited by Juan Francisco Rodriguez-Landa and Jonathan Cueto-Escobedo. London: InTechOpen, 2017. doi:10.5772/intechopen.69657.

Entringer, S., and E. S. Epel. "The Stress Field Ages: A Close Look into Cellular Aging Processes." *Psychoneuroendocrinology* 113, no. 104537 (2020). doi:10.1016/j.psyneuen.2019.104537.

Gallo, M., F. Gámiz, M. Perez-García, R. G. Del Moral, and E. T. Rolls. "Taste and Olfactory Status in a Gourmand with a Right Amygdala Lesion." *Neurocase: Behavior, Cognition, and Science* 20, no. 4 (2014): 421–33. doi:10.1080/13554794.2013.791862.

Grice, H. P. "Logic and Conversation." In *Readings in Language and Mind*, edited by H. Geirsson and M. Losonsky, 121–33. Oxford: Blackwell Publishers, 1996.

Guidi, J., M. Lucente, N. Sonino, and G. A. Fava. "Allostatic Load and Its Impact on Health: A Systematic Review." *Psychotherapy and Psychosomatics* 90, no. 1 (2021): 11–27. doi:10.1159/000510696.

Havermans, R. C., L. Vancleef, A. Kalamatianos, and C. Nederkoorn. "Eating and Inflicting Pain Out of Boredom." *Appetite* 85 (2015): 52–57. doi:10.1016/j.appet.2014.11.007.

Hoppe, K., and S. Tatkin. *Baby Bomb: A Relationship Survival Guide for New Parents*. Oakland: New Harbinger Publications, 2021.

Ivanov, V. Z., A. Nordsletten, D. Mataix-Cols, E. Serlachius, P. Lichtenstein, S. Lundström, P. K. E. Magnusson, R. Kuja-Halkola, C. Rück. "Heritability of Hoarding Symptoms across Adolescence and Young Adulthood: A Longitudinal Twin Study." *PLoS One* 12, no. 6 (2017): e0179541. doi:10.1371/journal.pone.0179541.

Jones, V. C. *The Hatfields and the McCoys*. Chapel Hill: University of North Carolina Press, 1948.

Kahneman, D. *Thinking, Fast and Slow*. New York: Farrar, Straus and Giroux, 2011.

Kohlberg, L., and R. A. Ryncarz. "Beyond Justice Reasoning: Moral Development and Consideration of a Seventh Stage." In *Higher Stages of Human Development: Perspectives on Adult Growth*, edited by C. N. Alexander and E. J. Langer, 191–207. Oxford: Oxford University Press, 1990.

Krusemark, E. A. "Physiological Reactivity and Neural Correlates of Trait Narcissism." In *Handbook of Trait Narcissism*, edited by Anthony D. Hermann, Amy B. Brunell, and Joshua D. Foster, 213–23. New York: Springer, 2018.

Lee, B. K. "Where Codependency Takes Us: A Commentary." *Journal of Gambling Issues* 29(2014): 1–5. doi:10.4309/jgi.2014 .29.12.

Lisansky Gomberg, E. S. "On Terms Used and Abused: The Concept of Codependency." *Drugs & Society* 3, no. 3–4 (1989): 113–132. doi: 10.1300/J023v03n03_05.

Lundstrom, J. N., J. A. Boyle, R. J. Zatorre, and M. Jones-Gotman. "Functional Neuronal Processing of Body Odors Differs from that of Similar Common Odors." *Cerebral Cortex* 18, no. 6 (2008): 1466–74. doi:10.1093/cercor/bhm178.

Mahler, M. S., writ. and dir. *The Psychological Birth of the Human Infant: The Separation-Individuation Process*. Franklin Lakes, NJ: Margaret S. Mahler Psychiatric Research Foundation, 1983. Videocassette (VHS), 50 min.

Martin, M., G. Sadlo, and G. Stew. "The Phenomenon of Boredom." *Qualitative Research in Psychology* 3, no. 3 (2006): 193–211. doi:10.1191/1478088706qrp066oa.

Mellody, P., and A. W. Miller. *Breaking Free: A Recovery Handbook for Facing Codependence*. New York: HarperCollins, 1989.

Miller, G. A., and S. Isard. "Some Perceptual Consequences of Linguistic Rules." *Journal of Verbal Learning and Verbal Behavior* 2, no. 3 (1963): 217–28. doi:10.1016/s0022–5371(63)80087–0.

Peifer, C., H. Schächinger, S. Engeser, and C. H. Antoni. "Cortisol Effects on Flow-Experience." *Psychopharmacology* 232, no. 6 (2015): 1165–73. doi:10.1007/s00213-014-3753-5.

Perone, S., E. H. Weybright, and A. J. Anderson. "Over and Over Again: Changes in Frontal EEG Asymmetry across a Boring Task." *Psychophysiology* 56, no. 10 (2019). doi:10.1111/psyp.13427.

Porges, S. W. *The Polyvagal Theory: Neurophysiological Foundations of Emotions, Attachment, Communication, and Self-Regulation*. New York: W. W. Norton & Company, 2011.

Sapolsky, R. M. *Behave: The Biology of Humans at Our Best and Worst*. New York: Penguin Books, 2017.

Saxbe, D. E., L. Beckes, S. A. Stoycos, and J. A. Coan. "Social Allostasis and Social Allostatic Load: A New Model for Research in Social Dynamics, Stress, and Health." *Perspectives on Psychological Science* 15, no. 2 (2020): 469–82. doi:10.1177/1745691619876528.

Schore, A. N. "The Right Brain Implicit Self: A Central Mechanism of the Psychotherapy Change Process." In *Unrepressed Unconscious, Implicit Memory, and Clinical Work*, edited by Giuseppe Craparo and Clara Mucci, 73–98. London: Routledge, 2017.

Serota, K. B., and T. R. Levine. "A Few Prolific Liars: Variation in the Prevalence of Lying." *Journal of Language and Social Psychology* 34, no. 2 (2015): 138–57. doi:10.1177/0261927X14528804.

Serota, K. B., T. R. Levine, and T. Docan-Morgan. "Unpacking Variation in Lie Prevalence: Prolific Liars, Bad Lie Days, or Both?" *Communication Monographs* 89, no. 3 (2022): 307–31. doi:10.1080/03637751.2021.1985153.

Siegel, D. *The Developing Mind: Toward a Neurobiology of Interpersonal Experience*. New York: Guilford Press, 1999.

Spitoni, G. F., P. Zingaretti, G. Giovanardi, G. Antonucci, G. Galati, V. Lingiardi. G. Cruciani, G. Titone, and M. Boccia. "Disorganized Attachment Pattern Affects the Perception of Affective Touch." *Scientific Reports* 10, no. 1 (2020): 9658. doi:10.1038/s41598-020-66606-5.

Tatkin, S. *We Do: Saying Yes to a Relationship of Depth, True Connection, and Enduring Love.* Louisville, CO: Sounds True, 2018.

———. *Wired for Love: How Understanding Your Partner's Brain Can Help You Defuse Conflicts and Spark Intimacy.* Oakland, CA: New Harbinger Publications, 2012.

Van Rosmalen, L., R. Van Der Veer, and F. Van Der Horst. "Ainsworth's Strange Situation Procedure: The Origin of an Instrument." *Journal of the History of the Behavioral Sciences* 51, no. 3 (2015): 261–84. doi:10.1002/jhbs.21729.

Weiss, R. *Prodependence: Moving beyond Codependency.* New York: Simon and Schuster, 2018.

———. "Prodependence vs. Codependency: Would a New Model (Prodependence) for Treating Loved Ones of Sex Addicts Be More Effective Than the Model We've Got (Codependency)?" *Sexual Addiction & Compulsivity* 26, no. 3–4 (2019): 177–90. doi:10.1080/10720162.2019.1653239.

Zald, D. H. "The Human Amygdala and the Emotional Evaluation of Sensory Stimuli." *Brain Research Reviews* 41, no. 1 (2003): 88–123. doi:10.1016/s0165-0173(02)00248-5.

Index

Note: Italicized page numbers indicate figures.

fighting dos and don'ts (*continued*)
  silence and nonresponses, 86, 90–91, 94
  taking a stand, 69–70
  taking care of self and other, 64–65
  thirds, comanagement of, 63
  transparency and, 63
  working the problem, not each other, 64
fighting words (example), 79
flow, 291–92, 305
friends, 168–72
  bringing into couple fold, 172, 211
  disagreements about, 210–11
  partner tells me to get more friends, 276–82
  as thirds, 168–72, 210–11
funerals, 60

gaslighting, 87, 170, 171
  defined, 257
gender-neutral language, 3
giving up, 269–70, 271
good faith, 44–45, 88, 171
goodwill, 44–45
governance, 6, 23, 256
  shared principles of, 12–14, 118, 208, 256, 313
gratitude, expressing, 41
Grice's maxims, 21–22
growth (complaint about), 133–45
guardrails, 7–10, 15, 41, 208, 208–9
  constructing, 31, 112, 227

See also agreements
guilt, blended families and, 234–35

happiness, 273, 317
  of parents and children, 213–14, 217
hoarding, 116–23
home, 281–82, 317
  one partner doesn't like, 156–61
honesty, 55
human condition, 19–33
human nature, 1–15, 104, 242, 281, 289
  overriding, 313–14

illness, 144, 194–202
  COVID pandemic, 76, 190–91, 282–83, 315–16
  partner is always sick, 194–202
  protecting child from, 75–83
  supporting your partner in, 59
inattentiveness, 156
independence, 270–71, 300
inequity, 98–99, 104–5, 248
influence, 36, 38, 131, *132*
  safety and, 36, 46, 267
information sharing, 209, 211, 249–51
  See also transparency
insecure attachment, 279, 284, 286
insecure functioning, 73, 132–33, 153
interdependence, 5–6, 132, 153, 179, 300, 312
  defined, 313

repetition (*continued*)

   loops (being in a loop), 26, 32, 95, 184–85, 239, 259

resistance, dealing with, 158

reward circuit, 175–76, 179, 182

road rage, 89–90

safety

   interpersonal, 36–38, 46

   responsibility for, 46

safety and security, 75–106, 203

   don't make decisions together, 99–105

   felt sense of, 46, 221

   partner bullies me, 90–99

   partner drives like a maniac, 83–90

   partner throws me under the bus, 203–9, 210

   partner won't protect our child from illness, 75–83

   seeking professional advice for, 82

   trust and, 130

secure attachment, 250, 286

secure functioning, 5–6, 197–98

   agreements and guardrails, 7–11

   defined, 5–6, 313

   fairness and justice, 237, 270, 312, 313

   leverage and, 270

   relationships, as pay to play, 58, 264

   rewards of, 312–14

   transparency and, 63, 209, 211, 249–50

vs. insecure functioning, 73, 132

secure functioning partners, 36–38, 197–98, 312–14

   decision-making and, 99

   doing the right thing, 270

   equal power of, 3, 5, 129, 232, 281

   happiness, responsibility for, 273

   interests and, 131–32

   personal will and, 45–46

   putting relationship first, 41, 63, 113, 164, 275–76, 313

   See also two-person system

security. *See* safety and security

sensation

   aversions, 292–94

   near senses, 292–94

sex, 285–312

   agreements about, 7–8

   alcohol or drugs and, 305

   arousal and, 287–89

   attachment and, 286–87

   attention and, 291–92, 299, 310–11

   brain and, 289–91

   cheating, and lack of trust, 56–57

   comparisons and expectations, 288–89

   contact maintenance and, 286–87

   device use to achieve orgasm, 189

   DIY sexual intake questions, 294–97

   flow and, 291–92, 305

   intimacy and, 294, 297

   monogamy, 55–56

   near senses and, 292–94

About the Author

S tan Tatkin, PsyD, MFT, is a clinician, researcher, teacher, and developer of A Psychobiological Approach to Couple Therapy® (PACT). He has a clinical practice in Calabasas, CA, and with his wife, Dr. Tracey Tatkin, cofounded the PACT Institute for the purpose of training other psychotherapists to use this method in their clinical practice.

In addition, Dr. Tatkin teaches and supervises family medicine residents at Kaiser Permanente in Woodland Hills, CA, and is an assistant clinical professor at the UCLA David Geffen School of Medicine, Department of Family Medicine. He is on the board of directors of Lifespan Learning Institute and serves as a member on Relationships First Counsel, a nonprofit organization founded by Harville Hendrix and Helen LaKelly Hunt.